The *Quick* Reference Guide

THIRD EDITION

Ralph M. Holmes

GLENCOE
McGraw-Hill

New York, New York   Columbus, Ohio   Woodland Hills, California   Peoria, Illinois

Library of Congress Cataloging-in-Publication Data

Holmes, Ralph M. (Ralph Miley), date
    The quick reference guide / Ralph M. Holmes. — 3rd ed.
        p.   cm.
    Includes index.
    ISBN 0-02-802526-1
        1. English Language—Rhetoric—Handbooks, manuals, etc.
2. English language—Rhetoric—Problems, exercises, etc.   3. English
language—Grammar—Handbooks, manuals, etc.   4. English language—
Grammar—Problems, exercises, etc.   5. English language—
Composition and excercises.   I. Title.
PE1408.H6717   1995
808'.042--dc20   94-20501

The Quick Reference Guide, Third Edition

Imprint 2000

Send all inquiries to:
Glencoe/McGraw-Hill
8787 Orion Place
Columbus, OH 43240

ISBN: 0-02-802526-1

 5 6 7 8 9 10 11 12 13 14 15   003   04 03 02 01 00

CONTENTS

UNIT 3

NUMBERS 35

UNIT 4

ABBREVIATIONS...................... 47

UNIT **5**

GRAMMAR

UNIT **6**

PHRASES, CLAUSES, SENTENCES, AND PARAGRAPHS

UNIT **7**

SPELLING AND WORD CHOICE

UNIT 8

THE WRITING PROCESS: PREWRITING AND DRAFTING ... 135

UNIT 9

THE WRITING PROCESS: REVISING, EDITING, AND FINAL DRAFTING ... 147

UNIT 10

REFERENCE SOURCES ... 157

UNIT **11**

UNIT **12**

UNIT **13**

APPENDIX **A**

APPENDIX **B**

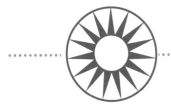

PREFACE

Technology has broadened writing opportunities for individuals in every environment including the office, classroom, and home. This third edition of *The Quick Reference Guide* has been completely revised to be of greater assistance to writers in all those environments—business, academic, and personal. The guide's major purposes include (1) serving as a ready writing reference for students and office workers and (2) providing a teaching/learning/reviewing tool for both classroom use and individual study.

Maintaining its original intent to be a clear, concise, ready reference, *The Quick Reference Guide* provides answers to questions most often asked in all kinds of writing situations. The finding devices built into the design—thumb index, table of contents, numbered topics, running heads, and index—enable easy location of major topics and subtopics. The convenient size and spiral binding allow easy handling and fold-back flexibility for ease in reading. The generous use of color helps label and highlight the major divisions in the content of the text.

New to this edition are two units covering the writing process, a dynamic system in which the writer follows the steps of prewriting, drafting, evaluating, revising, editing, and rewriting. This process enables the writer to develop a finished document—memo, letter, research paper, business report—that speaks properly to the intended audience.

To offer greater assistance in using today's technology, the expanded appendix now includes WordPerfect® commands (cursor movements and keystrokes for most basic functions in WordPerfect® software), DOS commands (basic DOS commands and their purposes), and a glossary of computer terms (terms and definitions related to computer literacy). Other useful appendix sections include grammatical terms, business and legal terms, alphabetic filing rules, and survival tips.

An especially helpful addition is a set of 26 worksheets designed to provide extra practice in using the reference guide and applying the content of each of the thirteen units. A pretest and a posttest help measure student progress. The worksheets provide practice in addition to that in the self-check exercises that conclude each unit in *The Quick Reference Guide*.

The Quick Reference Guide can be the basis for organized, directed classroom study as well as for casual, nonstructured, individual study. If a less detailed classroom study is desired, a "mini-course" can be developed around selected units.

Technology is encouraging change in the way writing has traditionally been done. Goals are to achieve higher levels of productivity and to use more fully the capabilities of computerized equipment. Where differences of opinion exist regarding rules or where the technology encourages methods other than those endorsed in the past, *The Quick Reference Guide* follows the most widely held interpretation or provides alternatives.

A Teacher's Manual, including keys to the worksheet exercises, is available for those who wish to use *The Quick Reference Guide* in a classroom setting. It provides teaching suggestions, "finding activities" to develop proficiency in using the materials, exercises for every unit for extra practice or evaluation, and answers to all the exercises in *The Quick Reference Guide*.

Special thanks go to those who offered suggestions to make this new edition a more effective reference tool—teachers, students, companies and organizations, and especially the editorial staff at Glencoe/McGraw-Hill.

To those who helped me develop an appreciation of language and how to use it effectively—special teachers like Mrs. Bessie G. Long (my fourth grade teacher who provided the initial spark)—I am truly grateful.

To my family—especially my wife, Billie, who has been a source of constant encouragement—I dedicate this edition of *The Quick Reference Guide*.

Ralph M. Holmes

PUNCTUATION

Punctuation provides clarity to writing. Punctuation marks serve as "traffic signals," telling the reader when to pause, when to stop, and even when to lend certain expression to words. Without punctuation, writing would be a meaningless jumble of words, and written communication would be impossible. The following punctuation rules are those most commonly used in written communication.

APOSTROPHE

1.1 With nouns, use an apostrophe to show ownership. Add an apostrophe and *s* ('s) to singular nouns and to plural nouns not ending in *s*.

> The doctor's diagnosis indicated the need for further treatment.
> The children's toys are stored neatly in the closet.

Add an apostrophe and *s* ('s) to proper nouns.

> The security guard found Timothy's wallet.
> The man removed Ross's books from the sidewalk.

If adding an extra syllable would make a word ending difficult to pronounce, add the apostrophe only.

> New Orleans' restaurants are known for their fine food.

Add only an apostrophe (') after plural nouns ending in *s*.

> The girls' debate team is having a successful year.

Add an apostrophe and *s* ('s) only to the final of two or more names to show joint ownership.

> Denise and Chan's performance brought down the house.

Use an apostrophe and *s* ('s) after each name when two or more persons possess something individually.

> Harry's and Lillian's coats are the same color.
> Everybody's favorite songs are sung on the recording.

1.2 Personal pronouns in the possessive case (*his, hers, its, ours, yours,* and *theirs*) and the relative pronoun *whose* do not need an apostrophe to show ownership.

> It is his book, not yours.
> Whose desk is this?

1.3 Use an apostrophe and *s* ('s) to show ownership for most indefinite pronouns (*one, everyone, everybody, somebody,* and so on).

> She tried to get everybody's approval of her dress.
> Somebody's notebook is lying in the hallway.

1.4 Use an apostrophe to replace letters or numbers in contractions.

> I can't go to the game if I don't finish my homework.
> The flood of '93 will never be forgotten.

1.5 Add an *s* to form the plural of words used as words, numbers, symbols, letters, and abbreviations with periods.

> The teacher said she would accept no *ifs, ands,* or *buts.*
> It is difficult to distinguish the *9s* from the *Ps.*
> Use *$s* for dollars and *#s* for pounds in the report.
> All the *CEOs* had *Ph.D.s* from large universities.

1.6 Use an apostrophe to indicate feet or minutes in technical writing. (In general writing, spell out the words *feet* and *minutes.*)

> 16' × 30'   [feet]
> The swimming pool will be 16' by 32'.   [feet]
> Trae ran the mile in four minutes.

1.7 Use apostrophes as single quotation marks for a quotation within a quotation.

> The doctor asked, "Have you read the article 'How to Gain Good Health' by Anna Wyatt?"

Spacing

1.8 Do not leave a space before or after an apostrophe used within a word.

> Marilyn couldn't go to the party.

Leave no spaces before, but one space after, an apostrophe at the end of a word.

The boys' team won the championship last year.

ASTERISK

1.9 Use an asterisk to refer to a footnote that appears at the bottom of a page.

Thomas Jefferson* wrote the Declaration of Independence.

_____

*(footnote)

1.10 Use five asterisks to indicate the omission of censored or unprintable material.

The director was so enraged with the group that she called them *****.

Spacing

1.11 If an asterisk is used as a footnote reference within the text, leave no spaces before but one space after the asterisk. If the asterisk falls at the end of the sentence, leave no space before but two spaces after the asterisk. In the footnote itself, do not space after the asterisk.

If asterisks show the omission of censored material, leave no spaces between the asterisks.

BRACE

1.12 Use a brace as a joining device in legal documents.

<u>Elizabeth Nye</u> ⎫
Plaintiff   ⎭

    vs.   ⎬

<u>Ronald Ziegler</u> ⎫
Defendant   ⎭

A brace can be made by using two or more right parentheses if the characters are not included in available fonts.

BRACKETS

1.13 Use brackets to enclose a writer's explanation, addition, or correction within a quotation.

> The law clerk discovered that the high court [U.S. Circuit Court] had ruled on the matter in 1993.

1.14 Use brackets to indicate an error or questionable word in a quotation by enclosing *sic*.

> The student wrote, "The principle [*sic*] called Ms. Jones to the office."

1.15 Use brackets to enclose parenthetical material within another parenthetical element.

> (The librarian cited *The World of Nature* [3rd edition] as the most current reference.)

Spacing

1.16 Brackets, like parentheses, are used to enclose material. Leave one space before the left bracket and one space after the right bracket (unless the bracket is immediately followed by a mark of punctuation).

COLON

1.17 Use a colon to introduce a list or a long statement that completes a sentence.

> Mr. Wilson said he needed the following art supplies: three brushes, two tubes of cleaner, and a package of wipes.
>
> Ambassador Hunter made the following observation: The world is a much better place because of the intervention that took place in that country.

1.18 Use a colon to separate hours and minutes in expressions of time.

> 9:37 a.m.   11:46 p.m.

1.19 Use a colon in proportions to represent the word *to*.

> 3:1 (*three to one*)   2.9:1 (*2.9 to one*)
>
> The formula required a ratio of 2:1 to obtain the proper mixture.

1.20 Use a colon after salutations in business letters using mixed (standard) punctuation.

Dear Ms. Valdez:	Ladies and Gentlemen:
Dear Sir or Madam:	Dear Mr. Johnson:

1.21 Use a colon to separate the originator's initials from those of the person keying the document in the reference initials line of a business letter if all capital letters are used.

BJH:SJE

1.22 Use a colon in footnotes and bibliography entries to separate the city of publication from the publisher's name as well as the volume number from the page number.

[1]Lydia Steinfeld, *The Jewish Question* (New York: Empire Publishing Co., 1991), p. 485.   [footnote]

Steinfeld, Lydia. *The Jewish Question.* New York: Empire Publishing Co., 1991. [bibliography]

Langston, Anthony. "The Way of the West." *Western Chronicles* 28:117–119. [volume]

Spacing

1.23 Do not leave a space before or after a colon used in expressions of time, proportions, reference initials, or volume/page references. In all other cases, do not leave a space before, but leave two spaces after a colon. A colon should always appear *outside* quotation marks or parentheses when they are used together.

The plane arrives at 12:23 p.m.
The combination of instruments sounded "odd": an oboe, a zither, and a cello.

COMMA

1.24 Use a comma to set off academic degrees. If found within a sentence, commas precede and follow the degree.

Lei Phong, Ph.D.
Merlin Greco, Ph.D., was named to the faculty.

A seniority designation following a person's name is not set off by commas unless that style is the individual's preference.

George Wilson Sr.   Ronald D. Whitworth III

1.25 Use a comma between two or more adjectives preceding and modifying the same noun.

The hikers were refreshed by the cool, bubbly water.
The meteorologist predicted stormy, unsettled weather.

1.26 Use a comma to set off appositives and appositive phrases. An *appositive* or appositive phrase is a noun or pronoun that explains, describes, or renames the noun or pronoun it follows.

Trudy Ransome, the lab technician, analyzed all the specimens.
The tour guide, Randy O'Quinn of Apex Travel, had a commanding presence.

1.27 Use a comma after the salutation in a friendly letter and after the complimentary close in all letters (except in business letters using open punctuation).

Dear Joe,   Sincerely,   Respectfully,   Yours truly,

1.28 Use a comma to separate the parts in dates and addresses. (Do not use a comma if only the month and year are given; do not use a comma between the state and ZIP Code.)

The address given is 127 Lake Street, Building 6, Des Moines, IA 50010.
They toured the city in June 1985; and, on April 1, 1986, the city suffered an earthquake.

1.29 Use a comma or commas to set off words of direct address.

Finish your assignment, Clarence, and you may leave early.
Al, will you make six photocopies of this page for me?

1.30 Use a comma to set off direct quotations.

Mrs. Chung announced, "This report is due in two weeks."
"When you prepare," Professor Levitz said, "your presentation will be much more professional."
"In the business world, market research is essential," Don said.

1.31 Use a comma to set off the abbreviation *etc.*

Randy ordered envelopes, copier paper, invoice forms, etc.
The dietician recommended apples, bananas, etc., for healthy snacks between meals.

1.32 The abbreviations *Inc.* and *Ltd.* in company names are not set off by commas unless that style is the known preference of the company.

> ATV Builders Inc.   Langston Ltd.
> Capitol Technical Services, Inc., is located in Phoenix.   [company preference]

1.33 Use a comma to separate three or more items in a series. Put a comma after each item except the last.

> The new school will install microcomputers in every classroom, photocopiers in every department, and fax machines in every office.
> The Mexican food was described as spicy, tangy, sizzling, and filling.

If all items in the series are joined by *and* or *or,* do not use commas to separate.

> The entertainer told the crowd to sing or clap or whistle.

1.34 Use a comma to separate thousands and millions in numbers of four or more digits.

> 8,643   77,481   433,792,045

1.35 Use a comma to separate two numbers in succession to avoid confusion.

> We ordered 21, 13 of which were placed on back order.
> In 1994, 23 percent of the students were enrolled in tech prep courses.

1.36 Use a comma to show the omission of understood or implied words or phrases.

> The first-hour class selected Diane; the second-hour class, Martha.
> The letter suggested paying half the bill immediately; the remainder, in three monthly installments.

1.37 Use a comma to set off parenthetical expressions and nonrestrictive phrases and clauses. Parenthetical expressions and nonrestrictive phrases and clauses are words, phrases, or clauses that add nonessential information or opinions to the meaning of the sentence.

> We were told, nevertheless, that the assignment was still due on Monday.
> The equipment, in any case, must always be turned off when not in use.
> The train, which always seemed to be very noisy, passed near the school.

1.38 Use a comma to separate the surname (last name) from the rest of the name when transposed (when the last name is placed first).

> Tryon Jr., William C.   Jerlo, Rich   Sanchez, Juan R., M.D.

1.39 Use a comma before coordinating conjunctions (*and, but, for, or, nor, yet*) that separate independent clauses in a sentence unless both clauses are very short—typically containing only subjects and verbs.

> We arrived on the scene on Monday, and we will leave today.
> Maxine keyed the report, but she was unable to print it.
> Al was not accepted, for he did not have the qualifications.
> Check the figures on the table, or inaccuracies may occur.
> She would not let us help, nor would she help herself.
> One child jumped and the other ran.

1.40 Use a comma to set off introductory words and phrases that cause a break in the reading of a sentence.

> Well, I think that eliminates any chance of winning.
> By the end of the day, we were ready to give up.
> Laughing out loud, she pointed to the missing page.

1.41 Use a comma to set off a dependent clause that begins a sentence.

> If we all work together, we can finish by noon.
> After Marie keyed the report, she proofread it for accuracy.
> When you meet with the counselor, be sure to ask about the tech prep program.

Spacing

1.42 Never leave a space before a comma. Generally, leave one space after a comma (unless the comma is used to separate thousands and/or millions within a number).

Always place a comma *inside* quotation marks. If a comma is used with parentheses or brackets, place the comma *outside*.

> "Consider the alternative," Janet said, "and I'm sure you will agree with our plan."
> Use the computer (in the lab), and you will save time.

DASH

1.43 Use a dash for emphasis or to indicate any kind of abrupt change in the sentence. Use a second dash at the end of the change if the sentence continues.

> The truth hurts—but was that really the truth?
> Janice said—actually shouted—that she passed the exam.

1.44 Use a dash to emphasize a parenthetical expression.

> Mr. Ristau—a remarkable scientist—will speak at the convocation.
> The examination—containing 350 questions—required three hours to complete.

1.45 Use a dash before an author's name that follows a quotation.

> A penny saved is a penny earned.—Franklin

Spacing

1.46 Do not space before or after a dash. On most keyboarding equipment, the dash is made with two hyphens.

DIAGONAL

1.47 Use a diagonal between two words to indicate that either or both are correct.

> The report/manuscript was thought to be too voluminous.
> You may phone and/or write me of your decision.

1.48 Use a diagonal to separate the numbers in the short form of a date to indicate month, day, and year.

> 11/10/94

1.49 Use a diagonal between two numbers or letters used to express a fraction, an abbreviation, or a period of time.

> The road race was 5 1/2 miles long.
> Mail a copy of your résumé c/o Deanna Wall.
> The tax returns were for 1993/1994.

1.50 Use a diagonal to separate the originator's initials from those of the person keying the document in the reference initials line of a business letter if all lowercase letters are used.

> bjh/vlc

Spacing

1.51 Do not leave a space before or after a diagonal.

ELLIPSIS

1.52 Use an ellipsis (three spaced periods) to indicate an intentional omission of one or more words in quoted material.

> "The matter is simple . . . let your conscience be your guide."
> "So live, that when your summons comes. . . ."

Spacing

1.53   When an ellipsis indicates an omission within a sentence, use three periods with a space before, between, and after each period.

When an ellipsis falls at the end of a sentence, use three periods and the closing punctuation mark. Place the first period immediately *after* the last word. Leave one space before, between, and after the next two periods. Then add the closing punctuation mark.

EXCLAMATION POINT

1.54   Use an exclamation point to express strong feelings or a command.

Stop shouting! I can hear you perfectly well!

Spacing

1.55   Leave two spaces after the exclamation point at the end of a sentence; do not leave a space before the exclamation point. Place an exclamation point *inside* the quotation mark only if the exclamation point is part of the quoted material. If it is not part of the quoted material, place the exclamation point *outside* the quotation mark.

When William heard the crash, he shouted, "Call 911 now!"
Watch out for that old "clunker"!

[Note: If a proportional font is used, leave one space after the exclamation point at the end of a sentence.]

HYPHEN

1.56   Use a hyphen to join the words of a compound adjective before the noun it modifies.

Harry works on a day-to-day basis.
A first-class plan is needed to ensure success.

1.57   Use a hyphen to show that two or more compound adjectives share the same base word.

The principal cancelled the ninth-, tenth-, and eleventh-grade classes.
Because of the weather, there was a two- to three-hour delay in leaving the terminal.

1.58   Use a hyphen in spelled-out compound numbers from 21 to 99.

eighty-six   one thousand nine hundred ninety-five

1.59 Use a hyphen with inclusive dates and numbers.

May 19-22, 1995   5-6 chapters   1941-1945   pages 1-99

1.60 Use a hyphen to divide a word between syllables at the end of a line.

To meet the virtually impossible deadline, the loyal office staff worked over-
time several evenings.

1.61 Use a hyphen with spelled-out fractions used as adjectives.

one-fourth share of the property
a two-thirds majority of the Senate
but two thirds of the Senate

1.62 Use a hyphen to join certain prefixes to words.

self-respect   all-inclusive   ex-officio

1.63 Use a hyphen to separate a prefix from a proper noun.

pro-American   ex-Yankee   non-Protestant

Spacing

1.64 Do not leave a space before or after a hyphen within either a word or a number.

PARENTHESES

1.65 Use parentheses to set off nonessential words, phrases, or clauses that further explain or emphasize a part of a sentence.

The FCC (Federal Communications Commission) rejected the request for a broadcasting license.

1.66 Use parentheses to set off dollar amounts in numbers in legal and business documents.

Anthony Garza agrees to pay Three Hundred Dollars ($300).

1.67 Use parentheses to indicate enumerated items in a sentence.

To be promoted, you must (1) be experienced, (2) have good work habits, and (3) be
ready to move.

1.68 Use parentheses in footnotes to set off the place of publication, the publisher, and the date.

> [2]Marilyn Quincy, *The Roanoke Story* (Raleigh: Tar Heel Publishers, 1994), p. 316.
> [3]John Hammond, "The First Settlers," *National Historical Quarterly* (April 1995), pp. 2–5.

1.69 Use parentheses to set off periods of time.

> The Great Depression (1930–1936) was a time of testing for the nation.

Spacing

1.70 Leave one space before the left parenthesis and one space after the right parenthesis.

If another punctuation mark applies to the complete sentence rather than the material enclosed in parentheses, place the punctuation mark *outside* the right parenthesis with no space between the two.

If the punctuation mark applies to the material enclosed in parentheses, place the punctuation mark *inside* the right parenthesis.

PERIOD

1.71 Use a period after a declarative sentence (a statement).

> Angelina removed her backpack from the locker.
> The bookstore will remain open until midnight this week.

1.72 Use a period after an imperative sentence (a command).

> Give those papers to the registrar immediately.
> Report to the gymnasium for your uniforms.

1.73 Use a period after a simple request.

> Will you please see if Jonathan is in the other room.
> Please tell Mr. Smith that I cannot attend the session.

1.74 Use a period after initials, academic degrees, and most abbreviations.

J. W. Baker	c.o.d.	Maxwell Tyler, Ph.D.
Ltd.	Oct.	Dr. Philip Ramsey

1.75 Use a period as a decimal point in dollar amounts, decimals, or percentages.

$49.18	0.4333	37.49%

1.76 Use a period after the numbers and letters in outlines and enumerations in the form of a vertical list.

    I. Location factors
       A. Traffic
       B. Public facilities
          1. Hospitals
          2. Schools
             a. Public
             b. Private
   1. Computers
   2. Printers
   3. Monitors
   4. Modems

Spacing

1.77 Leave two spaces after a period at the end of a sentence or in enumerated outlines.

Leave one space after the period at the end of an abbreviation or initial unless the period falls at the end of a sentence. In that case, leave two spaces.

Do not space after a period used as a decimal point or within an abbreviation.

Always place a period *inside* quotation marks.

Wanda replied, "I will see you next week."

Place a period *inside* an asterisk at the end of a sentence.

The latest report indicated that Mary had won the election.*

When material enclosed in parentheses or brackets appears at the end of a sentence, place the period *outside* the right parenthesis or bracket.

The center opened in 1989 (the year Sam finished Harvard).

If a complete, independent sentence is enclosed in parentheses or brackets, place the period *inside* the right parenthesis or bracket.

The Melbourne Company significantly increased its market share. (A copy of the annual report is enclosed.)

[Note: If a proportional font is used, leave one space after the period at the end of a sentence.]

QUESTION MARK

1.78 Use a question mark after a direct question.

Did you comply with her request?

Use a period after a polite request in the form of a question if you expect your reader to respond by acting.

Will you please comply with her request.

1.79 Use a question mark to express doubt.

The article relating to the Tech Prep program appeared in the August(?) issue of *Today's Educator.*

1.80 Use a question mark to indicate several short questions within one complete sentence.

Did Elaine submit the outline? the proposal? the report?

Spacing

1.81 Leave two spaces after a question mark at the end of a sentence and one space after a question mark within a sentence.

Can you meet the schedule for June? for July? for August?

Do not space before or after a question mark enclosed in parentheses and used to express doubt.

The country entered World War II in 1940(?).

Place a question mark *inside* quotation marks, parentheses, or brackets only when the question mark is part of the quoted or enclosed material.

Thomas asked, "Will he really attend the party?"
Did Thomas say, "I think he will attend the party"?
Wayne explained his plan again (was it really necessary the third time?) for the program committee.

[Note: If a proportional font is used, leave one space after the question mark at the end of a sentence.]

QUOTATION MARKS

1.82 Use quotation marks to enclose a direct quotation. Quotations of more than one paragraph have a quotation mark at the beginning of each paragraph and at the end of the *last* paragraph.

> "The furniture will arrive today," Ruth said.
> "Must you," Cynthia asked, "whistle while you work?"

1.83 Some sources use quotation marks to refer to a word itself.

> Joyce taught the children to properly pronounce "environment" in their science lesson.
> Please emphasize the word "safe" when you talk to new drivers.

[Note: Some sources prefer to use the underscore or italics to refer to a word itself.]

1.84 Use quotation marks to set off words used in unexpected ways, such as nicknames, slang, technical words, or unusual expressions.

> Lydia told Anthony to "dump" the files.
> James advised Tim to "stand tall" as he faced up to his problem.

1.85 Use quotation marks to enclose a definition or a foreign word.

> The "cursor" is used to indicate position on a computer screen.
> Jan wished everyone "bon appétit" as she served dessert.

1.86 Use quotation marks to indicate irony. Irony is the use of words to convey the opposite of their literal meaning.

> Wilma's "smile" was obviously not sincere.
> The young actor's "talent" was highly overrated.

1.87 Use quotation marks to enclose titles of articles, short stories, songs, poems, speeches, and chapters of books.

> The students were required to read the article "Preparing for Today's Technical World."
> Martha enjoyed reading "Going to Rome" from the collection of short stories.
> The most popular song was "River Town Blues."
> Perhaps the most widely known speech is Lincoln's "Gettysburg Address."
> Chapter 3, "Music Masters," is the best chapter in the book.

Spacing

1.88   Leave one space before the left quotation mark and one space after the right quotation mark unless the quotation mark falls at the end of the sentence. Leave two spaces after the quotation mark at the end of a sentence.

> Julius insisted that his "strategy" would work perfectly.
> Their suggestions were "interesting."

Always place quotation marks *outside* a period or a comma.

> Christina said, "It's time to depart."
> "Whenever you eat at Rachel's," Ruth said, "you get excellent service."

Always place the quotation marks *inside* a colon or a semicolon.

> The preceding class set the "standard": our class failed to match that standard.
> The team selected a "motto": "Never give up."

Place exclamation points and question marks *inside* quotation marks if they are actually part of the quoted material. Otherwise, place the exclamation points and question marks *outside* the quotation marks.

> The director asked, "Should the music soften at this point?"
> Will Randy say, "We should have won the game"?
> When Lucy received her paper from the teacher, she shouted, "Yes!"
> Don't touch that wire, or you'll be "zapped"!

[Note: If a proportional font is used, leave one space after the quotation mark at the end of a sentence.]

SEMICOLON

1.89   Use a semicolon to separate two or more closely related independent clauses in a compound sentence not joined by a conjunction.

> The research had been completed; the report had been written.
> Effort promotes success; success brings fulfillment.

1.90   Use a semicolon between the independent clauses of a compound sentence when they are joined by such words as *accordingly, consequently, hence, however, in fact, instead, moreover, otherwise, nevertheless, therefore, thus, whereas, yet,* and *so.* Place a comma *after* the joining word.

> Henry was delayed by the traffic; however, he still made it to his appointment on time.

1.91   Use a semicolon between the clauses of a compound sentence if either clause contains a comma.

> Liza keyed the deposition, the affidavit, and the contract; and she did so without error.
>
> The business plan was well formulated; it included market research, financial data, and risk analysis.

1.92   Use a semicolon between parts of a listing or a series when commas exist within the parts.

> Mr. Tate issued three directives: one for recording attendance; one for handling absences; and one for dealing with discipline, disputes, and criticism.

Spacing

1.93   Leave one space after, but not before, a semicolon. Place a semicolon *outside* quotation marks, parentheses, or brackets.

> John is a "tower of strength"; however, he broke down at the news of the disaster.
>
> The class held its reunion that year (1993); in addition, it held a special gathering shortly after to celebrate the school's centennial.

UNDERSCORE

1.94   Use the underscore to emphasize letters, numbers, symbols, or words.

> Write <u>yes</u> in those blanks that apply to you.
>
> The order was for <u>60</u> cases, not 600.
>
> Do <u>not</u> begin the exam until you've read the directions.

1.95   Use the underscore to indicate the titles of books, magazines, television programs, works of art, names of ships, plays, and newspapers.

> The library ordered six copies of <u>The New Age of Tech Prep</u>.
>
> Mae is an avid reader of the sports magazine <u>SportsWatch</u>.
>
> Ron served two years on the ship <u>H.M.S. Celestial</u>.
>
> Jonathan wrote an article for the <u>Daily Chronicle</u> newspaper.

1.96   Use the underscore to indicate foreign words and phrases.

> On every quarter is the inscription <u>E Pluribus Unum</u>.

1.97 Use the underscore to indicate italics in material to be set in type.

Many students read <u>Seventeen</u>, the fashion magazine.

The revival of the popular musical <u>Carousel</u> won several Tony Awards.

The sculpture <u>Madonna and Child</u> gave a serene feeling to the small sculpture garden.

Kathy Hogan Trocheck's mystery novel <u>Every Crooked Nanny</u> introduced Atlanta detective Callahan Garrity.

1.98 Italic type, if available, may be used in place of the underscore.

Many students read *Seventeen*, the fashion magazine.

The revival of the popular musical *Carousel* won several Tony Awards.

The sculpture *Madonna and Child* gave a serene feeling to the small sculpture garden.

Kathy Hogan Trocheck's mystery novel *Every Crooked Nanny* introduced Atlanta detective Callahan Garrity.

Spacing

1.99 Key an underscore as a solid line. Do not extend the underscore under other punctuation marks that are not part of the underscored material. Supply the correct punctuation in the following sentences.

SELF-CHECK EXERCISE 1, *UNIT 1*

....

_____

(Name)

Supply the correct punctuation in the following sentences.

1. Johns letter indicated that his doctors report would be sent to the insurance company.

2. Well Marie and Daniel duet won the talent contest but they didn't accept the award

3. The instructor asked Have you read the article Studying Works by Don Schuller

4. It was the decision of the court U.S. Supreme Court on Friday the speaker said to limit representation

5. Duane said he needed the following items 3 pencils 11 folders and 23 paper clips no later than 830 am

6. Charity Hargrove PhD spoke to the group in clear positive language reminding them to stand tall in times of trouble.

7. She gave her address as 16 Central Avenue Apt 3 Houston TX 50307

8. Arthur did you check to see if that figure of $77631 was correct in the Wilson Buildings Inc report

9. It was a difficult task nevertheless it needed to be done

10. Stop Your car is on fire

11. Mr Anthony the computer specialist developed a first class curriculum for the school

12. The FTC Federal Trade Commission ruled that the J C Marlowe Company Inc had not acted properly

13. The amount of $437 21 represented 16 95% of the total

14. The word indubitably is difficult for most people to pronounce

15. The title of Tonys speech was How Not To Get It Right

16. Phyllis left the campus early she was too ill to continue

17. On March 17 1995 Ruth began the task and she continued until she had completed the final report

18. Paul gave three reports one emphasizing employee morale one centering on employee work habits and one focusing on stress time management and incentives

19. The title of the book was Make Room for Me

20. The girls soccer team led by Tammy and Lani scored its goals in the first period

21. The total pages keyed were 13 11 of which contained errors

22. When the order finally arrived that it contained products produced in 1993 1994

23. Myra requested perhaps demanded that we stop talking

24. One third of the money goes to William but a one half share of that goes to Millicent

25. It requires a great deal of self denyal sic wrote Henry if you want to develop discipline

Supply the correct punctuation in the following memo.

TO: Ruby McFadden Data Processing Director

FROM: Tony Whitten National Sales Manager

DATE: May 16 1995

SUBJECT: Monthly Sales Reports

At the San Diego meeting of the regional sales managers I informed the group that in the future monthly sales reports would be provided showing the following information 1 equipment sales 2 service sales and 3 total sales I also indicated that we will accept any suggestions reported no later than June 30 1995 Will you design a format Ruby that will readily display specific concise sales data

In his address to the group our president Mr Mahoney said We must have more accurate sales data if we are to make appropriate projections As I study this matter I will need complete data for all sales representatives or perhaps for each sales representative by region Can you possibly provide this information

Would you also provide first second and third quarter sales figures for those representatives with sales of more than $750000 According to my recollection at least seven representatives have reached this goal

May I refer you to an article entitled Making the Most of Data which appeared in a recent issue of Data Processing I believe it presented a good case for providing solid data however I am not sure you will agree with the methods advocated

Check your answers in the back of the book.

UNIT

CAPITALIZATION

A writer's decision to capitalize is based, for the most part, on a set of established and accepted rules. Sometimes, however, writers use capitalization to emphasize and clarify and may not observe strict rules. In any case, the writer should strive for consistency within the text. The most commonly accepted and widely used capitalization rules follow.

ACADEMIC DEGREES

2.1   Capitalize a specific academic degree only when it immediately follows a person's name, whether the degree is spelled out or abbreviated.

> Marie introduced Matthew Larkin, Ph.D., as the newest member of the faculty.
> Laren Whiteside, Doctor of Philosophy, wrote a prize-winning novel.
> Jennifer's goal was to complete work on her master's degree.

ARMED FORCES

2.2   Capitalize the names of specific branches of the armed forces.

United States Army	United States Air Force
United States Navy	United States Coast Guard
the Marine Corps	Air National Guard

ASTRONOMICAL AND CELESTIAL BODIES

2.3   Capitalize names of planets, stars, constellations, and other celestial bodies except for *earth, sun,* and *moon.* Capitalize *earth, sun,* and *moon* only when used with other capitalized celestial bodies.

the Milky Way	Mars
Pluto	Rigel
Orion	Venus

Mrs. Ryan discussed the environments of Earth, Mars, and Venus.
We must understand the earth to better understand the moon.
The North Star was clearly visible to the astronauts.

FIRST WORDS

2.4 Capitalize the first word of a sentence.

The school board recommended a tech prep program to improve job skills.

2.5 Capitalize the first word of a direct quotation unless it is a fragmentary quotation or is closely woven into the sentence. Do not capitalize the first word in the continuation of a quotation.

The controller asked, "Have you finished the audit?"

The committee recommended a curriculum "heavy in technology."

"Your essay must be completed by Friday," said Mr. Smith, "if you wish to have it entered in the contest."

2.6 Capitalize the first word after a colon only when a complete sentence follows.

Carolyn recorded two inaccuracies: The total should have been $340, and the price for paper should have been $35.

Two reasons exist for William's demotion: poor work habits and procrastination.

2.7 Capitalize the first word of phrases meant to stand alone.

Now to the facts of the matter.
What a day for a picnic!

2.8 Capitalize the first word of each line in a poem unless the poet has deliberately used lowercase.

All that shines may not be bright,
Blighted with a doomsday fright.

2.9 Capitalize only the first word of divisions of outlines.

  I. Components of a tech prep program
    A. Articulation agreement
    B. Specifically developed curriculum
    C. Equal access of special populations
 II. Resources needed

2

2.10 Capitalize the first word of a resolution following the word *Resolved.*

Resolved: That August 6 be recognized as a day of prayer.

2.11 Capitalize the first word of a statement or a question included in a sentence without quotation marks.

My response was, This will never do.
His question was, Will this settle the matter?

BUSINESS NAMES

2.12 Capitalize the first and all important words in business names. Do not capitalize *the, and, of,* and other such words unless they are the first word of the business name.

National Tractor Company	Cafe on the Hillside
Bill's Bakery	The Heritage Inn
Jake's of Memphis	Jan and Joseph Caterers

2.13 Do not capitalize the words *company* and *corporation* used in place of the full name of a business.

Samantha worked for a company that produced parachutes.
The corporation provides annual performance reviews.

COMPASS POINTS

2.14 Capitalize points of the compass only when they designate specific areas of the country. Do not capitalize points of the compass when they are used simply to indicate direction.

Cold temperatures are the rule in the East and Northeast.

The Southwest is known for its easy style of living.

A tornado watch was in effect in the western section of the county.

The rescue team had to climb the east face of the mountain to reach the injured climber on South Pinnacle.

She lived for many years in western Massachusetts.

DATES

2.15 Capitalize days of the week, months of the year, holidays, and special events.

> The computer lab is available to all students on Monday and Wednesday of each week.
> January, February, and March are our most productive months.
> We celebrate Memorial Day each May.

2.16 Do not capitalize names of the seasons unless they are personified. (Personification is the giving of human qualities to inanimate objects or abstract ideas.)

> This area enjoys four seasons—spring, summer, fall, and winter.
> My favorite season is summer, closely followed by spring.
> "Oh, Autumn, how I long for your warm colors."

ETHNIC, RACIAL, AND NATIONAL REFERENCES

2.17 Capitalize terms that refer to ethnic groups, races, nationalities, cultures, and languages.

Arabic	English
Caucasian	Asian
Japanese	Polish
German	Spanish

2.18 Do not capitalize the words *blacks* or *whites*.

the blacks	the whites

GEOGRAPHIC TERMS

2.19 Capitalize names of specific continents, countries, states, cities, towns, streets, mountains, parks, bodies of water, and so on.

South America	Annapolis
Europe	the Indian Ocean
United States	Fifth Avenue
Somalia	the Black Mountains
Utah	Lake Superior

2.20 Do not capitalize terms such as *river, ocean, city,* and *state* when used alone or when they appear *before* a proper noun.

Popular vacation sites are frequently located near a river, lake, or ocean.
We visited the states of Virginia, Maryland, and Delaware on our vacation.
Jan left New York City and sailed alone across the ocean.

GOVERNMENTAL, POLITICAL, AND JUDICIAL UNITS

2.21 Capitalize the names of specific governmental, political, and judicial units.

The United States Senate	Department of Human Services
the Nebraska Legislature	Federal Trade Commission
the Supreme Court	Houston City Council
Democratic Party	the Circuit Court of Appeals

2.22 Do not capitalize the words *federal, state,* and *government* unless they are part of a proper noun.

We entered the state of Arizona early in the morning.
It is common knowledge that state employees have excellent benefits.
Mary was employed by the federal government as a case worker.
Daniel was told to report to the security office in the federal building.

HISTORICAL PERIODS, EVENTS, AND DOCUMENTS

2.23 Capitalize the names of historical, cultural, and geological periods.

the Stone Age	Middle Ages
the Renaissance	the Roaring Twenties

2.24 Capitalize the names of all important historical events.

Boston Tea Party	Battle of Gettysburg
Vietnam War	Desert Storm

2.25 Do not capitalize references to centuries or decades.

eighteenth century	the thirties

2.26 Capitalize the names of historical documents, treaties, acts, and laws.

Bill of Rights	U.S. Constitution
Treaty of Paris	the Eighteenth Amendment
Taft-Hartley Act	the Marshall Plan

2.27 Do not capitalize references to pending legislation or references used in place of the full name of legislation or treaties.

The town council is considering a zoning law.
The treaty was signed by six nations.

HYPHENATED WORDS

2.28 Capitalize the proper nouns or proper adjectives found in hyphenated words in a sentence.

pro-American   Japanese-speaking   mid-March holiday

Lee saw Senator-elect Carson speaking to the pro-Israeli delegation at the United Nations Building.

2.29 Capitalize the first letter of each word in a hyphenated word when used in titles or headings of reports, documents, and so on.

Mid-April Budget Report   Self-Esteem Seminar

LETTER PARTS

2.30 Capitalize the first and other important words in salutations, attention lines, and subject lines.

Dear Ms. Donahue	Members of the Association:
To Whom It May Concern	Attention: Mr. Don Zapata
Subject: Invoice No. 1746	

2.31 Capitalize only the first word in complimentary closes.

Cordially yours,   Sincerely yours,   Very truly yours,

NOUNS WITH NUMBERED OR LETTERED ITEMS

2.32 Generally, capitalize a noun appearing immediately before a number or letter.

Flight 968	Catalogue 20	Apt. 38
Chapter 37	Building A	Division 13

Janice referred to Appendix D for the information on statehood.

2.33 Do not capitalize *page, paragraph, line, note, size, step,* and *verse.*

Laura found the updated information she needed on page 68, paragraph 2, line 3.

ORGANIZATIONS

2.34 Capitalize the first word and all important words in names of organizations, institutions, schools, clubs, societies, and so on.

Young Republicans	Young American Artists
Rochester String Quartet	Louisiana State University
Owen High School	First United Methodist Church
Zion Temple	University of Mississippi

2.35 Do not capitalize *church, college, high school, hotel, library, theater, university,* or other such names unless they are part of a proper noun.

Our church is located next to a hotel.
A good university generally has an outstanding library.
The Sudbury Theater offers the latest films.

PROPER NOUNS AND PROPER ADJECTIVES

2.36 Capitalize proper nouns and proper adjectives. Proper nouns are words or initials that name a specific person, place, or thing. Proper adjectives are derived from proper nouns and modify another noun or pronoun.

Raymond T. Jenkins	New Bern, North Carolina
Washington Memorial	Darwinist theory [proper adjective]
Fort Knox	the Colorado Rockies
Hong Kong	Shakespearean drama [proper adjective]
USA	

2.37 Capitalize names of persons exactly as the individual prefers. Foreign names may not consistently follow a pattern of capitalization.

John McHenry	Mae MacBride	RayLee Van Husan
Myra de la Fontaine	R. T. LaDeaux	Thom vonRibbentrop
Marilyn LaRoquette	Celeste DeMille	VanDamme

2.38 Do not capitalize words derived from proper nouns that have taken on common usage. (Refer to the dictionary when in doubt.)

manila envelope	china platter	roman numerals
oriental rug	french dressing	plaster of paris

2.39 Capitalize the names of awards, monuments, planes, ships, and other specific events, places, or things.

U.S.S. Missouri	Vietnam Memorial	Pulitzer Prize

PUBLISHED MATERIALS

2.40 Capitalize the first word and all principal words in titles of published materials—books, plays, magazines, novels, paintings, works of art, newspapers, articles, poems, and software.

Gone With the Wind	"Promote Job Preparation"
The Daily Herald	*The Music Man*
Travel and Leisure	"Ode to Summer"
"Just Say No!"	*Mona Lisa*

RELIGIOUS TERMS

2.41 Capitalize names of deities and saints, titles and divisions of sacred writings, names of sacred and holy days, and names of religious groups.

God	Buddha	Christians	Jesus
Genesis	Yom Kippur	Jehovah	St. Peter
Catholics	the Holy Spirit	the Koran	Mormons
the Bible	Christmas	New Testament	Yahweh

SCHOOL SUBJECTS

2.42 Capitalize the names of specific course titles and school subjects that are languages. Do not capitalize the names of other academic subjects unless they contain a proper noun, a proper adjective, or are followed by a number.

> Dwayne's résumé indicated he had taken courses in computer science, European history, political science, and French.
>
> Juniors are required to take English III, Introduction to Business, American History, and Tech Prep I.
>
> Her parents wanted June to take courses in advanced mathematics and science.

TITLES

2.43 Capitalize titles and forms of address showing great respect.

Her Majesty	Your Excellency
The Honorable	Your Royal Highness
Your Honor	His Holiness
Mr. President	Madam Ambassador
His Eminence	The Very Reverend

2.44 Capitalize governmental, family, military, professional, and religious titles as well as nobility only if the title immediately precedes a person's name, is used in place of the name, or is in direct address.

President Harry S. Truman	Mayor Daly
Uncle Robert	the Andrews sisters
General Stonewall Jackson	King James I
Lady Diana	Professor Margaret Barkley
Dr. Ted Stoddard	Pope John
Rabbi Wertz	General Colin Powell

> My grandfather, a memorable individual, was named Napoleon Lafayette Hawthorne.
>
> Thad has a cousin, Lynn Welch, who is a general in the army.
>
> A queen receives her title through birth or marriage.
>
> My great aunt saw Maestro Stravinsky perform in Munich.
>
> May I present the Vice President of the United States.
>
> Robert wants to be the pastor of a church.
>
> Can you give me some help, Mother, with my homework.

TRADEMARKS AND BRAND NAMES

2.45 Capitalize specific brand names and words registered as trademarks.

Kodak	Oil of Olay	IBM PC
Canon	Kool-Aid	Intel
Milk Duds	Microsoft	Post Toasties

2.46 Because of wide use and acceptance, certain trademarks and brand names are no longer protected and need not be capitalized.

milk of magnesia   nylon   spandex   aspirin

2

_____

(Name)

Indicate the proper capitalization in the following sentences by placing three underlines under the letter to be capitalized.

Example: lloyd burson said, "we must make contact with the aerostar corporation by april 13, 1996."

1. the democratic party sponsored a giant rally in the spring; the republicans countered with a television appearance by a celebrity.

2. after receiving her bachelor's degree from capitol college, judith joined the marine corps.

3. the class in religion centered on a study of the bible, the koran, and the major religions of india.

4. mr. childs said, "the class will spend thanksgiving in the state of florida; then we will visit cities in the south along the mississippi river."

5. resolved: that june 16 be set aside as a day of celebration.

6. it was veterans' day; all federal workers were enjoying the holiday.

7. jay's reaction was, it's too good to be true.

8. in miss quick's history class, we studied the politics of the nineteenth century.

9. the town of winston was founded where the sunshine and chicopee rivers join.

10. maria goes to church every sunday and then immediately goes to the library to study.

11. during the gilded age, american history was marked by taming of the west and the rise of a new south.

12. hoyt, who served on the u.s.s. independence, visited the vietnam memorial to find the name of a friend.

13. she gave this reason for the equipment failure: the drive shaft on the machine developed a wobble.

14. you can find information about the chicago symphony on page 16, paragraph 3, lines 4 through 13.

15. larry and his japanese friend visited new england in autumn.

16. his majesty, william III, granted a mid-april holiday to all those serving in the british navy.

17. after writing the poem entitled "at the end of the day," angela frost submitted her poetry to the *new york times* for publication.
18. his grandfather was president of the company that supplied french dressing for governor-elect johnson's inauguration.
19. my uncle, harry jacobs, read *gone with the wind* while on flight 110 to portland.
20. the vietnamese refugees made many contributions in the west.

SELF-CHECK EXERCISE 2, *UNIT 2*

Read the following sentences, observing especially the underlined text. Write the correct capitalization for the underlined items on the blank lines below each sentence.

1. James Wilson, doctor of philosophy, wrote his dissertation on the comparison of the environments of venus, earth, and the moon.

   _____

   _____

   _____

2. It was ms. durkee who said, "the u.s. senate was responsible for that legislation."

   _____

   _____

   _____

3. Hal grew up in a small community in the midwest, in the town of west monroe.

   _____

   _____

   _____

4. Her adventure novels took place near the <u>atlantic ocean</u> and on the <u>mississippi and missouri rivers</u>.

_____

_____

_____

5. The <u>federal and state governments</u> appropriated funds for the restoration of the <u>vietnam war monument</u>.

_____

_____

_____

6. Randy referred to <u>catalogue 16, section 7, page 28</u> to find information about <u>oriental rugs and china platters</u>.

_____

_____

_____

7. Would you give me your opinion, <u>mother</u>, about the poem "<u>ode to the robins of the south</u>"?

_____

_____

_____

8. Mary Lynn Hunt, <u>president of the corporation</u>, gave two reasons for her success: <u>hard work and encouragement from her father</u>.

_____

_____

_____

9. The annual <u>fall festival</u> will be held on <u>friday, september 30</u> at the <u>theater in river city</u>.

_____

_____

_____

10. Ruby signed up for <u>french</u>, <u>drama</u>, and <u>algebra II</u>.

_____

_____

_____

Check your answers in the back of the book.

UNIT 3

NUMBERS

How does a writer determine whether to express a number in figures or words? While they vary somewhat depending on the nature of the writing, the following rules are generally accepted for expressing numbers in most forms of communication.

GENERAL RULES

3.1 In most written communication, spell out numbers that are expressed as one or two words (a hyphenated number like *thirty-one* counts as one word); use figures for others.

> While we will need twenty-seven copies of the exam by Tuesday, we need only eight copies today.
>
> More than 375 students attended the tech prep fair.

3.2 For most business writing, spell out numbers up to and including *ten*. Use figures for numbers larger than ten.

> The computer center requested five reams of computer paper, four boxes of envelopes, and nine printer ribbons.
>
> The advertisement brought in an additional 2,735 customers.
>
> The library reported 23,913 books in circulation during the month.

3.3 Within a short section of text, treat all related numbers consistently. If the largest number is written in figures, use figures for all.

> The counselor reported that 117 students took the SAT, 9 took the PSAT, and 273 took the Regents Exam in the last two years.

[Note: The number *two* in the above example is spelled out because it is not used in the same way as the other numbers.]

3.4 Always spell out a number that begins a sentence. If spelling the number is awkward because of its size, revise the sentence to eliminate the number as the first word.

Nineteen students agreed to participate in the experiment.
The computer center trained 1,125 students last year.   [*not* One thousand one hundred twenty-five students were trained by the computer center last year.]

3.5 Spell out approximate numbers and even hundreds, thousands, millions, billions, and so on.

Henry traveled for twenty-one days in Europe this summer.
The new trade law will supposedly create seven hundred fifty thousand new jobs.

[Note: Hyphenate compound numbers from 21 to 99 that are spelled out.]

3.6 Spell out ordinal numbers that can be written in one or two words. Use figures with the ordinal ending for larger numbers.

third   forty-second   ten-thousandth   225th

3.7 Express very large round numbers (millions, billions, and so on) in a combination of figures and words.

213 million   2.8 billion   23 trillion

3.8 Always use figures with abbreviations or symbols.

16 ft   99%
6 × 4 = 24   7 ml

3.9 Use a comma in numbers of four or more digits.

9,097   232,000   2,675,113

3.10 When two related numbers appear beside each other and one is part of a compound modifier, spell out the smaller number and use figures for the larger number.

We were told to provide seven 14-page documents.
Ms. Neilson placed an order for 367 four-copy invoice forms.

3.11   Use a comma to separate unrelated adjacent numbers written in figures or words.

> On page 178, 25 problems on dividends are provided.
> While the assembly began at two, three of the panel members did not arrive until much later.

ADDRESSES

3.12   Use figures to designate state, federal, and interstate highways.

> The Highway Department scheduled repairs for State Route 39, U.S. 30, and Interstate 64.

3.13   Spell out names of numbered streets up to and including *ten*. Use ordinal figures for numbered streets over ten.

> Eighth Avenue   Fourth Street
> 42nd Street   15th Avenue

3.14   Use figures for house and building numbers with the exception of *one*.

> 39 Timber Park Drive   19 East 21st Street
> 13165 Lincoln Parkway   One Market Avenue

3.15   Always use figures for ZIP Codes (separated from the state name by one space).

> Cincinnati, OH 45230   Asheville, NC 28805-4334

[Note: Place a hyphen after the fifth digit in a nine-digit ZIP Code.]

3.16   Use figures for apartment, rural delivery, post office box, and room numbers.

> Apartment 16   P.O. Box 93
> Room 302C   R.D. 2

AGES AND ANNIVERSARIES

3.17   In general, spell out ages.

> Bill's grandfather is eighty-eight years old.
> Mary's nine-year-old sister still requires a baby sitter.
> Although he is only six years old, Harvey plays the piano very well.

3.18 Use figures when an age is used in technical writing or when the age immediately follows a name.

> The subjects in the nutrition experiment were 11- and 12-year olds.
> Janene Crane, 13, is our top math student.

3.19 Use figures without commas for exact ages (when year, month, and days are given).

> RaeLynn was exactly 18 years 7 months and 2 days old.

3.20 Spell out ordinal numbers used in reference to birthdays and anniversaries if they can be written in one or two words. Use figures with the ordinal ending for larger numbers.

> Maria and Michael will celebrate their tenth wedding anniversary on Saturday.
> We will give Lynn a surprise party for her twenty-first birthday.
> The town council appointed a committee to plan for the 125th anniversary.

DATES AND TIMES

3.21 In correspondence, use figures for the date.

> February 13, 1995   13 February 1995   [military usage]
> On April 13, 1945, President Roosevelt died.

3.22 When the year is omitted from a date, do not express the day as an ordinal.

> His paper for the correspondence course was mailed on March 6.   [*not* March 6th]

3.23 A short form of the date is sometimes used for datelines in informal business communications and on some business forms.

> 8/24/95   8-24-95

3.24 In informal writing, the full number of a year may be abbreviated.

> The summer of '73 was marked by a large number of tornados.

3.25 Use figures for year dates preceded or followed by era designations. B.C. (*before Christ*) follows the year; A.D. (*anno Domini,* in the year of the Lord) precedes the year.

> 92 B.C.   A.D. 980

3.26 In legal documents, formal invitations, and proclamations, spell out dates or express them in figures as ordinals.

AFFIRMED this sixteenth day of May, nineteen hundred ninety-five.
AFFIRMED this 16th day of May, 1995.

3.27 Centuries and decades may be expressed in figures or words.

the 1700s   [*or* the seventeen hundreds]
the fourteenth century   the 30s

3.28 In general, spell out the time of day except when stating the exact time. Always spell out the time when using *o'clock.*

After working the night shift, Jan had breakfast at seven at her mother's house.
The school bell rings at exactly 8:15 each morning.
All staff must attend the orientation at eight o'clock.

3.29 Always use figures with *a.m.* or *p.m.* Do not use the words *evening, morning, afternoon,* or *o'clock* with *a.m.* or *p.m.*

All parents are invited to attend the 8:15 p.m. meeting to discuss the transfer of credits in the tech prep program.

Ciphers (*00*) are not used when expressing time on the hour.

The report must be on my desk no later than 3 p.m.   [*not* 3:00 p.m.]

[Note: The abbreviations *a.m.* and *p.m.* are generally not capitalized. In printed material, however, they may be shown in small capitals—A.M., P.M.]

3.30 Use the word *midnight* or *noon* when referring to twelve o'clock.

The study session begins at 6:30 p.m. and ends at 12 midnight.
We will meet for lunch at twelve o'clock noon.

3.31 In the 24-hour military system of time, use figures without *a.m.* or *p.m.*

0345 (*3:45 a.m.*)   2045 (*8:45 p.m.*)

DECIMALS, FRACTIONS, AND PERCENTAGES

3.32 Use figures for decimal numbers. Always place a zero before decimal fractions.

The average life of that product is 2.7 years.
The precise answer to the problem was 0.27387.

3.33 A series of fractions in a sentence is best understood when expressed in figures.

The winners received 1/8, 1/4, and 5/8 of the prize, respectively.

Spell out a fraction that appears alone in a sentence.

For her work in the project, Anna received a one-sixth share of the profits.

3.34 When keying a fraction that does not appear on the keyboard, use a diagonal between the two numbers.

1/6   5/16

When several fractions appear in the same sentence, do not mix fractions found on the keyboard and fractions made by using the diagonal.

Mr. Price asked what number could be divided by 1/2, 1/8, and 1/4.   [*not* ½, 1/8, and ¼]

3.35 Use figures for mixed numbers (numbers composed of whole numbers and fractions) except at the beginning of a sentence. When keying mixed numbers, leave one space between a whole number and the fraction. Never use a hyphen between a whole number and a fraction.

Michael purchased the stock at 37 5/16 and sold it for 40 3/16 a month later.

3.36 Hyphenate a spelled-out fraction used as a noun or an adjective unless an element of the fraction already contains a hyphen.

Don Wilson will use one-half of the profits for educational purposes.   [noun]
Each of the six holders of the winning lottery ticket will receive a one-sixth share. [adjective]
We've achieved fifteen thirty-seconds of our goal in just three months.

3.37 Spell out or use a decimal for percentages smaller than 1 percent. Spell out the word *percent*.

one-eighth of a percent   one-half of 1 percent
0.17 percent   0.777 percent

3.38 Use figures or a decimal for percentages of 1 percent or greater, unless the number begins a sentence.

The airline will grant a 25 percent discount on all tickets purchased seven days in advance.
Seven percent is the current interest rate on CDs.
The rate of inflation is currently pegged at 2.8 percent annually.

3

3.39 In a series of percents, the word *percent* follows the last figure in the series.

They quoted rates of 6, 8 1/2, 10 2/3, and 12 percent.

3.40 Use the percent symbol in tables and statistical matter.

1990	1993	1995
16%	10%	3%
43%	21%	5%

GOVERNMENT DESIGNATIONS

3.41 For specific governments, dynasties, and governing bodies, spell out numbers in ordinal form.

Fourth Republic   Third Reich   Seventh Dynasty

3.42 For political subdivisions, spell out in ordinal form numbers less than 100.

Third Circuit Court   Eighteenth Precinct
Eighty-Second Congress   Eighth Congressional District

3.43 For military units, spell out in ordinal form numbers less than 100.

Third Army   Twenty-Second Regiment
Fourth Battalion   Eighth Air Force

MONEY

3.44 Use figures for exact or approximate sums of money (with a dollar sign).

The mortgage called for a payment of $916.38 each month.
Sunita paid $29.16 for the textbook.
Mary's net worth was $236,919.16.
The salary was about $36,000 a year.

3.45 Use figures and words for very large amounts of money expressed in round numbers with a dollar sign.

$827 million $6.2 billion $19 1/2 trillion

3.46 Spell out, or use figures for, fractional amounts of large sums of money.

one-half of a million dollars
a half-million dollars *or* $500,000

3.47 Do not use a decimal point or ciphers (*.00*) with whole dollar amounts in a sentence.

Sarah left a tip of $13 for our waiter.   [*not* $13.00]
Randall paid $50 for his sweater while Tony bought one for $43.75.   [*not* $50.00]

3.48 For sums of money less than $1, use figures and the word *cents*. Do not use the dollar sign or decimal point unless related amounts require a dollar sign.

Lawrence smiled when he saw the dividend check was for only 68 cents.
Arturo paid $23.98 for a shirt, $14.50 for a tie, and only $.98 for a handkerchief.

3.49 Hyphenate a sum of money used as an adjective.

a 29-cent stamp   a $75-a-month raise

3.50 In legal documents, generally express amounts of money in both words and figures.

The buyer agrees to pay Seven Hundred Fifty-eight and 25/100 Dollars ($758.25).

3.51 Spell out indefinite sums of money.

a few hundred dollars   many millions of dollars

ORGANIZATIONS

3.52 Spell out in ordinal form all numbers that appear before the names of religious organizations.

Second Unitarian Church   First Assembly of God

3.53 Use figures for numbers designating local branches of unions and fraternal organizations.

VFW Post No. 75   Textile Workers Union No. 14

PLURALS OF NUMBERS

3.54 Form plurals of spelled-out numbers the same as plurals of other nouns.

Lynne asked for tens and twenties when she cashed the check.

3.55 To form the plurals of numbers written in figures, add *s*.

Millie, a good golfer, usually shoots in the 80s.
The skaters were required to include a series of figure 8s in their routines.

PUBLISHED MATERIALS

3.56 Use figures for numbers of pages, chapters, volumes, and so on. Use capitalized roman numerals for major divisions of a book.

A student found the error in Unit VI, Chapter 3, on page 28 of Volume 3.

QUANTITIES AND MEASUREMENTS

3.57 Use figures for distances unless they indicate fractional quantities.

The track team members were required to run 30 miles each week.
The distance from my house to the school is one-fourth mile.

3.58 Use figures for dimensions.

The piece of cloth measured 29 × 46 inches.
We have a 16′ × 32′ pool in our back yard.
Use a 2-inch top margin for the first page of your research paper.

3.59 Use figures for scientific measurements of distance, length, area, volume, pressure, and so on. No periods appear after abbreviations.

28 grams	110 volts
168 psi	96 meters
38 mi	2.617 cm

3.60 Use figures for quantities given in pints, quarts, bushels, and so on.

Maryanne purchased 3 quarts of milk and 2 pints of cream.
The agricultural market reported the sale of 13,000 bushels of corn.

3.61 Use figures for weights.

The truck weighed 4,667 pounds; the ball bearing weighed only 2 ounces.

3.62 Use figures for temperatures with the degree symbol (°). To express temperatures in Celsius, use the symbol °C.

The weather bureau reported a high temperature of 97° this afternoon.
Water freezes at a temperature of 0°C.

3

ROMAN NUMERALS

3.63 Use roman numerals to express volume and unit references in published materials. The general rule is that a letter before one of greater value subtracts from the value of the larger number; a letter after one of greater value adds to the value.

1	I	9	IX	17	XVII	70	LXX	600	DC
2	II	10	X	18	XVIII	80	LXXX	700	DCC
3	III	11	XI	19	XIX	90	XC	800	DCCC
4	IV	12	XII	20	XX	100	C	900	CM
5	V	13	XIII	30	XXX	200	CC	1,000	M
6	VI	14	XIV	40	XL	300	CCC	2,000	MM
7	VII	15	XV	50	L	400	CD	4,000	M$\overline{V}$
8	VIII	16	XVI	60	LX	500	D	5,000	$\overline{V}$

[Note: A dash over a roman numeral indicates that its original value is to be multiplied by 1000.]

SCORES AND VOTES

3.64 Use figures for scores of any kind and for results of elections.

The Bulls defeated the Suns by a score of 119–111.
Alonzo Witte won the tennis match 6–4, 6–7, 6–2.
Voters cast 80,264 votes in the last mayoral election.

SYMBOLS

3.65 Use the following symbols with expressions of numbers.

+	addition	8^2	exponent
&	ampersand (and)	′	feet, minutes
*	asterisk	″	inches, seconds
@	at or each	−	minus
[ ]	brackets	× or ·	multiplication
¢	cent(s)	#	number or pound
°	degree	¶	paragraph
$	dollar(s)	( )	parentheses
÷	division	/	per
£	English pound	%	percent
=	equals	:	ratio

(Name)

In the following sentences, circle the proper expression of the number.

1. WITNESSETH this (twelfth, 12th) day of April, nineteen hundred eighty-seven.

2. The guitar cost (two hundred twelve dollars and two cents, $212.02).

3. Her son is (four years, two months, and twelve days; 4 years 2 months and 12 days) old.

4. The race was (11, eleven) miles (four hundred, 400) yards long.

5. There are nearly (one-hundred twenty-one, 121) million people in the country.

6. The (3rd, Third) Reich met its downfall in 1945.

7. The (4, four) students began their journey, leaving at (eleven, 11 a.m.) in the morning from the hotel on Route (twenty, 20).

8. The analysis shows that there are (one point six, 1.6) grams of the foreign substance in the prescription.

9. Marilyn paid (38.00, $38) for the bicycle; she bought it at the (Fourth, 4th) Ward public auction.

10. Their offices are located at (1, One) Enterprise Place and (4, Four) Highland Avenue.

11. On May (fifth, 5), the heirs of the deceased received (one half, one fourth, and one fourth; 1/2, 1/4, and 1/4) of the estate, respectively.

12. She carried (four, 4) cameras, (19, nineteen) rolls of film, and (16, sixteen) flashbulbs in (two, 2) suitcases.

13. The cost of the building was (two hundred twenty-three million dollars, $223 million).

14. He is (six feet, three inches; 6′3″) tall; he weighs (one hundred eighty-three, 183) pounds.

15. On June 16, the Printers' Union No. (Sixteen, 16) voted (two hundred, 200) for the strike, (two hundred forty-one, 241) against.

16. The supervisor asked for (thirty-eight, 38) four-page booklets.

17. On April (22, 22nd) the Class of (Sixty-two, '62) held its (twenty-fifth, 25th) reunion.

18. The town hall blows the whistle at exactly (12 noon, 12 o'clock noon) every day.

19. (53%, Fifty-three percent) of those graduating went into business.

20. The stock market fell (28 1/2, 28-1/2) points in a matter of seconds.

Read the following letter. Circle any incorrect expressions of numbers.

May 23rd, 1993

Ms. Winnie Malone, Director
XYZ Company
1 Center Boulevard
Tampa, FL 33673-1404

Dear Ms. Malone

Seven days ago I wrote you concerning the accident involving
one of your drivers on 8th Avenue at 3:30 p.m. o'clock. 7
minutes after the accident, police officers from the Eleventh
Precinct arrived. They determined the distance between the
initial impact and the actual stopping point to be one hundred seventy-six feet. A total of 3 citations were issued to
your driver.

Damage to my car amounted to $750.00 as determined by esti-
mates from 3 repair shops. In addition, I paid $75.65 for a
rental car, which could have cost several $100 more. I was
given a 7 percent discount. I also incurred other expenses.
Because I was out of work for a while, I did not receive a
$25-a-month raise. In addition, my son Ronnie, twelve,
missed twenty-one days of school, almost 1/3 of the marking
period.

Most of the 21 witnesses to the accident are willing to testify. Your secretary told me to expect 7 ten-page documents
from your office to be returned by May 31st. This will be
difficult to do since it will take about 5 days just to read
the documents.

Please call me after 7 o'clock to discuss this matter.

Sincerely

Rhonda Wilson
Apartment Ten, State Route Nine
Tampa, FL 33673

Check your answers in the back of the book.

UNIT 4

ABBREVIATIONS

Abbreviations are shortened forms of words or phrases used to save space. As a rule, avoid using abbreviations because of the possibility of misunderstanding. Abbreviations may be acceptable when used traditionally, when called for in technical writing, or when necessary because of spacing problems.

To decide whether to abbreviate, follow what has been the custom, what is needed to maintain clarity, and what is needed for the degree of formality required. Do not use abbreviations for ordinary words in general writing or business communication.

The trend is away from the use of periods with many abbreviations. Where they have traditionally appeared, periods have been left in the examples that follow. Whatever you do, be consistent in using each category of abbreviation.

ACADEMIC DEGREES

4.1 Academic degrees that stand alone may be abbreviated except in very formal writing. Abbreviate academic degrees if they follow full names. Do not use titles such as *Mr., Mrs., Dr., Miss,* or *Ms.* when an academic degree follows a name.

Montgomery Jackson, Ph.D.   J. D. Bryan, M.D.

John received his M.A. degree last year.

4.2 A list of common abbreviations for academic degrees follows. A period, with no space after, follows each part of the abbreviation.

A.A.   Associate of Arts
B.A. *or*
A.B.   Bachelor of Arts
B.B.A.   Bachelor of Business Administration
B.C.E.   Bachelor of Civil (*or* Chemical) Engineering
B.D.   Bachelor of Divinity
B.L.S.   Bachelor of Library Sciences
B.S.   Bachelor of Science
D.B.A.   Doctor of Business Administration

D.D.	Doctor of Divinity
D.D.S.	Doctor of Dental Surgery (*or* Science)
D.Sc.	Doctor of Science
Ed.D.	Doctor of Education
J.D.	Doctor of Jurisprudence (Law)
L.H.D.	Doctor of Humanities
Litt.D.	Doctor of Letters
LL.B.	Bachelor of Laws
LL.D.	Doctor of Laws
M.A.	Master of Arts
M.B.A.	Master of Business Administration
M.D.	Doctor of Medicine
M.Ed.	Master of Education
M.S.	Master of Science
Ph.D.	Doctor of Philosophy
Th.D.	Doctor of Theology

ADDRESSES AND GEOGRAPHICAL TERMS

4.3 The following terms are sometimes abbreviated in addresses. Avoid abbreviating such words in inside addresses.

Ave.	Avenue	La. *or* Ln.	Lane	St.	Street
Bldg.	Building	Pkwy.	Parkway	Terr.	Terrace
Blvd.	Boulevard	Pl.	Place	Hgwy.	Highway
Ct.	Court	Rd.	Road	Tpk.	Turnpike
Dr.	Drive	Sq.	Square		

4.4 Always spell out names of countries and their states, territories, or possessions when they stand alone.

Great Britain   [*not* G. Brit.]   Germany   [*not* Ger.]

4.5 The following table contains the standard and two-letter abbreviations (used with ZIP Codes) for states, districts, and territories of the United States. (The following states do not have standard abbreviations: Alaska, Hawaii, Idaho, Iowa, Maine, Ohio, and Utah.)

State	Standard Abbreviation	Two-Letter Abbreviation
Alabama	Ala.	AL
Alaska	—	AK
Arizona	Ariz.	AZ
Arkansas	Ark.	AR
California	Calif.	CA
Colorado	Colo.	CO

State	Standard Abbreviation	Two-Letter Abbreviation
Connecticut	Conn.	CT
Delaware	Del.	DE
Florida	Fla.	FL
Georgia	Ga.	GA
Hawaii	—	HI
Idaho	—	ID
Illinois	Ill.	IL
Indiana	Ind.	IN
Iowa	—	IA
Kansas	Kans.	KS
Kentucky	Ky.	KY
Louisiana	La.	LA
Maine	—	ME
Maryland	Md.	MD
Massachusetts	Mass.	MA
Michigan	Mich.	MI
Minnesota	Minn.	MN
Mississippi	Miss.	MS
Missouri	Mo.	MO
Montana	Mont.	MT
Nebraska	Nebr.	NE
Nevada	Nev.	NV
New Hampshire	N.H.	NH
New Jersey	N.J.	NJ
New Mexico	N. Mex.	NM
New York	N.Y.	NY
North Carolina	N.C.	NC
North Dakota	N. Dak.	ND
Ohio	—	OH
Oklahoma	Okla.	OK
Oregon	Oreg.	OR
Pennsylvania	Pa.	PA
Rhode Island	R.I.	RI
South Carolina	S.C.	SC
South Dakota	S. Dak.	SD
Tennessee	Tenn.	TN
Texas	Tex.	TX
Utah	—	UT
Vermont	Vt.	VT
Virginia	Va.	VA
Washington	Wash.	WA
West Virginia	W. Va.	WV
Wisconsin	Wis.	WI
Wyoming	Wyo.	WY

4

State	Standard Abbreviation	Two-Letter Abbreviation
Districts and Territories of the United States		
District of Columbia	D.C.	DC
Federated States of Micronesia	—	FM
Guam	Guam	GU
Marshall Islands	—	MH
Northern Mariana Islands	—	MP
Puerto Rico	P.R.	PR
Virgin Islands	V.I.	VI

4.6 Do not abbreviate *Fort, Mount, Point,* or *Port* in place names. Use the abbreviation *St.* for *Saint* in place names.

Fort Riley	Mount Mitchell
Port Huron	St. Louis

4.7 The following list includes the standard and two-letter abbreviations for Canadian provinces.

Province	Standard Abbreviation	Two-Letter Abbreviation
Alberta	Alta.	AB
British Columbia	B.C.	BC
Manitoba	Man.	MB
New Brunswick	N.B.	NB
Newfoundland	Nfld./Newf.	NF
Northwest Territories	N.W.T.	NT
Nova Scotia	N.S.	NS
Ontario	Ont.	ON
Prince Edward Island	P.E.I.	PE
Quebec	P.Q. *or* Que.	PQ
Saskatchewan	Sask.	SK
Yukon Territory	Y.T. *or* Yuk.	YT

4

BROADCASTING STATIONS

4.8 To abbreviate radio and television broadcasting stations and networks, use capital letters without periods or spaces.

WMIT	WABC	KRLD
KOA-TV	KISS-FM	ABC
CBS	NBC	PBS

COMPANY NAMES

4.9 The following abbreviations are often used as part of company names.

Bro.	Brother	Inc.	Incorporated
Bros.	Brothers	Ltd.	Limited
Co.	Company	Mfg.	Manufacturing
Corp.	Corporation	Mfrs.	Manufacturers

COMPASS POINTS

4.10 To abbreviate compass points, use capital letters without periods or spaces.

N	North	NW	Northwest
S	South	SW	Southwest
E	East	NNE	North by Northeast
W	West	SSE	South by Southeast
NE	Northeast	NNW	North by Northwest
SE	Southeast	SSW	South by Southwest

COMPUTER TERMINOLOGY

4.11 Use capital letters without periods or spaces for the following common computer terms.

AI	Artificial Intelligence
ALU	Arithmetic Logic Unit
ASCII	American Standard Code for Information Interchange
BASIC	Beginner's All-Purpose Symbolic Instruction Code
BBS	Bulletin Board Service
Bit	Binary Digit
CAD	Computer-Aided Design
CAI	Computer-Aided Instruction
CAM	Computer-Aided Manufacturing
CD-ROM	Compact Disk-Read Only Memory
COBOL	Common Business-Oriented Language
COM	Computer Output to Microfilm (*or* Microfiche)
CPU	Central Processing Unit
CRT	Cathode-Ray Tube
DAT	Digital Audiotape
DOS	Disk Operating System
DTP	Desktop Publishing
EBCDIC	Extended Binary Coded Decimal Interchange Code

4

EDP	Electronic Data Processing
FORTRAN	Formula Translator
GB	Gigabyte
GUI	Graphical User Interface
I/O	Input/Output
K	Kilobyte (1024 bytes)
LAN	Local Area Network
MB	Megabyte
MICR	Magnetic Ink Character Recognition
MIDI	Musical Instrument Digital Interface
MIS	Management Information System
OCR	Optical Character Recognition
PC	Personal Computer
RAM	Random-Access Memory
ROM	Read-Only Memory
VDT	Video-Display Terminal
WAN	Wide Area Network
WORM	Write Once Read Many
WYSIWYG	What You See Is What You Get

DATES AND TIMES

4.12 In text, spell out names of months and days of the week. They may be abbreviated, however, in tables and footnotes. When abbreviating months and days, use the following.

Months of the Year

Jan.	January	July *or* Jul.	July
Feb.	February	Aug.	August
Mar.	March	Sept. *or* Sep.	September
Apr.	April	Oct.	October
May	May	Nov.	November
June *or* Jun.	June	Dec.	December

Days of the Week

Sun.	Sunday	Thurs. *or* Thu.	Thursday
Mon.	Monday	Fri.	Friday
Tues. *or* Tue.	Tuesday	Sat.	Saturday
Wed.	Wednesday		

4.13 Abbreviate time periods of the day as follows.

a.m.	before noon	[*ante meridiem*]
p.m.	after noon	[*post meridiem*]

4.14   To abbreviate the time zones in the continental United States, use capital letters without periods or spaces.

CST	Central Standard Time	MST	Mountain Standard Time
DST	Daylight Saving Time	PST	Pacific Standard Time
EST	Eastern Standard Time	EDT	Eastern Daylight Time

4.15   Other abbreviations associated with time are as follows, some of which are written without periods.

A.D.	*anno Domini* [in the year of our Lord]	min	minute
		mo	month
B.C.	before Christ	sec	second
d	day	yr	year
hr	hour		

GOVERNMENT AGENCIES

4.16   To abbreviate well-known government agencies, use capital letters with no periods or spaces.

BIA	Bureau of Indian Affairs
CAB	Civil Aeronautics Board
CIA	Central Intelligence Agency
CIC	Consumer Information Center
CPSC	Consumer Product Safety Commission
CSC	Civil Service Commission
EEOC	Equal Employment Opportunity Commission
EPA	Environmental Protection Agency
FAA	Federal Aviation Administration
FBI	Federal Bureau of Investigation
FCC	Federal Communications Commission
FDA	Food and Drug Administration
FDIC	Federal Deposit Insurance Corporation
FHA	Federal Housing Administration
FPC	Federal Power Commission
FRB	Federal Reserve Bank (*or* Board)
FRS	Federal Reserve System
FSLIC	Federal Savings and Loan Insurance Corporation
FTC	Federal Trade Commission
GAO	General Accounting Office
GPO	Government Printing Office
GSA	General Services Administration
HHS	Department of Health and Human Services
HUD	Department of Housing and Urban Development
ICC	Interstate Commerce Commission
INS	Immigration and Naturalization Service

4

IRS   Internal Revenue Service
MBDA   Minority Business Development Agency
NASA   National Aeronautics and Space Administration
NIST   National Institute of Standards and Technology
NIE   National Institute of Education
NLRB   National Labor Relations Board
NRC   Nuclear Regulatory Commission
NSC   National Security Council
OMB   Office of Management and Budget
PHS   Public Health Service
ROTC   Reserve Officers' Training Corps
SBA   Small Business Administration
SEC   Securities and Exchange Commission
SSA   Social Security Administration
SSS   Selective Service System
TVA   Tennessee Valley Authority
USA   United States Army
USAF   United States Air Force
USCG   United States Coast Guard
USDA   United States Department of Agriculture
USIA   United States Information Agency
USMC United States Marine Corps
USN   United States Navy
VA   Veterans' Administration

MEASUREMENT UNITS

4.17 Spell out measurement units except in scientific or technical writing. The following abbreviations generally represent standard units of measure. Abbreviations of units of measure are the same in the singular and plural form. Generally, abbreviate units of measure without periods.

Length

in	inch	rd	rod (5½ yd)
ft	foot (12 in)	mi	mile (5,280 ft)
yd	yard (3 ft)		

Area

sq in	square inch	sq rd	square rod (30¼ sq yd)
sq ft	square foot (144 sq in)	sq mile	(640 acres)
sq yd	square yard (9 sq ft)		

Volume

cu in	cubic inch
cu ft	cubic foot (1,728 cu in)
cu yd	cubic yard (27 cu ft)

Weight

gr	grain	lb	pound (16 oz)
dr	dram (27.344 gr)	cwt	hundredweight (100 lb)
oz	ounce (16 dr)	t	ton 2,000 lb)

Dry Measure

pt	pint	pk	peck (8 qt)
qt	quart (2 pt)	bu	bushel (4 pk)

Liquid Measure

oz	fluid ounce	gal	gallon (4 qt)
pt	pint (16 fl oz)	bbl	barrel (31.5 gal)
qt	quart (2 pt)		

METRIC MEASUREMENTS

4.18 To abbreviate metric measures, do not use periods.

Length

mm	millimeter	dam	dekameter (10 m)
cm	centimeter (10 mm)	hm	hectometer (10 dam)
dm	decimeter (10 cm)	km	kilometer (10 hm)
m	meter (10 dm)		

Area

mm^2	square millimeter	dam^2	square dekameter (100 m^2)
cm^2	square centimeter (100 mm^2)	hm^2	square hectometer (100 dam^2)
dm^2	square decimeter (100 cm^2)	km^2	square kilometer (100 hm^2)
m^2	square meter (100 dm^2)		

Volume

mm^3	cubic millimeter	dam^3	cubic dekameter (1,000 m^3)
cm^3	cubic centimeter (1,000 mm^3)	hm^3	cubic hectometer (1,000 dam^3)
dm^3	cubic decimeter (1,000 cm^3)	km^3	cubic kilometer (1,000 hm^3)
m^3	cubic meter (1,000 dm^3)		

4

Weight

mg	milligram	dag	dekagram (10 g)
cg	centigram (10 mg)	hg	hectogram (10 dag)
dg	dekigram (10 cg)	kg	kilogram (10 hg)
g	gram (10 dg)		

Capacity

ml	milliliter	dal	dekaliter (10 l)
cl	centiliter (10 ml)	hl	hectoliter (10 dal)
dl	dekiliter (10 cl)	kl	kiloliter (10 hl)
l	liter (10 dl)		

4.19 The following are metric equivalents of several standard measurements.

1 in	= 2.54 cm		1 pt	= 0.47 l
1 ft	= 0.305 m		1 qt	= 0.95 l
1 yd	= 0.914 m		1 gal	= 3.79 l
1 mi	= 1.609 km			
1 sq in	= 6.5 cm^2		1 oz	= 28.35 g
1 sq ft	= 0.09 m^2		1 lb	= 0.45 kg
1 sq yd	= 0.8 m^2		1 t	= 1,000 kg
1 A	= 4,047 m^2			
1 cu in	= 16.4 cm^3			
1 cu ft	= 0.03 m^3			
1 cu yd	= 0.8 m^3			

4.20 The following are standard equivalents of several metric quantities.

1 mm	= 0.04 in		1 ml	= 0.034 oz
1 cm	= 0.4 in		1 cl	= 0.34 oz
1 m	= 39.37 in		1 l	= 2.1 pt; 1.06 qt; 0.26 gal
1 km	= 0.6 mi		1 g	= 0.035 oz
1 cm^2	= 0.16 sq in		1 kg	= 2.2 lb
1 m^2	= 10.8 sq ft; 1.2 sq yd			
1 cm^3	= 0.06 cu in			
1 m^3	= 35.3 cu ft; 1.3 cu yd			

4

NAMES
. . . .

4.21 As a general rule, do not abbreviate the given names of individuals.

James [*not* Jas.] Wilson   Margaret [*not* Marg.] Martinez

4.22 Use no periods when referring to persons by initials only.

JFK	John Fitzgerald Kennedy
FDR	Franklin Delano Roosevelt
HRC	Hillary Rodham Clinton

ORGANIZATIONS

4.23 To abbreviate well-known organizations, use capital letters with no spaces or periods.

AAA	American Automobile Association
ABA	American Bankers Association; American Bar Association
ABC	American Broadcasting Company
ACLU	American Civil Liberties Union
AFL-CIO	American Federation of Labor and Congress of Industrial Organizations
AIB	American Institute of Banking
AICPA	American Institute of Certified Public Accountants
AMA	American Medical Association; American Management Association
AMEX	American Stock Exchange
AMS	Administrative Management Society
AP	Associated Press
ASCAP	American Society of Composers, Authors, and Publishers
ASE	American Stock Exchange
AT&T	American Telephone and Telegraph Company
BBB	Better Business Bureau
BBC	British Broadcasting Corporation
CBS	Columbia Broadcasting System
GOP	Grand Old Party (Republican)
IBM	International Business Machines
ILGWU	International Ladies' Garment Workers' Union
MADD	Mothers Against Drunk Driving
NAACP	National Association for the Advancement of Colored People
NAM	National Association of Manufacturers
NATO	North Atlantic Treaty Organization
NBC	National Broadcasting Company
NCR	National Cash Register
NEA	National Education Association
NEA	National Endowment for the Arts
NIMH	National Institute of Mental Health
NPR	National Public Radio
NOW	National Organization for Women
NYSE	New York Stock Exchange
OPEC	Organization of Petroleum Exporting Countries
PAC	Political Action Committee

4

PBS	Public Broadcasting System
PTA	Parent-Teacher Association
PTO	Parent-Teacher Organization
RCA	Radio Corporation of America
SPCA	Society for the Prevention of Cruelty to Animals
SADD	Students Against Driving Drunk
UN	United Nations
UNESCO	United Nations Educational, Scientific, and Cultural Organization
UNICEF	United Nations International Children's Emergency Fund
WHO	World Health Organization
YMCA	Young Men's Christian Association
YWCA	Young Women's Christian Association
ZOA	Zionist Organization of America

4.24 Generally, spell out a company or organization name when first used; then abbreviate the name in the remainder of the writing if the abbreviation is well known.

The *American Telephone and Telegraph Company* is one of the largest communication companies in the country. *AT&T,* as it is sometimes called, provides long-distance service in most areas.

SCIENTIFIC TERMS

4.25 The following are common scientific abbreviations.

A	ampere	FM	frequency modulation
A	angstrom Unit	ft-lb	foot-pound
a.c. *or* AC	alternating current	hp	horsepower
AM	amplitude modulation	°K	degree Kelvin
at wt	atomic weight	kW	kilowatt
avdp.	avoirdupois	m.p.	melting point
bar.	barometer	mph	miles per hour
bp	boiling point	neg.	negative
Btu	British thermal unit	psi	pounds per square inch
°C	degree Celsius	R	roentgen
	(centigrade)	r.p.m.	revolutions per minute
cal	calorie	sp gr	specific gravity
cc	cubic centimeter	std.	standard
d.c. *or* DC	direct current	T	temperature
dB	decibel	V	volt
deg	degree	W	watt
°F	degree Fahrenheit	wt	weight

TITLES

4.26 Do not abbreviate civil, military, or religious titles preceding surnames (last names) only.

General Ridgeway   [*not* Gen. Ridgeway]
Senator Dole   [*not* Sen. Dole]
Monsignor Radewicz   [*not* Mgr. Radewicz]

4.27 Civil, military, or religious titles preceding full names may be abbreviated.

Gen. Colin Powell   Fr. John O'Donnell
Sen. Nancy Kassebaum   Adm. J. William Kime

4.28 Always abbreviate social titles.

Mr.	Mister	Messrs.	Messieurs (plural of *Mr.*)
M.	Monsieur	Mmes.	Mesdames (plural of *Madame* and *Mrs.*)
Mrs.	Mistress	Mses. *or* Mss.	(plural of *Ms.*)
Mme.	Madame	Misses	(plural of *Miss*)
Ms.	Miss *or* Mrs.	Dr.	Doctor
Mlle.	Mademoiselle		

[Note: The title *Miss* is not an abbreviation and is not followed by a period. Never use the title *Ms.* with a woman's husband's name (i.e., *Ms. Bruce Hurst* is incorrect).]

4.29 Abbreviate seniority titles (*Jr.* for *Junior* and *Sr.* for *Senior*) that follow full names.

John F. Kennedy Jr.   Mr. Wayne Wilson Maclin Sr.

Use *Esq.* only with a preceding full name or name with initials. No title should precede the form *Esq.*

Landrun R. Thames, Esq.

COMMON ABBREVIATIONS

4.30 Except in technical or scientific writing, most terms should generally be written in full. In situations where space is limited or for ease in notetaking in lecture classes, shortened forms of terms may be useful. The following is a list of common abbreviations not found in the preceding sections.

abbr.	abbreviation	cont.	continued
abr.	abridged	CPA	certified public
a/c	account current		accountant
acct.	account	CPS	certified profes-
admin.	administration		sional secretary
advt.	advertisement	cr.	credit, creditor
agt.	agent, agreement	cust.	customer
AI	Artificial Intelligence	d.b.a. *or* DBA	doing business as
a.k.a.	also known as	dept.	department
amt.	amount	disc.	discount
anon.	anonymous	dist.	district
ans.	answer	div.	dividend, division,
AP	accounts payable		divisor
approx.	approximate	doz.	dozen
appt.	appoint, appointment	dr.	debit, debtor
apt.	apartment	ea.	each
AR	accounts receivable	ed.	edition, editor
ar.	arrive, arrival	e.g.	*exempli gratia*
ASAP	as soon as possible		(for example)
asgmt.	assignment	enc. *or* encl.	enclosure
Assn.	Association	e.o.m.	end of month
asst.	assistant	Esq.	Esquire
ATM	automatic teller machine	est.	estimated
att.	attachment	ETA	estimated time of arrival
Attn.	Attention	et al.	*et alii* (and others)
atty.	attorney	etc.	*et cetera* (and so forth)
avg.	average	ex.	example
bal.	balance	exec.	executive, executor
B/F	brought forward	exp.	expense
bk.	book	fed.	federal
B/L	bill of lading	ff.	and the following pages
bldg.	building	FIFO	first in, first out
B/S	bill of sale	fig.	figure
c	copy	f.o.b.	free on board
cap.	capital, capitalize	frt.	freight
cat.	catalogue	FY	fiscal year
CD	certificate of deposit *or*	FYI	for your information
	compact disc	govt.	government
CEO	chief executive officer	HMO	health maintenance
CFO	chief financial officer		organization
ch. *or* chap.	chapter	hq.	headquarters
chg.	charge, change	ibid.	*ibidem* (in the same place)
c.i.f.	cost, insurance, and	i.e.	*id est* (that is)
	freight	incl.	including, inclusive
c.l.	carload	ins.	insurance
c/o	in care of	int.	interest
c.o.d. *or* COD	collect (*or* cash) on	intl.	international
	delivery	inv.	invoice

IOU	I owe you	RD	rural delivery
IQ	intelligence quotient	recd.	received
ital.	italic	ref.	reference
jour.	journal	Rep.	Representative, Republican
J.P.	justice of the peace		
k	carat	req.	require, requisition
lat.	latitude	reqd.	required
L/C	letter of credit	rm.	ream, room
lc	lowercase	R.N.	registered nurse
LIFO	last in, first out	rpm	revolutions per minute
long.	longitude		
max.	maximum	RR or R.R.	railroad, rural route
mdse.	merchandise	r.s.v.p.	respond, if you please
memo	memorandum	rte.	route
mfg.	manufacturing	SASE	self-addressed stamped envelope
mfr.	manufacturer		
mgr.	manager	sec.	secretary
min.	minimum	sp.	spelling, special
misc.	miscellaneous	spec.	specification
mkt.	market	SRO	standing room only
mpg	miles per gallon	St.	saint
mph	miles per hour	std.	standard
N/30	net in 30 days	steno	stenographer
N.A.	not applicable, not avail-able, North America	stmt.	statement
		sub.	substitute
no.	number	subj.	subject
nos.	numbers	supt.	superintendent
opt.	optional	tbs. or tbsp.	tablespoon
orig.	original	tchr.	teacher
O/S	out of stock	tech.	technical
OTC	over the counter	tel.	telegraph, telegram, telephone
p., pp.	page, pages		
par.	paragraph	temp.	temperature
payt.	payment	tkt.	ticket
PBX	private branch (telephone) exchange	TM	trademark
		treas.	treasury, treasurer
pd.	paid	tripl.	triplicate
PERT	program evaluation and review technique	tsp.	teaspoon
		TV	television
pkg.	package	TWX	teletypewriter exchange
PO	purchase order	typo.	typographical
P.O.	post office	typw.	typewriter
ppd.	postpaid, prepaid	Univ.	university
pr.	pair	UPC	universal product code
P.S.	postscript	val.	value
pt.	point, part, port	var.	variable, variety
qr.	quarter	VDT	video display terminal
qty.	quantity	ver.	verse, version

4

VHF	very high frequency
VIP	very important person
vol.	volume
vou.	voucher
VP	vice president
vs.	versus (legal)
wd.	word
whsle.	wholesale
wk.	week
wkly.	weekly
w/o	without
wt.	weight
uc	uppercase
UFO	unidentified flying object
UHF	ultrahigh frequency
yr.	year
yrs.	yours
ZIP	Zone Improvement Plan

ABBREVIATIONS FOUND IN SOURCES

4.31   The following is a list of abbreviations commonly found in sources for research papers and reports.

© *or* c	copyright; as in ©*1995* to show date of copyright
c., ca	approximately; as in *1839 c.* or *ca 1839*
cf.	compare; as in *cf. Monroe Doctrine*
ed.	editor, edited, or edition; as in *ed. Ronald Jones*
e.g.	for example; as in *e.g., the rings around Saturn*
et al.	and other people; as in *John F. Mason et al.*
f., ff.	following pages; as in *p. 636ff.*
ibid.	in the same place as preceding source; as in *ibid., Mason, p. 116*
i.e.	that is; as in *i.e., the report of May 16*
loc. cit.	in the place cited; as in *Mason, loc. cit.*
N.B.	note well; as in *N.B. Mason article*
op. cit.	in the work cited; as in *Mason, op. cit., p. 173*
p., pp.	page or pages; as in *pp. 173-74*
sic	thus, or as it was written; as in *"I'd rather dye [sic] than admit I was wrong"*

Do not underscore or italicize *loc. cit., op. cit.,* or *ibid.* in their use as sources.

4

_____

(Name)

Indicate which of the following abbreviations or expressions correctly represent the words in parentheses by writing *C* in the blank. For incorrect items,
write the corrected abbreviation or expression in the blank.

1. M.A. (Master of Arts)   _____

2. Gen. Thompson (General Thompson)   _____

3. Calif. *and* CA (California)   _____

4. P.R. *and* PI (Puerto Rico)   _____

5. B.C. *and* BC (British Columbia)   _____

6. Brots. (Brothers)   _____

7. NNW (North by Northeast)   _____

8. CPR (Central Processing Unit)   _____

9. OCR (Optical Character Recognition)   _____

10. Sept. or Se. (September)   _____

11. Wed. (Wednesday)   _____

12. F. B. I. (Federal Bureau of Investigation)   _____

13. ft (foot)   _____

14. pi (pint)   _____

15. Adm. Lynn J. White (Admiral Lynn J. White)   _____

16. mr (meter)   _____

17. F.A.N. (Frank A. Nelson)   _____

18. Rev. McNamara (Reverend McNamara)   _____

19. i.e. (that is)   _____

20. sic (thus)   _____

SELF-CHECK EXERCISE 2, *UNIT 4*

Using correct abbreviations, rewrite the following examples in the blanks.

1. (inside address)

   Mister John White

   1721 First Av.

   New Orleans, LO 70183

   _____

   _____

   _____

2. Ft. Riley is located in Kans.

   _____

3. John works for station W.N.I.T. in Boston, MS.

   _____

4. Eliz. Wortham received her PHD last Aug.

   _____

5. Doctor John T. Smith, Junior lives on West Blvd.

   _____

6. Miss Henrietta White, Ed.D. is from G. Brit.

   _____

7. (envelope address)

   Acme Glass Comp.

   1900 Center Rd.

   Jacksonville, FA 45333

   _____

   _____

   _____

SELF-CHECK EXERCISE 3, *UNIT 4*

_____

(Name)

Write the full names of the following computer-related abbreviations.

1. AI   _____

2. CPU   _____

3. DOS   _____

4. LAN   _____

5. RAM   _____

SELF-CHECK EXERCISE 4, *UNIT 4*

Write the correct abbreviations or terms in the following spaces.

 1. British Thermal Unit _____

 2. direct current   _____

 3. as soon as possible _____

 4. Association   _____

 5. automatic teller machine _____

 6. c   _____

 7. tsp.   _____

 8. hp   _____

 9. mph   _____

10. cont.   _____

11. superintendent   _____

12. Certified Public Accountant _____

13. department _____

14. Esquire _____

15. et cetera _____

16. VP _____

17. weekly _____

18. estimated time of arrival _____

19. without _____

20. year _____

Check your answers in the back of the book.

UNIT 5

GRAMMAR

A knowledge of the rules of grammar will enable you to speak and write more effectively. The following rules are those most commonly observed in general writing and in business communication.

ADJECTIVES

5.1 An *adjective* is a word that describes or modifies a noun or pronoun by telling which one, what kind, or how many.

Mona wore *red* shoes and a *blue* sweater with *three* stripes.
An *icy, wintry* wind whistled through the *wide* cracks in the cabin.
Many suggestions were made regarding the handling of *customer* complaints.
This fabric is typically used on *that* kind of coat.

5.2 A *proper adjective* is either an adjective derived from a proper noun or a proper noun used as an adjective. As with a proper noun, a proper adjective is capitalized.

During our *African* safari, we drank a lot of *English* tea.
The *Japanese* railway system is one of the world's finest.

5.3 A *predicate adjective* follows a linking verb (*am, is, are, was, were, been, being, appear, become, feel, seem, taste,* and others) and describes the subject of the sentence.

Donna Jean is very *organized*.
The dessert tasted *delicious*.

5.4 *Articles* (*a, an,* and *the*) are the most frequently used adjectives. *A* and *an* are *indefinite articles* and refer to something in a general category or group.

She saw *a* vase on display that she wanted.
Janice waited *an* hour before she left for class.

5

Use *a* before words beginning with a consonant or consonant sound. Use *an* before words beginning with a vowel or vowel sound.

a drink   *an* apple   *an h*our
a bowl   *an o*range

5.5 A *compound adjective* consists of two or more words combined to form a single descriptive adjective. A compound adjective is generally hyphenated only if it immediately precedes the noun it modifies.

The teacher used an *easy-to-hard* arrangement of questions on the examination.
The teacher arranged the questions on the examination from *easy to hard.*

5.6 Adjectives are often used to compare two or more persons or things. To make comparisons, adjectives have different forms or degrees. The three degrees of comparison are the positive, the comparative, and the superlative.

Positive	Comparative	Superlative
fast	faster	fastest
hot	hotter	hottest

5.7 Use the *positive degree* when no comparison is being made. The adjective modifies only one person or thing.

Rudy is a *good* swimmer.
The sun was *hot* during the middle of the day.

5.8 Use the *comparative degree* to compare two persons or things. To form the comparative degree of most adjectives, add *-er* to the positive form.

Annette is a *fast* reader.   [positive]
Jack is a *faster* reader than Annette.   [comparative]

To form the comparative degree of most adjectives having more than two sylla- bles and of most adjectives that end in *-ful* or *-less*, use either the word *more* or *less* with the positive form.

Daniel is *more studious* than Rudy.
Dennis is *less careful* on the road than Elaine.

5.9 Use the *superlative degree* to compare three or more persons or things. To form the superlative degree of most adjectives, add *-est* to the positive form.

Annette is a *fast* reader.   [positive]
Jack is a *faster* reader than Annette.   [comparative]
Tony is the *fastest* reader of the three.   [superlative]

To form the superlative degree of most adjectives that have more than two syllables and of most adjectives that end in *-ful* or *-less*, use either the word *most* or *least* with the positive form.

Daniel is the *most studious* boy in school.
Jan is the *least creative* writer in the class.

5.10   Some adjectives show the comparative and superlative degrees in irregular ways, as shown in the following examples. Consult a dictionary when you are unsure of the correct form.

Positive	Comparative	Superlative
bad	worse	worst
good	better	best
many	more	most

ADVERBS

5.11   An *adverb* is a word that modifies or changes the meaning of a verb, an adjective, or another adverb. Adverbs tell when, where, how, and to what extent. Many adverbs are formed by adding the suffix *-ly* to an adjective.

Ross responded *immediately* to the question with an excellent answer.   [when]
William slid *sideways* down the icy street in his car.   [where]
Lucille *intently* stared at the picture of the woman.   [how]
Aileen was *very much* indebted to Susan for her kindness.   [to what extent]

5.12   Adverbs, like adjectives, can be used to compare two or more things. They, too, have three degrees: positive, comparative, and superlative.

Positive	Comparative	Superlative
hard	harder	hardest
tactfully	more tactfully	most tactfully

5.13   Use the *positive degree* when no comparison is being made.

Julian runs *fast.*

5.14   Use the *comparative degree* when two things or persons are being compared. To form the comparative degree of most adverbs, add *-er* to the positive degree or use either the word *more* or *less* with the positive degree.

Julian runs *faster* than Franco.
Of the two students, Lana submits her assignments *more promptly.*

5

5.15 Use the *superlative degree* when comparing more than two things or people. To form the superlative degree, add *-est* to the positive form or use either the word *most* or *least* with the positive degree.

> Of all the weight lifters at the health club, Al is the *strongest*.
> Lela's solo was the *most technically* correct.
> Anthony's routine was the *least skillfully* performed.

CONJUNCTIONS

5.16 A *conjunction* is a word that joins words, phrases, or clauses. Three types of conjunctions are coordinating, correlative, and subordinating.

5.17 A *coordinating conjunction* joins two or more words, phrases, or clauses of equal rank. The coordinating conjunctions are *and, but, for, or, nor, yet,* and *so.*

> The registrar's office *and* the residence halls will open on Monday *and* Tuesday. [joins two nouns]
> You must go through the front door *and* into the bedroom. [joins two phrases]
> Larry worked late into the night, *yet* he was not able to complete the assignment. [joins two independent clauses]

5.18 *Correlative conjunctions* are used in pairs to connect words, phrases, or clauses of equal rank. Commonly used correlative conjunctions are listed below.

either/or	both/and
neither/nor	not only/but also
whether/or	

> *Neither* Lisa *nor* Susan will appear on the program.
> Joseph *not only* proofread the report but also corrected the errors.

5.19 A *subordinating conjunction* begins dependent clauses and joins them to independent clauses. Commonly used subordinating conjunctions follow.

after	because	in order that	unless
although	before	since	until
as	for	so that	when
as if	if	than	where
as soon as	inasmuch as	that	wherever
as though	in case	though	while

> *Although* the outline was carefully prepared, the paper did not follow it adequately.
> Sharon needs to master French *so that* she can understand the language during her year in France.
> The class picnic was postponed until Friday *inasmuch* as it rained on Monday.

INTERJECTIONS

5.20   An *interjection* is a word that expresses very strong feelings, emotions, or sudden reactions. An exclamation point follows an interjection.

Stop! That car is running the red light!
Hooray! The superintendent declared a holiday for winning the championship.

5

NOUNS

5.21   A *noun* is a word that names a person, place, thing, or idea. A noun can be classified as a common noun, a proper noun, a concrete noun, an abstract noun, or a collective noun according to the type of thing it names.

5.22   A *common noun* names a person, place, thing, or idea in a general class.

boy	violin	village
house	minute	report

Mr. Willis purchased a *computer* for every *employee* in the *department.*

5.23   A *proper noun* names a particular person, place, or thing. Proper nouns are always capitalized.

Karen Shaeffer	Charlotte	Fashions Unlimited
Professor Smith	Pacific Ocean	Stetson University

Dr. Marilyn Stein is an obstetrician at *Cedars Hospital.*

5.24   A *concrete noun* refers to something that can be perceived directly.

Irene wore a stunning *dress.*
The *sunset* is certainly beautiful.

5.25   An *abstract noun* refers to an idea or concept, something that can be thought about but cannot be seen directly.

Honesty, truthfulness, and *loyalty* are important personal qualities.

5.26   A *collective noun* refers to a group of people, animals, or things.

audience	committee	family	pack
bunch	company	flock	savings
city	crowd	herd	series
class	faculty	nation	troop

The *crowd* listened intently as the coach spoke about the *team.*

5.27 A collective noun almost always refers to a group that the speaker considers to be acting as one unit. Use a singular verb when a collective noun acts as one unit.

> The *crew* meets each day before beginning work.
> The *ensemble* practices twice each week.

5.28 If a collective noun refers to a group in which the speaker considers the members to be acting individually, use a plural verb.

> On some occasions, the *squad have been asked* to stay for additional practice.
> The *council were pleased* to be recognized for their efforts.

[Note: Use of a plural verb with a collective noun occurs infrequently. A clearer way to write this type of sentence is to include the word *members*.]

> On some occasions, the squad members have been asked to stay for additional practice.
> The council members were pleased to be recognized for their efforts.

5.29 Expressions of fractions, time, measure, weight, and volume are usually singular and require a singular verb. Use a plural verb if the amount is thought of as separate units.

> *Four fifths* of the day *is spent* in class.
> *Six months is needed* to finish the manuscript.
> *Four fifths* of the students *make* excellent grades.

PREPOSITIONS

5.30 A *preposition* is a word that is used to join and show the relationship of a noun or pronoun to another part of the sentence. Commonly used prepositions follow.

about	below	including	over
above	beneath	inside	past
across	beside	into	through
after	between	like	to
against	beyond	near	toward
along	by	next	under
among	down	of	until
around	during	off	up
as	except	on	upon
at	for	onto	with
before	from	out	within
behind	in	outside	without

News *of* a tech prep curriculum was received *by* the students *with* great interest.
Mary entered the figures *in* the ledger *on* her desk.

5.31 A *prepositional phrase* is a group of words consisting of a preposition, a noun or pronoun, and, usually, a modifier.

Prepare your outline *in good form on one page* and place it *in a folder.*
Sign your name *beside the X* and return the form *within two days.*

5.32 A prepositional phrase that modifies a noun or pronoun is called an *adjective phrase.* (The prepositional phrase describes the noun or pronoun.)

The student *with the highest score* was Lenny Michaels.   [modifies *student*]

5.33 A prepositional phrase that modifies an adjective, adverb, or verb is called an *adverb phrase.*

Martha was very active *in student organizations.*   [modifies *active*]
Jonathan writes concisely and creatively *in every composition assignment.*   [modifies *concisely* and *creatively*]
John placed his report *in the basket.*   [modifies *placed*]

PRONOUNS

5.34 A *pronoun* is a word used to replace or refer to a noun.

5.35 A *personal pronoun* refers to a particular person or thing. A personal pronoun is usually referred to in terms of person (first, second, or third), number (singular or plural), gender (masculine, feminine, or neuter), and case (nominative, objective, or possessive).

Person

5.36 By changing its form, a personal pronoun can indicate whether the pronoun refers to the speaker (first person), to the person or thing spoken to (second person), or the person or thing spoken of (third person). The following chart shows the pronouns that are used with first, second, and third person.

Person	Singular	Plural
First	I, me, my, mine	we, us, our, ours
Second	you, your, yours	you, your, yours
Third	he, she, it, him, her, his, hers, its	they, them, their, theirs

Number

5.37   A personal pronoun usually has either a singular or a plural form (number). A *singular* form indicates only one person or thing. A *plural* form indicates two or more people or things. The pronoun *you,* however, is used for both the singular and the plural form.

> *I* asked Martha to explain the passage to *me.*   [singular]
> Please explain to the three of *them* why Al was late.   [plural]
> The mother told *her* son, "*You* must always tell the truth."   [singular]
> The principal said to the graduating class, "*You* must look to the future."   [plural]

Gender

5.38   *Gender* refers to the sex of the pronoun. Only third-person personal pronouns can be classified by gender. The masculine pronouns are *he, his,* and *him.* The feminine pronouns are *she, hers,* and *her.* The pronoun *it* is of neuter gender and refers to things that are neither masculine nor feminine.

All other personal pronouns (*I, you, your, our, ours, they, their,* and *them*) are referred to as common-gender pronouns because they can be either masculine or feminine.

Case

5.39   Depending on their use in sentences, pronouns can be in the nominative, objective, or possessive case.

5.40   The personal pronouns *I, he, she, we,* and *they* are always in the nominative case. They are used either as subjects or as predicate nominatives (also called *subject complements*) of sentences.

> *I* learned very quickly to update skills constantly.   [subject]
> Looking ahead, *we* planned for an alternate date.   [subject]
> It was *he* who was asked to give the report.   [predicate nominative]

5.41   The personal pronouns *me, him, her, us,* and *them* are in the *objective case* and are used as the objects of verbs and prepositions.

> The instructor asked *them* not to make any changes in the report.   [object of verb *asked*]
> After discussing the plan with *us,* he agreed to make the needed changes.   [object of preposition *with*]

5.42   The personal pronouns *my, mine, your, yours, his, hers, its, our, ours, their,* and *theirs* are in the *possessive case* and are used to show ownership. The possessive form of personal pronouns does not require an apostrophe.

> *His* paper was read to the class yesterday.   [shows ownership of *paper*]
> Team members received *their* awards at the banquet.   [shows ownership of *awards*]

5.43   The personal pronouns *you* and *it* can be in either the nominative case or the objective case, depending on how they are used in the sentence.

> While writing the report, *you* must be careful to provide accurate information.   [subject; nominative case]
>
> *It* is I who must make the decision.   [subject; nominative case]
>
> Melody will go with *you* to the contest.   [object of preposition *with*; objective case]
>
> While reading the essay, Mr. Johnson marked *it* for typographical errors.   [object of verb *marked*; objective case]

Agreement

5.44   The noun to which the pronoun refers is known as its *antecedent*. Personal pronouns must agree with their antecedents in number and gender.

> Mr. Jamison stood to give *his* report to the advisory committee.   [The pronoun his refers to its antecedent, *Mr. Jamison*, which is singular in number and masculine in gender.]
>
> The judges compiled *their* scores in the contest.   [The pronoun *their* refers to its antecedent, *judges*, which is plural in number and common in gender.]
>
> The automobile blew *its* left tire as it ran over the rocks.   [The pronoun *its* refers to the antecedent, *automobile*, which is singular in number and neuter in gender.]

5.45   When referring to two or more antecedents joined by the word *and*, use a plural pronoun.

> *Miss Lee and Mr. Loring* presented *their* arguments to the jury.

5.46   When two titles refer to the same person, use a singular pronoun.

> The *president and chief executive officer* presented *her* recommendations to the stockholders.   [The president and chief executive officer are the same person.]

5.47   When two titles refer to two different persons, use a plural pronoun.

> The *author and* the *editor* indicated *they* needed more time to study the recommendation.   [The author and the editor are two different persons.]

The word *the* used before each title is usually an indication of two different persons.

5.48   When two or more singular antecedents are joined by *or* or *nor*, use a singular pronoun.

> Neither Ray *nor* Tom left *his* books on the receptionist's desk.

5.49 When adjectives such as *each, every, many a,* and *an* are used with two or more antecedents joined by *and,* use a singular pronoun.

Each driver and loader was informed of *his or her* new responsibilities.

Every manager, supervisor, and worker contributed part of *his or her* paycheck to the Special Olympics.

5.50 Antecedents of common gender may be dealt with in a number of ways. A combination of masculine and feminine pronouns may be used.

The *applicant* will sign *his or her* name on the employment form.

The *winner* will receive *his* or *her* award following the announcement of the results.

The constant use of *his or her,* however, tends to become a burden to the reader. The preferable alternative is to rewrite the sentence to eliminate the singular pronoun.

To increase *his or her* level of productivity, a *manager* must constantly look for shortcuts.

To increase *their* level of productivity, *managers* must constantly look for shortcuts.

Indefinite Pronouns

5.51 *Indefinite pronouns* refer to a nonspecific person or thing. The indefinite pronouns include *everybody, somebody, anybody, everyone, someone, anyone, one, every one, any one, each, either, neither, nothing,* and *another.* These indefinite pronouns require the singular form of the verb when used as subjects of sentences.

Every one of the operators *is* well qualified.

Either of the opinions *was* defensible.

When the indefinite pronouns *both, few, several, many,* and *others* are used as a subject, they take the plural form of the verb.

Several of the sources of information *were thought* to be out of date.

Both of the career paths in the curriculum *were* attractive to Mike.

The indefinite pronouns *some, none, any, all,* and *most* may take either the singular or plural form of the verb when used as a subject, depending on the meaning of the sentence.

Any time left after the examination *is* to be used for study.

None of the first drafts *were approved* by Mrs. Jones.

Some of the checks *were stapled* to the envelopes.

Interrogative Pronouns

5.52 *Interrogative pronouns* are used to ask questions. They include *who, whom, whose, which,* and *what.*
Who is always used as a subject or a predicate nominative and is always in the nominative case.

Who is responsible for seeing that the doors are locked?   [subject]

Whom is always used as the object of a verb or a preposition. It is always in the objective case.

Whom did Wilson vote for in the election?   [object of *for*]

To determine whether to use *who* or *whom,* substitute *he/she* for *who* and *him/her* for *whom* in the sentence. If *he* or *she* fits, then *who* is correct. On the other hand, if *him* or *her* fits, *whom* is correct.
Use *whose* to show ownership. It is always in the possessive case.

Whose research paper was the basis of the discussion?   [shows possession of *research paper*]

Use *which* and *what* as subjects or objects of verbs or prepositions in sentences. They may be in the nominative or objective case.

Which is the better dictionary?   [subject]
What would the council *think* of our suggestions?   [object of *would think*]

Relative Pronouns

5.53 *Relative pronouns* are used to join subordinate clauses to antecedents. Follow the same rules for determining the case of relative pronouns as described for personal pronouns. The relative pronouns *who, whom,* and *whose* refer to people. *Which* refers to animals and things. *That* refers to animals or things. *That* may also refer to a person when the reference is impersonal.

Lanny Monroe is the *technician who* will repair the computer.

Lanny Monroe, whom you saw in the hallway, will repair the computer.

The *report, which* was submitted yesterday, was approved by the supervisor.

The physician's assistant completed the *diagnosis that* was initiated by Dr. Jones.

The *candidate who* wins will have a difficult task.

The *candidate that* wins will have a difficult task.   [impersonal]

VERBS

5.54 A *verb* is a word that shows action, condition, or a state of being.

The angry child *slammed* the door shut.   [action]
The schedule *appears* to have been met.   [condition]
The author of the article *is* William Smith.   [state of being]

A verb may be a single word or a phrase of two or more words. A *verb phrase* includes the main verb with one or more helping, or auxiliary, verbs. The following are common *helping verbs:*

be	been	might	shall
am	have	ought	will
is	has	can	do
are	had	could	does
was	may	should	did
were	must	would	

Don *is* at home until later today.
The reports *should be completed* by Wednesday afternoon.
They *must reserve* the conference hall for the exhibit.

In certain situations, helping verbs may function as the main verb of a sentence.

Mary *was* unavailable to assist John with his speech.

The parts of a verb phrase are often separated by other words.

Louise *did* not *believe* the figures were accurate.   [*not* is an adverb]

Principal Parts of Verbs

5.55 All verbs have three principal parts: the present, the past, and the past participle. Use these parts to form the various tenses in sentences.

To form the past and the past participle of most verbs, add *-d* or *-ed* to the present form.

Present	Past	Past Participle
agree	agreed	agreed
call	called	called

5.56 Some verbs, however, are irregular. That is, to form the past and past participle forms of some verbs, change the spelling or keep the same spelling for all three parts.

The following list shows the principal parts of common irregular verbs.

Present	Past	Past Participle
arise	arose	arisen
awake	awoke/awaked	awoke/awaked
be/am/is/are	was/were	been
become	became	become
begin	began	begun
bite	bit	bitten
blow	blew	blown
bring	brought	brought
build	built	built
buy	bought	bought
catch	caught	caught
choose	chose	chosen
come	came	come
cut	cut	cut
do	did	done
draw	drew	drawn
drink	drank	drunk
drive	drove	driven
eat	ate	eaten
fall	fell	fallen
feed	fed	fed
feel	felt	felt
fight	fought	fought
find	found	found
fly	flew	flown
forget	forgot	forgotten
freeze	froze	frozen
get	got	got/gotten
give	gave	given
go	went	gone
grow	grew	grown
hang (execute)	hanged	hanged
hang (suspend)	hung	hung
have	had	had
hide	hid	hidden
hold	held	held
hurt	hurt	hurt
keep	kept	kept
know	knew	known

5

Present	Past	Past Participle
lay	laid	laid
lead	led	led
leave	left	left
lend	lent	lent
lie	lay	lain
lose	lost	lost
make	made	made
meet	met	met
pay	paid	paid
ride	rode	ridden
ring	rang	rung
rise	rose	risen
run	ran	run
say	said	said
see	saw	seen
sell	sold	sold
shake	shook	shaken
shine	shone	shone
sing	sang	sung
sink	sank/sunk	sunk
sit	sat	sat
speak	spoke	spoken
spring	sprang	sprung
stand	stood	stood
steal	stole	stolen
strike	struck	struck/stricken
swear	swore	sworn
swim	swam	swum
swing	swung	swung
take	took	taken
tear	tore	torn
tell	told	told
throw	threw	thrown
wear	wore	worn
write	wrote	written

Some patterns exist in the ways these verbs form the past and the past participle. However, memorize these verbs or consult a dictionary when you are in doubt.

Tense

5.57 The *tense* of a verb tells when some action happened or when something existed. Tense tells time. The English language has six basic tenses: present, past, future, present perfect, past perfect, and future perfect.

5.58 The *present tense* indicates an action occurring now, an action regularly done, or something that is a general truth. Use the present form of the verb for the present tense.

Laurie *jogs* regularly three times a week.
Randolph *is* an accomplished pianist.

Use the present tense also to show a future action when the time is specified.

The team *leaves* next Wednesday for Barcelona.

5.59 The *past tense* indicates an action or condition completed in the past. Use the past form of the verb for the past tense.

Mark *enrolled* in the technical drawing course at the local community college.
The holidays *were* difficult for those away from home.

5.60 The *future tense* indicates an action that has not yet occurred but that will happen in the future. Use *shall* or *will* plus the present form of the verb for the future tense.

The study group *will meet* at the library on Tuesday.
We *shall try* to meet the publication deadline.

5.61 The *present perfect tense* indicates an action that has been completed at some indefinite time in the past. Use *have* or *has* plus the past participle of the verb for the present perfect tense.

All of the new students *have completed* the orientation.
Ms. Whitcombe *has recommended* the adoption of a tech prep curriculum.

5.62 The *past perfect tense* indicates an action completed in the past before another action, also in the past. Use *had* plus the past participle of the verb for the past perfect tense.

Charles *had returned* to work by the time I arrived.

5.63 The *future perfect tense* indicates an action begun in the past that will be completed in the future before some other action. Use *will have* or *shall have* plus the past participle of the verb for the future perfect tense.

Mr. Felton *will have retired* by October 15.
I *shall have completed* my research for the work by tomorrow morning.

Voice

5.64 A verb is in *active voice* when the subject of the sentence directs or performs the action.

The computer operator *loaded* the new software into the system. [The subject is *operator*; the active verb, *loaded*.]

[Note: Active verbs are generally preferred in most writing because they are more forceful and express more action.]

5.65 A verb is in *passive voice* when the subject of the sentence receives the action.

The new software *was loaded* into the system by the computer operator. [The subject is *software*; the passive verb, *was loaded*.]

Agreement of Subject and Verb

5.66 Subjects and verbs must agree in person and number. Singular subjects of sentences require singular verbs. Singular, present-tense verbs generally end in *s*.

A good research *paper requires* much revision.
The *university closes* for spring vacation next week.

Some singular subjects may be separated from the verb by phrases that contain a plural noun; nevertheless, a singular verb is required.

Phillip Dwyer, accompanied by two business associates, *flies* to New York every week.
The *list* of the courses for tech prep *is* now available.

5.67 Plural nouns used as subjects require plural verbs. Plural verbs do not generally end in *s*.

Good research *papers require* much revision.

Plural subjects that are separated from the verb by phrases that contain a singular noun nevertheless take a plural verb.

The three *parts* of his report *were* rather confusing.
All *technicians* at the center *are tested* annually.

5.68 Most subjects that consist of two or more words are called *compound subjects*. A compound subject joined by *and* needs a plural verb.

The *sales staff* and the *manager were opposed* to the advertising campaign.
Ms. Lane and *Mr. Perez are* the new biologists.

[Note: When the parts of a compound subject refer to the same person or thing, use a singular verb.]

The *president* and *chairman* of the board *is* Ms. Fernandez.

5.69 A compound subject that consists of singular subjects joined by *or* or *nor* takes a singular verb.

Either the *president* or the *vice president is* to preside at the meeting.
Neither *Wilson* nor his *instructor was attending* the session.

5.70 When a singular subject and a plural subject are joined by *or* or *nor*, the verb agrees with the nearer subject.

Either the accountant or the *auditors have inspected* the records.
Either the auditors or the *accountant has inspected* the records.

5

Gerunds

5.71 A *gerund* is a verb form that ends in *-ing* and is used as a noun. Gerunds, like nouns, can be subjects, objects, and predicate nominatives.

Walking is an excellent way to burn calories.   [subject]
The student senate was opposed to *smoking* in the dormitories.   [object of preposition *to*]
To Levi, the hardest part of the trip is *packing*.   [predicate nominative]

A *gerund phrase* is a gerund and any modifiers it may have.

Going to class seemed like a good idea.

Nouns or pronouns used to modify gerunds should always be in the possessive case.

Monroe's whistling caused heads to turn in the library.
My father wanted to know about *my spending* so much money.

Infinitives

5.72 An infinitive is a verb form that usually consists of the word *to* plus a verb.

Zane wanted *to finish* the lesson early.

Infinitives may be used as nouns, adjectives, or adverbs. Avoid splitting the parts of an infinitive by not putting words between *to* and the verb.

The annual staff was asked *to* promptly *prepare* the layouts.   [split infinitive]
The annual staff was asked *to prepare* the layouts promptly.

Participles

5.73 A *participle* is a verb form used as an adjective to describe nouns and pronouns.

> *Relying* on his judgment, Mr. Sanchez decided not to make the purchase. [describes Mr. Sanchez]
>
> The person *reading* the paper is Marilyn.

Incorrect placement of participles results in confusion. Such incorrect placement is referred to as a "dangling" participle. Place participles as close to the words they describe as possible to avoid confusion.

> *Reading* very carefully, the report was edited by Linda. [Can the report be reading very carefully?]
>
> *Reading* very carefully, Linda edited the report.

_____

(Name)

Fill in the missing verb form in the following chart.

Present	Past	Past Participle
1. grow	_____	grown
2. _____	_____	driven
3. choose	chose	_____
4. hang (suspend)	_____	hung
5. lay	_____	laid
6. _____	lay	lain
7. eat	_____	eaten
8. lead	_____	_____
9. _____	swam	_____
10. shake	shook	_____
11. _____	sang	_____
12. tell	_____	told
13. _____	got	_____
14. run	_____	_____
15. lose	_____	_____
16. leave	_____	left
17. _____	began	begun
18. freeze	froze	_____
19. have	_____	_____
20. _____	drank	_____

Using the abbreviations listed below, label the part of speech of each italicized word in the sentences that follow.

adj	(adjective)	inf	(infinitive)	prep	(preposition)
adv	(adverb)	int	(interjection)	pro	(pronoun)
conj	(conjunction)	n	(noun)	v	(verb)

       pro   prep   n   adv

Example: *They* were told *by* the *instructor* to stay *late.*

1. *Sharon* is the *tallest* player *on* the squad.

2. *Yikes!* I just twisted *my* ankle *when* I fell to the *floor.*

3. In her desire *to win,* Marian lost sight of the ideal of *fairness.*

4. The foreman *explained* his plan *as* the workers waited *patiently.*

5. We *completed* the report on time even though it *required* a *great* effort.

Rewrite the following paragraphs, selecting the correct word from those given in parentheses.

Our class (was, were) noisy as (it, they) waited for Mrs. Lonnigan to arrive. "The unexpected storm and icy streets (has, have) caused her to be late," said Anthony. Leslie, the (louder, loudest) of the Baker twins, asked for quiet in the room. Ray, the class monitor, sharpened (his, their) pencil, checked the students' papers, and wrote down some figures.

Nancy said it was (her, she) who took the phone call about Mrs. Lonnigan's accident. Randy asked, "(Who, Whom) did you say took responsibility for the accident?" Nancy did not know, but indicated that the police officers and the sheriff said (he, they) wanted more time (to more thoroughly investigate, to investigate more thoroughly).

Check your answers in the back of the book.

UNIT 6

PHRASES, CLAUSES, SENTENCES, AND PARAGRAPHS

Effective written communication is composed of words, phrases, clauses, sentences, and paragraphs. Each element plays an important role in conciseness, clarity, and completeness. A knowledge of each of these elements and how to utilize them effectively will strengthen one's ability to communicate.

PHRASES

A *phrase* is a group of two or more words that does not contain a subject and a verb. The entire phrase acts as a single part of speech and may be a verb, prepositional, participial, gerund, infinitive, or appositive phrase.

Phrases expand basic sentence patterns and help create more vivid and expressive writing. Phrases add description, detail, and elaboration to ideas. They turn choppy, awkward sentences into smoothly flowing expressions that are enjoyable to read and easy to understand. Writers should use phrases liberally to improve their communication.

Verb Phrases

6.1 A *verb phrase* is the main verb plus one or more helping, or auxiliary, verbs. Common helping verbs are *be, am, is, are, was, were, been, have, has, had, may, must, ought, can, might, could, would, should, shall, will, do, does,* and *did.*

> Rachel *will key* the report for the Tech Prep Committee.
> No one *should leave* the building during the storm.
> All essays *must be turned* in no later than Monday.

6.2 The parts of the verb phrase may be separated from the main verb.

> Elizabeth *would* not *accept* the position.
> The Council *will* surely *meet* before the holidays.
> When *did* you first *learn* about the accident?

Prepositional Phrases

6.3 A *prepositional phrase* is a group of words that begins with a preposition and generally ends with a noun or a pronoun. The noun or pronoun that ends the phrase is known as the *object of the preposition.*

The bus goes *by my house* each day.
The field *of health care* is expanding nationally.
The class went *into the city* to observe the trial.

6.4 A prepositional phrase generally acts as an *adjective* or an *adverb*. When it acts as an adjective, a prepositional phrase modifies a noun or a pronoun.

The technicians *from the hospital* arrived yesterday. [adjective phrase modifying noun *technicians*]
The ushers *in red coats* directed the crowd. [adjective phrase modifying noun *ushers*]
Our school has been the location *of many sports events.* [adjective phrase modifying noun *location*]
Which *of the many choices* will I make? [adjective phrase modifying pronoun *which*]

6.5 When a prepositional phrase acts as an adverb, it modifies a verb, an adjective, or another adverb.

Rudy wrote his English paper *with great care.* [adverb phrase modifying verb *wrote*]
Before every game Beth practices faithfully. [adverb phrase modifying verb *practices*]
The class walked *to the computer lab.* [adverb phrase modifying verb *walked*]
The examination should be easy *for you.* [adverb phrase modifying adjective *easy*]
You are keying much too fast *for accurate copy.* [adverb phrase modifying adverb *fast*]

Participles and Participial Phrases

6.6 A *participle* is a verb form that acts as an adjective. All present participles end in *-ing*. Most past participles end in *-ed*. Other past participles may have different forms.

A *sailing* ship visited the city harbor.
The owner decided to purchase a *used* computer.
Mrs. Smythe asked about the *torn* page in the report.

6.7 A *participial phrase* contains a participle and any complements or modifiers. Participial phrases add variety to sentences and provide important information to the reader.

We heard the two boys *shouting in the room.*
The printer, *running steadily,* spewed out the report.
Covered with chalk dust, the chalkboard was unusable.
Wrinkled by repeated misuse, the pages in the book were falling out.

6.8 A participial phrase appearing at the beginning of a sentence is usually followed by a comma. A participial phrase in the middle or at the end of a sentence is set off by commas only if the phrase is not needed to understand the meaning of the sentence.

Having run all day, the photocopier began to falter.
Coach Ryan, *shouting instructions furiously,* sat at the end of the bench.
Wyatt drove the length of the court, *dribbling constantly* as he ran.

Gerunds and Gerund Phrases

6.9 A *gerund* is a verb form ending in *-ing* that acts as a noun. Gerunds, like nouns, can be used as subjects, objects, and predicate nominatives.

Jogging is a favorite pastime of many.   [gerund as subject]
Marilyn loves *hiking* in the mountains of Virginia.   [gerund as object of verb]
Wilson can improve his skill by *practicing.*   [gerund as object of preposition]
Dr. Whiting's hobby is *cooking* for his friends.   [gerund used as predicate nominative]

6.10 A *gerund phrase* contains a gerund and any complements or modifiers. Gerund phrases are useful in describing and explaining an activity or process.

Very careful planning is necessary for good execution.
Shannon hates *working late at night.*
May received a ticket for *parking in an illegal zone.*
The club's greatest achievement was *winning the service award.*

Infinitives and Infinitive Phrases

6.11 An *infinitive* is a verb form that usually consists of *to* and a verb. Infinitives act as nouns, adjectives, or adverbs.

To succeed is Anthony's primary concern in life.
Diane had the strength *to continue.*
Mr. Tatum's group came *to celebrate* the victory.

6.12 An *infinitive phrase* contains an infinitive and any complements and modifiers.

The group wanted *to finish quickly.*
To do his very best was Juan's goal in the class.
It was a great honor *to tell Marie of her award.*

6

Appositives and Appositive Phrases

6.13   An *appositive* is a noun or pronoun placed next to another noun or pronoun to explain, describe, or rename. Use commas to set off an appositive or appositive phrase that is not essential to the meaning of the sentence.

> My friend *Nathan* is a computer expert.
> Oxygen, *an element,* is colorless and odorless.
> It was Wilton *himself* who made the mistake.

6.14   An *appositive phrase* contains an appositive and any complements and modifiers.

> Take your application to the Administration Building, *the building located in the very center of the campus.*
> My friend's computer, *a very fast model loaded with features,* will run all kinds of software.
> John Wilson, *a talented student,* is the spokesperson for the group.

When there are commas within the material to which the appositive refers, other punctuation may be preferable in place of commas.

> John, Susie, and Raye—*all talented students*—are the leaders of the group.

CLAUSES

A *clause* is a group of words having a subject and a predicate that is used as part of a sentence. Those clauses that express a complete statement and can stand alone are known as *independent clauses.* Those that do not express a complete statement and cannot stand alone are known as *subordinate* (or *dependent*) clauses.

6.15   Every sentence must contain at least one independent clause containing a subject and a predicate. A sentence may contain more than one independent clause usually joined by *and, but, or, nor,* or *for.*

> Janet gave me the figures. I keyed the report.
> Janet gave me the figures, *and* I keyed the report.
> The disaster team worked quickly, *for* it was a matter of life and death.
> We worked until midnight, *but* we were unable to finish.

6.16   A *subordinate clause* (or *dependent clause*) has a subject and a predicate but cannot stand alone. A subordinate clause must be attached to an independent clause to make sense. The following are examples of subordinate clauses.

> who operated the video equipment
> which was her favorite subject
> when they operate as they should
> as soon as we receive the information

6.17 Combined with an independent clause, subordinate clauses support and expand the sentence.

> John was the staff member *who operated the video equipment.*
> Mary excelled in French, *which was her favorite subject.*
> Computers are wonderful tools *when they operate as they should.*
> *As soon as we receive the information,* we'll complete the report.

6.18 Subordinate clauses act as adjectives, adverbs, or nouns. An *adjective clause* modifies a noun or pronoun and usually follows the word it modifies. Adjective clauses are introduced by *who, whom, whose, that, which, when,* and *where.*

> Our principal is an individual *who is able to make decisions.*
> An article *that I enjoyed reading* is "Our Computing World."
> Marion is one *whose generosity exceeds her means.*
> The computer was invented in a time *when it was difficult to process data rapidly.*

6.19 The relative pronoun is sometimes omitted at the beginning of an adjective clause.

> Gwen gives a presentation on food preparation *I would love to hear.*   [The relative pronoun *that* is omitted.]

6.20 An *adverb clause* modifies a verb, an adjective, or an adverb. An adverb clause tells *when, where, how, why,* and *to what extent.* Use adverb clauses to explain or clarify why something happens or why people take certain actions.

> Margaret practices her keyboarding *when she has time.*
> *Wherever Ken goes,* he takes his notebook computer with him.
> The team played *as if it were the last game of the year.*
> Raye applied for the position *because she was qualified.*
> *Since the report is due Monday,* I must work tonight.
> Walter can run faster *than I can run.*

6.21 *Elliptical (incomplete) adverb clauses* omit part of the clause. The part of the clause that is omitted is understood.

> Mary can key much faster than I (*can key*).
> While (*I was*) reaching for the box, I tore my shirt.

6.22 A *noun clause* is used as a subject, direct object, object of a preposition, or predicate nominative. A noun clause may begin with *how, that, what, whatever, when, where, which, whichever, who, whom, whoever, whose,* or *why.*

> *Whoever writes the best essay* will win the prize.
> Mr. Lawson discussed *how the project will be completed.*
> Here is a draft of *what we project for next year.*
> Lynnette is *who will lead us in the parade.*
> *How we got the job done* is still a mystery.
> Mark wrote *whatever came into his mind at the moment.*

6

SENTENCE STRUCTURE

A *sentence* is a group of words expressing a complete thought, an independent clause. Obviously, groups of related sentences combine to convey messages. Clearly developed sentences define, clarify, expand, inform, and persuade, among other things. A knowledge of the mechanics of sentences is imperative to a creative writer.

Simple Sentences

6.23 A simple sentence has two basic parts, a *subject* and a *predicate*. The *simple subject* is the key or principal word or group of words that tells what a sentence is about. To determine the simple subject, ask *who?* or *what?* about the action expressed by the verb in the sentence.

> The *man* in the black coat ran out the back door. [answers question *who ran out the back door*]
>
> Our new *copier* makes excellent full-color copies. [answers question *what makes copies?*]

The *simple predicate* tells what the subject does or what is done to the subject. To determine the simple predicate, ask what action is taken by the subject.

> The man in the black coat *ran* out the back door. [tells what action the subject took]
>
> Our new copier *makes* excellent full-color copies. [tells what the subject does]

6.24 The *complete subject* is composed of the simple subject and the words that modify it. The modifiers help to expand the meaning of the sentence.

> *The course in anthropology* helped define humanity.
> *The first recipient of the scholarship* was Mae Jones.

6.25 A *compound subject* is composed of two or more simple subjects joined by a conjunction and having the same verb. The joining conjunctions are generally *and* and *or.*

> *Wilton and Sara* worked as a team on the project.
> *The gray sweater or the green pullover* looks best.
> *The teachers, the students, and the parents* applauded the action of the school board.

6.26 A *compound predicate* (or *compound verb*) is composed of two or more verbs or verb phrases joined by a conjunction and having the same subject.

> Everyone at the rally *clapped and shouted at the news.*
> Technical skills *were taught and reinforced in the class.*
> Rachel *will compile the data, prepare the tables, and key the document.*

6.27 In most sentences, the subject precedes the verb; however, some exceptions exist. Sometimes, in the case of a command or a request, the subject *you* is omitted but understood.

(You) Stand up immediately and give a response.
(You) Please try to get to class on time.

6.28 Sometimes a sentence is written in inverted order to add emphasis. In that case, the predicate comes before the subject.

On the floor beside the computer lay *two crumpled pages of the report.*
Just outside the courtroom stood *the two victims.*

6.29 When the word *there* or *here* begins a sentence, the predicate usually comes before the subject followed by a form of the verb *to be.* (*There* and *here* are very unlikely to be the subject.)

There are *several reasons for the failure.*
Here is *a full report on the matter.*

Complements

6

6.30 A *complement* is a word or group of words in the predicate needed to complete the meaning of the subject and the verb. The four types of complements are *direct objects, indirect objects, object complements,* and *subject complements.*

Subject	Verb	Complement
Harry	won	the contest. [direct object]
The class	sent	me a sympathy card. [indirect object]
The jury	found	him innocent. [object complement]
Lillian	is	president of her class. [subject complement]
The teacher	was	very creative in her lectures. [subject complement]

6.31 A *direct object* answers the question *what?* or *whom?* after an action verb.

James carried *a large box of chocolates* to Mrs. Long.
Dr. Danielson asked *Mark* to wait in his office.

6.32 An *indirect object* answers the question *to whom?* or *for whom?* the action of the verb was done.

The accounting office gave *Johnny* credit for the payment.
Stan loaned *his friend* a large sum of money.

6.33 A *subject complement* may be either a *predicate nominative* or a *predicate adjective.* A predicate nominative follows a linking verb and further identifies the subject.

Computer operators are *specialists in data retrieval.*
Professor Layne was *a Rhodes Scholar.*

6.34 A *predicate adjective* follows a linking verb and further describes the subject.

Students in tech prep programs become *knowledgeable about technology.*
Nutrition specialists should be *healthy role models.*

Types of Sentences

6.35 There are four kinds of sentences: *declarative, imperative, interrogative,* and *exclamatory.* A *declarative sentence* makes a statement and ends with a period.

Poor posture can cause injuries on the job.
Good writing skills pay big dividends.

6.36 An *imperative sentence* makes a request or gives a command. *You* is the understood subject, and the imperative sentence usually ends with a period.

Please give me your papers no later than April 5.
Pick that book off the floor immediately.

6.37 An *interrogative sentence* asks a question and ends with a question mark.

What is the best plan of action?
When do you need to receive the report?

6.38 An *exclamatory sentence* expresses strong feeling or emotion and ends with an exclamation mark.

The curtains are on fire!
What a fantastic idea!

Sentence Classifications

6.39 Sentences may also be classified according to their structure. There are four different sentence structures: *simple, compound, complex,* and *compound-complex.* A *simple sentence* has only one independent clause. Although it has only one main clause, a simple sentence can have a compound subject or a compound verb or both. It can also have modifiers and complements that can expand and enhance the meaning of the sentence.

Computers compile data.
Computers and printers compile and print data.   [compound subject, compound verb]
Computers and printers, used properly, compile and print data efficiently.   [compound subject, compound verb, modifiers]
Powerful computers and high-speed printers, used properly, compile huge amounts of information and print mountains of data rapidly and efficiently.   [compound subject, compound verb, modifiers, and complements]

6.40 A *compound sentence* has two or more independent clauses joined by a semicolon or by a coordinating conjunction (*and, but, or, nor, yet,* or *for*) preceded by a comma.

> He has served for seven years; it is time for a change.
> Josh has studied word processing, and now he is ready to go to work.
> You must learn a lot about technology, or you may have difficulty getting a good job.
> The printer is now working, but it will print only three pages per minute.

6.41 A *complex sentence* has one independent clause and one or more subordinate (or dependent) clauses.

> I studied Japanese because I wanted to work in Japan.
> While taking courses in health care, I got a job at a nursing home.
> If Sally will study harder, she can make better grades so that she can try out for track.

6.42 A *compound-complex sentence* has more than one independent clause and at least one subordinate clause.

> Writing effectively is an important skill, and students must practice that skill if they are to develop competency.
>
> Bill and Marie completed the assignment, and they were pleased since there was still time to go to the movies.
>
> If you will give me the data, I can finish the report; and I will have it at the office tomorrow since it is needed for the staff meeting.

6.43 A *sentence fragment* is a group of words that is missing a subject or a verb or has been punctuated improperly to give the appearance that it is a complete sentence. A sentence fragment does not express a complete thought.

Fragment:	Nathan took accounting last year. And passed the course.
Sentence:	Nathan took accounting last year and passed the course.
Fragment:	Modern technology many hours on the job.
Sentence:	Modern technology saves many hours on the job.
Fragment:	Good jobs today require many skills. That one can get through good training programs.
Sentence:	Good jobs today require many skills that one can get through good training programs.

6.44 A *run-on sentence* is two or more complete sentences sometimes joined by a comma or no punctuation rather than a period, semicolon, or conjunction. Such sentences should be avoided.

Run-on:	Lana works as a lab technician, Henry is training to be a machinist.
Revised:	Lana works as a lab technician. Henry is training to be a machinist.
Run-on:	It has rained all afternoon it will probably rain tomorrow, too.
Revised:	It has rained all afternoon; it will probably rain tomorrow, too.
Run-on:	Sam wants to play basketball his grades must improve.
Revised:	Sam wants to play basketball, but his grades must improve.

PARAGRAPHS

A *paragraph* is a group of related sentences that present one major idea. A paragraph is generally made up of a topic sentence stating the main idea followed by supporting sentences. As a general rule, single sentences are not written as paragraphs.

A paragraph may sometimes stand alone as an independent piece of writing. More often, however, a group of related paragraphs combine to build a longer composition such as a letter, memo, research paper, or report. In a complete composition, paragraphs both convey information within themselves and relate to and support the other paragraphs in the writing.

6.45 Depending on the writer's purpose in developing a document, paragraphs generally inform or explain, persuade, describe, or relate a series of events in some kind of order.

Expository Paragraphs

6.46 An *expository paragraph* provides information, explains a process, or defines a concept. Expository paragraphs tend to be objective and straightforward in their presentation. They may be developed using facts, examples, definitions, or cause and effect.

6.47 An expository paragraph may use facts to support the main idea expressed in the topic sentence. The following is a portion of such a paragraph.

> The Regulators took it upon themselves to settle the crisis. To begin with, a group of 150 regulators started a riot in Hillsborough. They attacked the presiding judge and the lawyers in the courtroom, disrupting court proceedings. They seated their own judge and held their own mock court. Within days they had completely disrupted the state's judicial system.

6.48 An expository paragraph may use examples to explain a point more clearly or to illustrate the main idea. The following is an example.

> During the Civil War, goods in the South became scarce and prices rose rapidly. A disrupted transportation system caused grave shortages in basic essentials. A barrel of flour that cost $18 in 1862 cost $500 in 1865. Bacon increased in price from $.33 to $7.50 a pound. Wheat prices rose from $3 to $50 a bushel.

6.49 An expository paragraph may also use a definition with supporting details of that definition. The following is an example.

> The term *part-time employee* is defined in this report as any Apex Corporation personnel who works on site no more than 20 hours per week. *On site* refers to the manufacturing facilities located in Worthington. Part-time employees, while being paid normal wage scales designated for full-time employees, receive reduced benefits from the corporation and do not participate in the company retirement program.

6

6.50   Finally, an expository paragraph may use cause and effect. Such an approach generally tells why something happened or is true or the consequences of an event. The following is an example.

> Sales increased dramatically for the Apex Corporation during the first quarter of this year. The increase could be attributed to the introduction of three new industrial waste products. There was also a significant increase in the demand for air pollution systems. Finally, the effects of the new advertising campaign initiated late last year were being felt.

Persuasive Paragraphs

6.51   A *persuasive paragraph* generally states the writer's opinion and supports that position with convincing evidence in the form of facts or examples. The following is an example.

> Arbitration is an excellent alternative to litigation. Using a third party known as an arbitrator, arbitration is generally much more flexible in its procedures than those in a lawsuit. Both sides in the dispute are able to present their views in a more relaxed environment than in a courtroom. The rules to be adhered to are often determined and agreed upon by both parties in the arbitration, contrary to the rules of litigation, which are fixed and inflexible and do not permit change by the litigants.

Descriptive Paragraphs

6.52   A *descriptive paragraph* uses language that appeals to the senses of the reader and generally centers on a single person, event, place, or thing. An example follows.

> The meeting room was at once imposing and foreboding, depending on your particular point of view. In the very center of the room stood a tall, darkly stained, bare, three-legged stool mounted on a circular platform a full foot above floor level. The stool was bathed in a strong white light aimed from a single spotlight positioned directly above. Around three sides of the platform in the otherwise dimly lighted room sat large, oak-framed arm chairs that could easily have come from a medieval castle. Either a recitation from a master or an inquisition of an apprentice seemed about to begin.

6.53   A *narrative paragraph* relates a series of events or tells a story. An example follows.

> The prize-winning orator's success story was one of struggle and perseverance. As a young girl she was plagued with a terrible stuttering problem, being barely able to utter a complete sentence without faltering badly. With hard work, long practice, and the help of a dedicated teacher, she slowly overcame the problem, although at moments of great stress the stuttering tried its best to reassert itself. Though her participation in numerous oratorical competitions brought mostly disappointment and many last-place finishes, it also fired a hardness and dedication that eventually forged her into a skilled debater and an engrossing extemporaneous speaker.

6

Topic Sentences

6.54 The topic or opening sentence in a paragraph should clearly express the main idea. The main idea should be broad enough to require more than one supporting sentence in the paragraph, but not so broad that it cannot be developed properly in the normal length of a paragraph. Finally, it should grab the reader's interest and encourage further reading.

Topic Sentence Too Vague
Some workers are rather slow in doing their work.

Topic Sentence Too Limited
The data entry operators on the Wilson 500 computers were very slow keyboarders.

Topic Sentence Too Broad
Workers tend to be generally unproductive in the communications center.

More Appropriate Topic Sentence
The data entry operators, though they seemed to work hard, were unable to produce an acceptable number of documents during a shift.

Supporting Sentences

6.55 Sentences that support the topic sentence should provide enough detail to further define, explain, or expand the main idea. Supporting sentences should not include ideas other than those already expressed in the topic sentence. Rather, they should add to the clarity of the topic sentence, reaffirm its main idea, and not in any way defeat its purpose.

6.56 Supporting sentences are generally placed in some logical order of support. For example, they may be placed in chronological order, showing the order of occurrence of events. They may be shown in order of increasing or decreasing importance. They may even be devised to show contrast or comparison. In any event, every supporting sentence in the paragraph should relate clearly to and reinforce the topic sentence.

Evaluating Paragraphs

6.57 Paragraphs, like entire compositions, should be evaluated carefully to ensure their effectiveness. The following questions may be asked.

1. Is the main idea expressed by the topic sentence absolutely clear to the reader?
2. Is the main idea expressed by the topic sentence able to be covered within the limits of a normal length paragraph?
3. Will the topic sentence interest the reader and entice him or her to read further?
4. Is the main idea developed properly by the supporting sentences?
5. Is the language difficult, dull, or uninteresting?
6. Is the main idea reaffirmed in the paragraph?

SELF-CHECK EXERCISE 1, *UNIT 6*

(Name)

In each of the following sentences, identify the underlined phrases. Above the phrase, write *V* for verb phrase, *PR* for prepositional phrase, *PP* for participial phrase, *G* for gerund phrase, *I* for infinitive phrase, and *A* for appositive phrase.

1. Shawn <u>will give</u> his report <u>before the advisory committee</u>.

2. <u>Swimming steadily</u>, Ted reached the dock <u>in two hours</u>.

3. <u>Going home at Thanksgiving</u> is a favorite memory <u>of mine</u>.

4. Racquel, <u>my friend</u>, <u>would have been</u> an excellent teacher.

5. <u>Running laps</u> was just something <u>to do in my spare time</u>.

6. It was Harriet herself who wanted <u>to share</u> the news.

7. Tim was best known for <u>setting the record</u> <u>in the mile</u>.

8. <u>Worn around the edges</u>, the tires <u>must be removed</u>.

9. <u>To make the highest score</u> was Richard's goal.

10. Jacqueline, <u>the girl in red</u>, loves <u>hiking in the woods</u>.

SELF-CHECK EXERCISE 2, *UNIT 6*

The following sentences describe a campus incident. Read the sentences to get an idea of the scene. Then rewrite the sentences, expanding each by adding at least one prepositional phrase.

1. Tommy was walking to class.

_____

2. He was carrying a bookbag.

_____

3. It was seven o'clock.

_____

4. He approached the classroom building.

_____

5. He stopped.

_____

SELF-CHECK EXERCISE 3, _UNIT 6_

Complete the following statements about paragraphs by filling in the blanks with the appropriate word or phrase.

1. A(n) _____ paragraph provides information, explains a process, or defines a concept.

2. A(n) _____ is a group of related sentences that presents one major idea.

3. An expository paragraph that tells why something happened or is true has been developed using a(n) _____ approach.

4. A(n) _____ paragraph states the writer's opinion and supports that opinion with convincing evidence.

5. A(n) _____ paragraph relates a series of events or tells a story.

6. The _____ in a paragraph expresses the main idea.

7. _____ in a paragraph provide detail to further define, explain, or expand the main idea.

8. A(n) _____ paragraph uses language that appeals to the senses of the reader.

9. _____ are generally not written to stand alone as a paragraph.

10. Paragraphs, like entire compositions, should be _____ carefully to be sure they are effective.

SELF-CHECK EXERCISE 4, *UNIT 6*

. . . .

_____

(Name)

Identify the following sentences by writing *D* for declarative, *I* for imperative, *IN* for interrogative, *E* for exclamatory, *R* for run on, or *F* for sentence fragment in the blanks at the right of the sentences.

1. Please give me the directory. _____

2. Should I have asked for another chance? _____

3. In every instance in which I tried. _____

4. Watch out for that speeding truck! _____

5. Tammy gave Lee the book he took it home. _____

6. It was very cold last evening. _____

7. Will you have the report ready tomorrow? _____

8. Never in my wildest dreams. _____

9. Stand in front of the class. _____

10. Never give up your dreams. _____

SELF-CHECK EXERCISE 5, *UNIT 6*

. . . .

Identify the following sentences by writing *S* for simple, *CX* for complex, *CD* for compound, or *CCX* for compound-complex.

1. Robert and Peggy prepared the report and made the presentation before the class on Monday. _____

2. Since he took French last year, Jan has wanted to go to France. _____

3. The advisory committee attended the meeting, and the members made several recommendations. _____

4. John registered for classes in Spanish, algebra, and journalism; and he paid his tuition since it was due by the end of the month. _____

5. Running fast to catch the train, John slipped on the ice and broke his arm. _____

6. Rachel took a course in medical technology, and now she plans to become a nurse. _____

7. Learning to write memos, letters, and reports helped Marta get a better job as a communications specialist. _____

8. If you expect to work in international marketing, you must learn about other customs and cultures. _____

9. You must set the timer and turn on the switch before you leave the room. _____

10. Make ten copies of the report; take the report to the office. _____

Check your answers in the back of the book.

SPELLING AND WORD CHOICE

While today's electronic technology can help produce acceptable documents, many instances remain in which limitations of technology and exceptions to rules require the writer's judgment. A rich vocabulary and a thorough knowledge of prefixes, suffixes, plural formation rules, word division rules, and hyphenation rules can help produce quality documents and save time when checking written work. The discipline of referring to a dictionary and lists of frequently misspelled words and frequently used words can also be beneficial.

THE DICTIONARY

The dictionary is an invaluable tool for those who want to be understood. Even the best wordsmiths need help from time to time with the spelling, definition, and pronunciation of a word.

Abridged dictionaries, sometimes called "college dictionaries," contain more than 150,000 entries and provide enough specific word information for most students and general users. Unabridged dictionaries contain as many as 500,000 entries and provide much more detailed word information.

A dictionary entry usually contains many elements, including definitions, division into syllables, preferred spelling, pronunciation, part of speech, plurals, capitalized forms, synonyms, antonyms, and word histories. The following entry is from *Merriam Webster Collegiate Dictionary,* Tenth Edition.

tech•nol•o•gy \-jē\ *n, pl* **-gies** [Gk *technologia* systematic treatment of an art, fr. *technē* art, skill + *-o-* + *-logia* -logy] (1859) **1 a:** the practical application of knowledge esp. in a particular area: ENGINEERING 2 <medical ~> <semiconductor ~> **b :** a capability given by the practical application of knowledge <an automobile's fuel-saving ~> **2 :** a manner of accomplishing a task esp. using technical processes, methods, or knowledge <new *technologies* for information storage> **3 :** the specialized aspects of a particular field of endeavor <educational ~> — **tech•nol•o•gist** \-jist\ *n*

PREFIXES

• •

7.1 *Prefixes* are word beginnings that form new words from base words. Knowing the meaning of prefixes may help you determine the meaning of words and their spelling. The most common prefixes, their meanings, and some examples follow.

ante- (before)
  antebellum
  antedate
anti- (against)
  antidote
  antihistamine
bi- (two)
  biannual
  bimonthly
circum- (around)
  circumspect
  circumvention
co- (together)
  cohabitate
  cooperate
contra- (opposite; against)
  contradict
  contravene
counter- (opposing)
  counterfeit
  countermand
de- (removal; reversal)
  debarkation
  debrief
dis- (lack of)
  disadvantage
  disappearance
ex- (removal; former; out)
  exclude
  exhume
extra- (beyond)
  extrasensory
  extraterrestrial
fore- (before; front)
  foremost
  forenoon
hyper- (excessive)
  hypercritical
  hyperthyroid
inter- (between)
  interlock
  intervention

intra- (within)
  intrastate
  intravenous
micro- (very small)
  microcosm
  microscope
mid- (middle)
  midnight
  midsummer
mis- (wrongness; opposite)
  miscalculate
  misdemeanor
mono- (one; single)
  monogram
  monotone
multi- (many)
  multiethnic
  multimillionaire
non- (not)
  nonfiction
  nonmetallic
out- (external; excel)
  outskirts
  outstanding
over- (excessive)
  overblown
  overcompensate
post- (after)
  postnatal
  postpone
pre- (before)
  prehistoric
  prejudge
pro- (favor)
  pro-American
  prorevolutionary
re- (again)
  rearrange
  rebound
semi- (half of; partly)
  semifinal
  semimonthly

7

sub- (below)
   subtotal
   subtropical
super- (above)
   superpower
   superscript
trans- (across)
   transmission
   transportation

tri- (three)
   tricolored
   trifocal
un- (opposite of)
   ungrateful
   unhappy

SUFFIXES

7.2 *Suffixes* are word endings that form new words from base words. Knowing the meaning and spelling of suffixes will help you expand your vocabulary. Common suffixes, their meanings, and some examples follow.

-able, -ible (capable of being)
   comprehensible
   serviceable
-age (connection with; place)
   heritage
   lineage
-ard, -art (one who)
   laggard
   braggart
-ate (rank, office; act on)
   delegate
   relegate
-ation (action; result)
   occupation
   ruination
-cy (state; condition)
   militancy
   efficiency
-dom (state; condition)
   freedom
   kingdom
-ee (receiver)
   employee
   payee
-ence (fact; condition)
   evidence
   residence
-er, -or (one who does or makes; that which)
   baker
   creditor

-ful (abundance, having characteristics)
   artful
   plentiful
-hood (state; condition)
   brotherhood
   statehood
-ian (resembling; skilled in)
   Jeffersonian
   electrician
-ism (act, practice, process)
   journalism
   socialism
-ist (believer)
   capitalist
   realist
-less (lack of)
   fearless
   hopeless
-ly (resembling; in a specified manner)
   hopefully
   motherly
-ment (act of; state of)
   appeasement
   contentment
-ness (state; quality; condition)
   fondness
   closeness
-tion (action; process)
   absorption
   transaction

7

-tude (quality; state)   -ure (result; means)
    gratitude   culture
    multitude   censure

FORMING PLURALS

Most nouns take different forms to indicate singular or plural number. The singular form indicates only one person, place, or thing. The plural form indicates more than one person, place, or thing. The following rules relate to the formation of plurals of nouns. When in doubt about the formation of a plural, consult a dictionary.

7.3 Most nouns form their plurals by adding s to the singular form.

Singular	Plural
machine	machines
collar	collars
door	doors

7.4 Most nouns that end in s, z, x, ch, or sh form their plurals by adding es to the singular form.

Singular	Plural
bus	buses
mix	mixes
wrench	wrenches
bush	bushes

7.5 Some nouns ending in s are always plural and have no singular form.

earnings	goods	thanks
proceeds	series	winnings

Some nouns ending in s are always singular and have no plural form.

news   headquarters

7.6 Nouns that end in y preceded by a consonant form their plurals by changing the y to i and adding es.

Singular	Plural
efficiency	efficiencies
spy	spies
family	families

Nouns that end in *y* preceded by a vowel form their plurals by adding *s*.

Singular	Plural
attorney	attorneys
valley	valleys

7.7 Most nouns that end in *ʃ* or *ʃe* form their plurals by changing the *ʃ* or *ʃe* to *v* and adding *es*.

Singular	Plural
self	selves
life	lives
loaf	loaves

Some nouns that end in *ʃ* or *ʃe* form their plurals simply by adding *s*.

Singular	Plural
chief	chiefs
roof	roofs
safe	safes

7.8 Most nouns that end in *o* preceded by a vowel form their plurals by adding *s* to the singular form.

Singular	Plural
radio	radios
studio	studios
stereo	stereos

Most nouns that end in *o* preceded by a consonant form their plurals by adding *es* to the singular form.

Singular	Plural
veto	vetoes
hero	heroes
tomato	tomatoes

Exceptions to this rule include the following:

piano	pianos
memo	memos

7

Some nouns ending in *o* form their plurals by adding either *s* or *es*.

Singular	Plural
motto	mottos *or* mottoes
zero	zeros *or* zeroes

Note: There are many exceptions to the rules for forming plurals of nouns ending in *o*. Check your dictionary when you are unsure of the correct spelling.

7.9 Some nouns form their plurals by changing a letter or letters within the singular form or by adding a special ending.

Singular	Plural
foot	feet
woman	women
child	children
ox	oxen

7.10 Some words derived from other languages use special endings to form their plurals.

Singular	Plural
datum	data
alumnus	alumni
alumna	alumnae
curriculum	curricula
medium	media

7.11 Some nouns retain the same form for both singular and plural.

Singular	Plural
fish	fish
quail	quail
sheep	sheep

7.12 Compound nouns written as single words form their plurals in the regular way.

Singular	Plural
metalworker	metalworkers
cupful	cupfuls
bookshelf	bookshelves

Hyphenated compound nouns generally form their plurals by changing the main word in the compound to the plural form.

Singular	Plural
attorney-at-law	attorneys-at-law
sister-in-law	sisters-in-law

7.13 Most surnames (last names) are made plural by adding *s*.

Singular	Plural
Campbell	Campbells
O'Calligan	O'Calligans

Surnames ending in *s, x, ch, sh,* or *z* are made plural by adding *es*.

Singular	Plural
Jones	Joneses
Fox	Foxes
Stitz	Stitzes

Note: When forming the plural of a proper name, never change the original spelling of the name.

Singular	Plural
O'Reilly	O'Reillys [*not* O'Reillies]
Tallman	Tallmans [*not* Tallmen]

7.14 The plurals of numbers, letters, symbols, and words used as words are formed by adding an *s*.

There were seven *36s* given for the answer to the math problems.
Michael wrote a string of *xs* across the page.
The proofreader found too many *thems* in one sentence.

SPELLING AND WORD DIVISIONS

7.15 The following list contains over 2,000 words frequently used in general writing and business communication. The list is arranged alphabetically and shows acceptable word division points. Shown in color are 500 most frequently misspelled words. Intensive practice on these words can help eliminate many spelling errors and increase productivity.

A

ab-bre-vi-a-tion
abil-ity
aboard
ab-rupt
ab-sence
ab-so-lute
ab-sorp-tion
abun-dant
aca-dem-ically
ac-cept
ac-cept-able
ac-cep-tance
ac-cepted
ac-cess
ac-ces-si-ble
ac-ci-den-tally
ac-cli-mated
ac-com-mo-da-tion
ac-com-pa-ni-ment
ac-com-plish
ac-com-plish-ment
ac-cor-dance
ac-cord-ing
ac-cord-ingly
ac-count
ac-count-ing
ac-credi-ta-tion
ac-cu-mu-lated
ac-cu-racy
ac-cu-rate
achieve
achieve-ment
ac-knowl-edge
ac-knowl-edg-ment
ac-quired
ac-qui-si-tion
ac-tive
ac-tivi-ties
ac-tiv-ity
ac-tual
ac-tu-ally
ad-di-tion
ad-di-tional
ad-dress
ad-e-quate
ad-ja-cent
ad-just-ment

ad-min-is-tered
ad-min-is-tra-tion
ad-min-is-tra-tive
ad-min-is-tra-tor
ad-mis-sion
ad-mit-tance
ad-mit-ted
ado-les-cent
adop-tion
ad-vance
ad-van-tage
ad-van-ta-geous
ad-ven-ture
ad-ver-tise-ment
ad-ver-tis-ing
ad-vice
ad-vise
ad-vi-sory
af-fair
af-fect
af-fi-da-vit
af-fir-ma-tive
af-ter-noon
against
agen-cies
agency
agenda
agent
agree
agree-ment
ag-ri-cul-ture
ahead
aide
air-craft
al-le-giance
al-li-ance
al-lot-ting
al-low
al-low-ance
al-most
al-pha-bet-ical
al-ready
al-ter-nate
al-ter-na-tive
al-though
alumnae
alumni
al-ways

among
amount
am-pli-fied
analy-sis
ana-lyze
an-ni-hi-late
an-nounced
an-nounce-ment
an-nual
anony-mous
an-other
an-swer
an-tici-pate
any-one
any-thing
apart-ment
apolo-get-ically
apolo-gize
ap-pa-ra-tus
ap-par-ent
ap-pear
ap-pli-ca-ble
ap-pli-cant
ap-pli-ca-tion
ap-plied
ap-plies
ap-ply
ap-pointed
ap-point-ment
ap-praisal
ap-pre-ci-ate
ap-pre-cia-tion
ap-proach
ap-pro-pri-ate
ap-proval
ap-prove
ap-proxi-mately
ar-chive
area
around
ar-range
ar-range-ment
ar-rival
ar-rive
ar-ti-cle
ask-ing
as-pect
as-sem-bly

7

as-sess
as-sess-ment
asset
as-sign
as-sign-ment
as-sist
as-sis-tance
as-sis-tant
as-sis-ting
as-so-ci-ate
as-so-cia-tion
as-sume
as-sum-ing
as-sump-tion
as-sur-ance
as-sure
at-mo-sphere
at-tach
at-tach-ment
at-tempt
at-tend
at-ten-dance
at-ten-tion
at-ti-tude
at-tor-ney
at-tor-neys
at-trac-tive
au-di-ence
au-dit
au-thor-ity
au-tho-ri-za-tion
au-tho-rized
auto
au-to-matic
au-to-mat-ically
au-to-mo-bile
aux-il-iary
availa-bil-ity
avail-able
av-er-age
avoid
award
aware
aw-fully

B

back-ground
bal-ance

bal-lot
bank-ing
bank-rupt
ban-quet
bar-bar-ian
ba-sic
ba-si-cally
ba-sis
batch
beau-ti-ful
be-came
be-cause
be-come
be-com-ing
be-fore
be-gan
beg-gar
be-gin
be-gin-ning
be-half
be-hav-ior
be-hind
be-lieve
bene-fi-cial
bene-fit
best
bet-ter
be-tween
be-yond
bi-an-nual
bib-li-og-ra-phy
bid-der
bid-ding
billed
bill-ing
blas-phemy
blood
blue-print
board
book-keep-ing
bot-tom
bou-le-vard
brace-let
bracket
branch
break-down (n)
break down (v)
break-fast

brief
briefly
bring
broad
bro-chure
bro-ken
bro-ker
brought
bub-ble
bud-get
buf-fet
build
build-ing
built
bul-le-tin
bu-reau
burial
busi-ness
busi-nes-ses
buy-ing

C

ca-ble
cal-cu-la-tion
cal-en-dar
call-ing
came
cam-ou-flage
cam-paign
cam-pus
can-cel
can-celed
can-cel-la-tion
can-di-date
can-not
ca-pa-bili-ties
ca-pac-ity
capi-tal
car-bu-re-tor
ca-reer
care-ful
care-fully
cari-ca-ture
car-ried
car-rier
car-ri-ers
carry
car-ry-ing

7

cash
cash-ier (n)
cata-log
ca-tas-tro-phe
cate-go-ries
cate-gory
ceil-ing
cel-lar
ceme-tery
cen-ter
cen-tral
cer-tain
cer-tainly
cer-tifi-cate
cer-tifi-ca-tion
cer-ti-fied
chain
chair-man
chair-per-son
chair-woman
chance
change
change-able
chang-ing
chan-nel
chap-ter
charge
chart
chas-sis
check
check-ing
chem-ical
chief
chil-dren
choice
choose
cho-sen
chronic
church
cir-cu-la-tion
cir-cum-stance
citi-zen
civil
claim
claim-ant
clari-fi-ca-tion
class
class-room

clear-ance
clearly
cler-ical
clerk
cli-ent
clinic
clin-ical
closed
clos-ing
coach
code
col-lapse
col-lected
col-lec-tion
col-lege
color
co-los-sal
com-bi-na-tion
com-ing
com-ment
com-mer-cial
com-mis-sion
com-mis-sioner
com-mit-ment
com-mit-ted
com-mit-tee
com-mon
com-mu-ni-cate
com-mu-ni-ca-tion
com-mu-nity
com-pact
com-pa-nies
com-pan-ion-ship
com-pany
com-para-tive
com-pared
com-pari-son
com-pen-sa-tion
com-pe-ti-tion
com-peti-tive
com-peti-tor
com-plaint
com-ple-ment
com-plete
com-pletely
com-plet-ing
com-ple-tion
com-plex

com-pli-ance
com-ply
com-po-nent
com-pre-hen-sive
com-pres-sor
com-puter
con-ceiv-able
con-cept
con-cern
con-cern-ing
con-clu-sion
con-crete
con-di-tion
con-do-min-ium
con-duct
con-duct-ing
con-fer-ence
con-fi-dence
con-fi-dent
con-firm
con-gratu-la-tions
con-gress
con-gres-sional
con-gress-man
con-gress-woman
con-junc-tion
con-nec-tion
con-nec-tor
con-nois-seur
con-sci-en-tious
con-sen-sus
con-sent
con-se-quently
con-ser-va-tion
con-sider
con-sid-er-able
con-sid-er-ably
con-sid-er-ation
con-sis-tent
con-stant
con-struc-tion
con-sul-tant
con-sul-ta-tion
con-sult-ing
con-sumer
con-tact
con-tain
con-tain-ing

con-tain-ment
con-tent
con-tinu-ation
con-tinue
con-tinu-ing
con-tinu-ous
con-tract
con-trac-tor
con-trib-ute
con-tri-bu-tion
con-trol
con-tro-versy
con-ve-nience
con-ve-nient
con-ven-tion
con-ver-sa-tion
con-ver-sion
con-veyer
co-op-er-ate
co-op-era-tion
co-op-era-tive
co-or-di-nate
co-or-di-nat-ing
co-or-di-na-tion
co-or-di-na-tor
cop-ies
copy
cor-ner
cor-po-rate
cor-po-ra-tion
cor-rect
cor-rec-tions
cor-re-spon-dence
cost
costly
could
coun-cils
coun-sel
coun-sel-ing
coun-sel-ors
count
coun-ter-feit
coun-tries
coun-try
county
cou-ple
course
court

cover
cov-er-age
crash
cre-ate
crea-tive
credit
cred-ited
crimi-nal
cri-te-ria
crit-ical
cross
cross-ing
cru-elty
cur-rent
cur-rently
cur-ricu-lum
cus-to-dial
cus-tody
cus-tomer
cy-cle

D

daily
dam-age
data
dated
dead-line
deal
dealer
deal-ing
dean
death
de-ba-cle
debit
deca-dent
de-ceit-ful
de-cide
de-ci-sion
deck
de-cline
de-duc-ti-ble
de-duc-tion
deed
deemed
de-fen-dant
de-fense
def-er-ence
de-ferred

de-fined
defi-nitely
de-gree
delay
de-lete
de-liver
de-liv-ery
de-mand
dem-on-strate
de-part-ment
de-part-men-tal
de-part-ments
de-pen-dent
de-posit
depth
de-scen-dant
de-scribe
de-scribed
de-scrip-tion
de-sign
des-ig-nated
de-sir-able
de-sire
desk
de-spair
de-tail
de-te-rio-ra-tion
de-ter-mi-na-tion
de-ter-mine
de-ter-min-ing
det-ri-men-tal
dev-as-ta-tion
de-velop
de-vel-op-ment
de-vel-op-men-tal
de-vice
de-vise
de-vote
dif-fer-ence
dif-fer-ent
dif-fi-cult
dif-fi-cul-ties
dif-fi-culty
di-lemma
dili-gence
din-ner
di-rect
di-rec-tion

7

di-rec-tions
di-rectly
di-rec-tor
dis-abili-ties
dis-abil-ity
di-sas-ter
di-sas-trous
dis-charge
dis-closed
dis-clo-sure
dis-count
dis-cov-ered
dis-crimi-na-tion
dis-cuss
dis-cuss-ing
dis-cus-sion
dis-play
dis-posal
dis-po-si-tion
dis-sat-is-fied
dis-tance
dis-trib-ute
dis-tri-bu-tion
dis-trict
di-vi-sion
docu-ment
docu-men-ta-tion
dol-lar
do-mes-tic
dou-ble
doubt
draft
drain
draw-ing
dress-ing
drill-ing
drive
driver
dur-ing
du-ties

E
ear-lier
ear-li-est
early
earn-ings
earth
eas-ier

eas-ily
eco-nom-ics
econ-omy
ec-stasy
edi-tion
edi-to-rial
edu-ca-tion
edu-ca-tional
ef-fect
ef-fec-tive
ef-fec-tively
ef-fec-tive-ness
ef-fi-ciency
ef-fi-cient
ef-fi-ciently
ef-fort
ei-ther
elect
elec-tion
elec-tri-cal
elec-tronic
ele-ment
ele-men-tary
ele-ments
eli-gi-bil-ity
eli-gi-ble
elimi-nate
elimi-nated
else
em-bar-rass-ment
em-blems
emer-gency
em-pha-sis
em-pha-size
em-ployed
em-ployee
em-ployer
em-ploy-ers
em-ploy-ment
en-able
en-close
en-clos-ing
en-cour-age
en-deavor
en-ergy
en-force-ment
en-gage
en-gine

en-gi-neer
en-gi-neer-ing
en-joy
enor-mous
enough
en-rolled
en-roll-ment
en-sure
en-ter
en-ter-tain-ment
en-thu-si-as-ti-cally
en-tire
en-tirely
en-ti-tle
en-trance
en-try
en-ve-lope
en-vi-ron-ment
en-vi-ron-men-tal
equal
equip-ment
er-ror
es-pe-cially
es-pi-o-nage
es-sence
es-sen-tial
es-tab-lish
es-tab-lish-ing
es-tate
es-ti-mate
etc.
evalu-ate
evalu-ation
even
eve-ning (n)
even-ing (v)
event
ever
every
every-one
every-thing
evi-dence
evi-dent
ex-actly
ex-ami-na-tion
ex-am-ine
ex-am-ined
ex-am-ple

ex-ceed
ex-cel-lent
ex-cept
ex-cep-tion
ex-cep-tional
ex-cess
ex-ces-sive
ex-change
ex-clu-sive
exe-cuted
ex-ecu-tive
ex-empt
ex-hibit
ex-ist
exist-ing
ex-pand
ex-pan-sion
ex-pect
ex-pected
ex-pen-di-ture
ex-pense
ex-pen-sive
ex-pe-ri-ence
ex-per-tise
ex-plain
ex-plained
ex-pla-na-tion
ex-plore
ex-po-sure
ex-press
ex-press-ing
ex-tend
ex-ten-sion
ex-ten-sive
ex-tent
ex-tra
ex-tremely

F

fa-cili-tate
fa-cili-ties
fa-cil-ity
fac-tor
fac-ulty
fail
failed
fail-ure
fair

fairly
fa-mil-iar
fami-lies
fam-ily
farm
fas-ci-na-tion
fas-ter
fa-ther
fa-vor
fa-vor-able
fea-si-bil-ity
fea-si-ble
fea-ture
fed-eral
feed-back
fel-low
femi-nine
field
fif-teen
fifth
fig-ure
files
fil-ing
fill-ing
film
fi-nal
fi-nally
fi-nance
fi-nan-cial
fi-nan-cier
fi-nanc-ing
find-ings
fin-ished
firm
first
fis-cal
fis-sion
fixed
fix-ture
flag
flexi-bil-ity
flex-ible
floor
flow
fluid
fo-cus
folder
fol-low

fol-lowed
fol-low-ing
fol-low-up
foot-ball
force
fore-cast
fore-clo-sure
for-eign
for-feit
form
for-mal
for-mat
for-mer
for-mula
forth-com-ing
for-ward
found
foun-da-tion
four
fourth
frame
free
freight
fre-quently
fresh-men
friend
fuel
ful-fill
fully
func-tion
func-tional
fund
fun-da-men-tal
fund-ing
fur-nish
fur-nished
fur-ni-ture
fur-ther
fur-ther-more
fu-ture

G

gain
gal-axy
gaso-line
ga-ther
gauge
gen-eral

7

gen-er-ally
gen-er-ated
gen-era-tion
get-ting
given
giv-ing
goes
going
goods
gov-ern-ment
grade
gradu-ate
gradu-at-ing
gram-mar
grand
grant
great
greater
great-est
greatly
gross
ground
group
growth
guar-an-tee
guest
guid-ance
guide
guide-lines
gym

H

half
ham-mer
hand-book
handi-capped
han-dle
han-dled
han-dling
hand-outs
hap-pen
happy
ha-rass
hav-ing
head-quar-ters
health
hear
heard

hear-ing
heavy
help-ful
help-ing
hereby
he-redi-tary
hesi-tate
higher
high-est
highly
high-way
hin-drance
hired
his-tor-ical
his-tory
hold-ing
hole
holi-day
hope-fully
hori-zon-tal
hos-pi-tal
hos-pi-tali-za-tion
hos-pi-tals
ho-tel
hour
hourly
house
house-hold
hous-ing
how-ever
hu-man
hun-dred
hy-poc-risy

I

idea
ide-ally
iden-ti-fi-ca-tion
iden-ti-fied
iden-tify
iden-ti-fy-ing
ill-ness
im-me-di-ate
im-me-di-ately
im-pact
im-ple-ment
im-ple-men-ta-tion
im-ple-ment-ed

im-ple-ment-ing
im-pli-ca-tion
im-por-tance
im-por-tant
im-pressed
im-pres-sion
im-prove
im-prove-ment
im-prov-ing
in-ade-quate
in-cen-tive
inches
in-ci-dence
in-ci-dent
in-clude
in-clud-ing
in-come
in-cor-rect
in-crease
in-creas-ing
in-curred
in-deed
in-de-pen-dent
in-dex
in-di-cate
in-di-cat-ing
in-di-ca-tor
in-dis-pens-able
in-di-vid-ual
in-duce-ment
in-dus-trial
in-dus-try
in-evi-ta-ble
in-fla-tion
in-flu-en-tial
in-form
in-for-mal
in-for-ma-tion
in-for-ma-tive
ini-tial
ini-ti-ated
ini-tia-tive
in-ju-ries
in-jury
in-no-cence
input
in-quir-ies
in-quiry

7

in-scribe
in-side
in-spec-tion
in-stall
in-stal-la-tion
in-stalled
in-stall-ment
in-stance
in-stead
in-sti-tu-tion
in-structed
in-struc-tion
in-struc-tional
in-struc-tor
in-stru-ment
in-sur-ance
in-sure
in-sured
in-te-gral
in-te-gra-tion
in-tel-lec-tual
in-tel-li-gence
in-tend
in-ten-sive
in-tent
in-ten-tion
in-ter-est
in-ter-ested
in-ter-est-ing
in-ter-fere
in-terim
in-te-rior
in-ter-nal
in-ter-na-tional
in-ter-pre-ta-tion
in-ter-roga-to-ries
in-ter-state
in-ter-view
in-tro-duce
in-tro-duced
in-tro-duc-tion
in-ven-to-ries
in-ven-tory
in-ves-ti-gate
in-vest-ment
in-vi-ta-tion
in-vite
in-voice

in-volve
in-volve-ment
in-volv-ing
ir-rele-vant
ir-re-sist-ible
is-su-ance
is-sue
item
itin-er-ary
it-self

J

join
joint
judg-ment
ju-di-cial
ju-nior
ju-ris-dic-tion
jus-tice
jus-ti-fi-ca-tion
ju-ve-nile

K

keep-ing
know-ing
knowl-edge
known

L

lab
la-bel
la-bor
labo-ra-tory
la-bo-ri-ous
lan-guage
large
larger
larg-est
later
lat-eral
lat-est
lay-off (n)
lay off (v)
lead
leader
lead-er-ship
learn

learned
learn-ing
lease
least
leave
leav-ing
le-gal
leg-is-la-tion
leg-is-la-tive
lei-sure
length
less
let-ter
level
lia-bil-ity
lib-eral
li-brary
li-cense
lien
life-time
light
likely
limit
limi-ta-tions
limi-ted
listed
list-ing
lit-era-ture
liti-ga-tion
lit-tle
live-li-hood
liv-ing
load
load-ing
loan
lo-cal
lo-cated
lo-ca-tion
longer
look-ing
lose
loss
lost
lower
low-est
lunch
lun-cheon
luxu-ri-ous

7

M

ma-chine
maga-zine
mag-nifi-cent
mail
mail-ing
main-tain
main-tained
main-tain-ing
main-te-nance
major
ma-jor-ity
mak-ing
mal-func-tion
ma-li-cious
man-age-ment
man-ager
man-ag-ing
man-ner
ma-neu-ver
man-ual
manu-fac-turer
manu-script
many
marked
mar-ket
mar-ket-ing
mas-ter
match
ma-te-rial
ma-ter-nity
mathe-mat-ics
mat-ter
maxi-mum
maybe
meals
mean-ing-ful
meant
mean-time
me-chan-ical
mecha-nism
media
med-ical
me-dio-cre
meet-ing
meet-ings
mel-an-choly
mem-ber

mem-ber-ship
memo-ran-dum
men-tal
men-tally
men-tion
mer-chan-dise
mes-sage
metal
meta-phor
me-ter
method
mid-dle
might
mile
mile-age
mili-tary
mil-lion
min-ia-ture
mini-mum
min-ing
min-is-try
mi-nor
min-ute (n)
mi-nute (adj)
mis-cel-la-neous
mis-chie-vous
miss-ing
mis-sion
mo-bile
model
mod-ern
mod-est
modi-fi-ca-tion
modi-fied
mo-ment
money
moni-tor
moni-tor-ing
month
monthly
moral
morn-ing
mort-gage
most
mother
mo-tion
mo-tor
mounted

move
move-ment
mov-ing
mul-ti-ple
mu-nici-pal
mu-sic
mu-tual
mu-tu-ally
my-self
mys-te-ri-ous

N

na-ive
name
na-tion
na-tion-ally
natu-ral
na-ture
nearly
nec-es-sary
ne-ces-sity
nega-tive
nei-ther
net-work
neu-rotic
never
news-let-ter
night
none
non-print
nor-mal
nor-mally
north
noth-ing
no-tice
no-ti-fi-ca-tion
no-ti-fied
no-tify
nu-clear
nui-sance
num-ber
nu-mer-ous
nurse

O

obe-di-ence
ob-jec-tives
ob-tain

ob-tained
ob-tain-ing
ob-vi-ous
ob-vi-ously
oc-ca-sion
oc-cu-pancy
oc-cu-pants
oc-cu-pa-tion
oc-cu-pa-tional
oc-cur
oc-curred
of-fer
of-fered
of-fer-ing
of-fice
of-fi-cer
of-fi-cial
off-set
of-ten
omit-ting
once
on-go-ing
only
opened
open-ing
op-er-ate
op-er-at-ing
op-era-tion
op-era-tional
op-era-tor
opin-ion
op-por-tu-ni-ties
op-por-tu-nity
op-po-si-tion
op-tion
or-der
or-dered
or-di-nance
or-di-nary
or-ga-ni-za-tion
or-gani-za-tional
ori-en-ta-tion
ori-gin
origi-nal
origi-nally
other
oth-er-wise
our-selves

out-line
out-pa-tient
out-ra-geous
out-side
out-stand-ing
over
over-all
owned
owner

P

pack-age
packet
pack-ing
page
paid
paint-ing
pam-phlet
panel
paper
pa-per-work
para-graph
pa-raly-sis
par-cel
par-ent
par-ents
park-ing
pa-role
par-tici-pant
par-tici-pate
par-tici-pat-ing
par-tici-pa-tion
par-ticu-lar
par-ticu-larly
par-ties
party
pas-time
pa-tient
pay
pay-able
pay-ing
pay-ment
pay-roll
ped-es-tal
pen-alty
pend-ing
peo-ple
per

per-ceive
per-cent
per-cent-age
per-form
per-for-mance
per-formed
per-haps
pe-riod
per-ma-nent
per-mis-sion
per-mit
per-mit-ted
per-sis-tent
per-son
per-sonal
per-son-ally
per-son-nel
per-spi-ra-tion
per-tain-ing
per-ti-nent
pe-ti-tion
phar-macy
phase
phe-nome-nal
phi-los-o-phy
phone
photo
pho-to-graph
phys-ical
phy-si-cian
pick
pic-ture
piece
pi-lot
place
place-ment
plac-ing
plain-tiff
plan
plan-ning
plant
pla-teau
play
pleas-ant
please
pleas-ure
plus
pocket

7

point
pole
po-lice
poli-cies
pol-icy
po-lit-ical
poli-ti-cian
popu-lar
popu-la-tion
por-tion
po-si-tion
posi-tive
pos-ses-sion
pos-si-bil-ity
pos-si-ble
pos-si-bly
post
post-age
postal
po-ten-tial
pounds
power
prac-ti-cal
prac-tice
pre-ced-ing
pre-domi-nant
pre-fer
pre-limi-nary
prem-ises
pre-mium
prep-a-ra-tion
pre-pare
pre-pared
pre-par-ing
pre-scrip-tion
pres-ence
pres-ent (n)
pre-sent (v)
pre-sen-ta-tion
pre-sented
pre-sent-ing
pres-ently
presi-dent
press
pres-sure
pre-sump-tion
preva-lent
pre-vent

pre-ven-tion
pre-vi-ous
pre-vi-ously
price
pric-ing
pri-mar-ily
pri-mary
prin-ci-pal
prin-ci-ple
print
print-ing
prior
pri-or-ities
pri-or-ity
pri-vate
privi-lege
privi-leges
prob-able
prob-ably
prob-lem
pro-ce-dure
pro-ceed
pro-ceed-ings
pro-cess
pro-cess-ing
pro-duce
pro-duc-ing
prod-uct
pro-duc-tion
pro-duc-tive
pro-duc-tiv-ity
pro-fes-sional
pro-file
profit
prof-it-able
pro-gram
pro-gram-mer
pro-gram-ming
prog-ress (n)
pro-gress (v)
pro-hi-bi-tion
proj-ect (n)
pro-ject (v)
pro-mote
pro-mo-tion
prompt
promptly
pro-pa-ganda

propa-gate
pro-per
prop-erly
prop-er-ties
prop-erty
proph-esy
pro-posal
pro-pose
pros-pect
pro-spec-tive
pro-tect
pro-tec-tion
proud
prove
pro-vide
pro-vid-ing
pro-vi-sion
psy-chi-at-ric
psy-chol-ogy
pub-lic
pub-li-ca-tion
pub-lic-ity
pub-lish
pub-lisher
pub-lish-ing
pu-pils
pur-chase
pur-chas-ing
pur-pose
pur-su-ant
pur-sue
put-ting

Q

quali-fi-ca-tion
quali-fied
qual-ify
qual-ity
quan-tity
quar-ter
quar-terly
ques-tion
ques-tion-naire
quickly
qui-etly
quite
quota
quo-ta-tion

R

ra-dio
raise
range
rap-idly
rate
rather
rat-ing
ra-tio
reach
re-ac-tion
read
read-ily
read-ing
ready
re-al-ize
re-ally
rear
rea-son
rea-son-able
rea-son-ably
re-bel-lion
re-call
re-ceipt
re-ceive
re-ceiv-ing
re-cent
re-cently
re-cep-tion
rec-og-ni-tion
rec-og-nize
rec-om-mend
rec-om-men-da-tion
rec-om-mended
rec-om-mend-ing
rec-ord (n)
re-cord (v)
re-corded
re-cord-ing
re-cov-ery
re-cruit-ment
re-duce
re-duc-tion
reel
re-fer
ref-er-ence
ref-er-enced
re-fer-ral

re-ferred
re-flect
re-fund
re-gard
re-gard-ing
re-gard-less
re-gion
re-gional
reg-is-ter
reg-is-tered
reg-is-tra-tion
regu-lar
regu-larly
regu-la-tion
re-hearsal
re-im-burse-ment
re-lated
re-la-tion
re-la-tion-ship
rela-tive
rela-tively
re-lease
re-li-able
re-lief
re-lieve
re-lo-ca-tion
re-main
re-main-der
re-main-ing
re-mem-ber
remi-nis-cent
re-moval
re-move
re-new
re-newal
rent
rental
re-pair
re-place
re-place-ment
re-ply
re-port
re-port-ing
rep-re-sent
rep-re-sen-ta-tive
rep-re-sent-ing
re-quest
re-quest-ing

re-quire
re-quire-ment
re-quir-ing
re-search
res-er-va-tion
re-serve
resi-dence
resi-dent
resi-den-tial
reso-lu-tion
re-solve
re-sort
re-source
re-spect
re-spec-tive
res-pi-ra-tory
re-spond
re-spond-ing
re-sponse
re-spon-si-bili-ties
re-spon-si-bil-ity
re-spon-si-ble
res-to-ra-tion
re-straint
re-sult
re-sulted
re-sult-ing
ré-sumé (n)
re-sume (v)
re-tail
re-tain
re-tarded
re-tire-ment
re-turn
re-turn-ing
re-vealed
reve-nue
re-view
re-view-ing
re-vised
re-vi-sion
re-ward-ing
right
risk
role
roof
round
route

7

rou-tine
rule
run-ning

S

safety
said
sal-a-ries
sal-ary
sale
sales-man
sales-per-son
sales-woman
sam-ple
sand
sat-is-fac-tion
sat-is-fac-tory
sat-is-fied
sat-isfy
save
sav-ings
sce-nario
sched-ule
sched-ul-ing
school
sci-ence
sci-en-tific
scope
score
search
sea-son
sec-ond
sec-ond-ary
sec-re-tarial
sec-re-tar-ies
sec-re-tary
sec-tion
sec-tor
se-cured
se-cu-ri-ties
se-cu-rity
seek-ing
seems
seg-ment
se-lect
se-lec-tion
sell
sell-ing

se-mes-ter
semi-nar
sen-ate
sena-tor
send-ing
se-nior
sense
sen-sory
sen-ti-ment
sepa-rate
sepa-rately
sepa-ra-tion
se-quence
se-ries
se-ri-ous
se-ri-ously
ser-vice
serv-ing
ses-sion
set-ting
set-tle-ment
sev-enth
sev-eral
shale
shall
share
shar-ing
sheet
shift
ship-ment
shipped
ship-ping
shop
short
shortly
should
shoul-der
show-ing
shown
siege
sign
sig-na-ture
signed
sig-nifi-cance
sig-nifi-cant
sig-nifi-cantly
sign-ing
si-lent

simi-lar
sim-ple
sim-plify
sim-ply
sin-gle
site
situ-ation
size
skill
slide
slightly
slip
small
smal-ler
snow
so-cial
so-ci-ety
soft
soft-ware
soil
sold
so-licit
so-lici-ta-tion
solid
so-lu-tion
solve
sol-vent
some
some-one
some-thing
some-time
some-times
some-what
sorry
sound
source
sour-ces
south
sou-ve-nir
space
speak
speak-ers
spe-cial
spe-cific
spe-cifi-cally
speci-fi-ca-tion
speci-fied
speci-men

speech
speed
spend
spend-ing
spent
spirit
spir-itual
spoke
spon-sor
spon-sored
sports
spring
square
staff
staff-ing
stage
stairs
stamp
stan-dard
stand-ing
start
start-ing
state
state-ment
sta-tion
sta-tis-ti-cal
sta-tis-tics
sta-tus
stat-ute
statu-tory
steel
step
still
stock
stock-hold-ers
stop
stor-age
store
sto-ries
storm
story
stra-te-gic
street
strength
stress
strong
strongly
struc-tural

struc-ture
stub-born
stu-dent
stud-ied
study
style
sub-com-mit-tee
sub-ject
sub-mis-sion
sub-mit
sub-mit-ted
sub-mit-ting
sub-se-quent
sub-se-quently
sub-stan-tial
sub-stan-tially
suc-cess
suc-cess-ful
suc-cess-fully
suc-ces-sion
such
suf-fi-cient
sug-gest
sug-ges-tion
suit
suit-able
sum
sum-mary
sum-mer
su-per-cede
su-per-in-ten-dent
su-per-vi-sion
su-per-vi-sor
su-per-vi-sory
sup-plied
sup-plier
sup-plies
sup-ply
sup-port
sup-press
sur-charge
sure
sur-face
sur-gery
sur-plus
sur-vey
sus-cep-ti-ble
sus-pen-sion

syn-ony-mous
sys-tem

T

table
tak-ing
talk
talk-ing
tank
tape
tar-get
tar-iff
task
tax
teach
teacher
team
tech-ni-cal
tech-nique
tech-nol-ogy
tele-phone
tele-vi-sion
tem-pera-ment
tem-pera-ture
tem-po-rary
ten-ants
ten-dency
ten-sile
ten-ta-tive
term
ter-mi-nal
ter-mi-na-tion
test
test-ing
text
thank
theft
their
theme
them-selves
theo-ret-ical
thera-pist
ther-apy
there
there-af-ter
thereby
there-fore
thing

7

think
this
thor-oughly
those
though
thought
thou-sands
thrift
through
through-out
thus
tick-ets
tim-bers
time
timely
title
today
to-gether
tol-er-ance
toll
tool
topic
tor-nado
total
to-tally
touch
toward
town
track
trade
tra-di-tional
traf-fic
trag-edy
train
train-ing
trans-ac-tion
tran-scend
trans-fer
trans-ferred
tran-sis-tor
tran-si-tion
trans-par-ent
trans-por-ta-tion
trans-pose
travel
treat
treat-ment
trees

trial
trou-ble
truck
true
truly
trust
trust-ees
try-ing
tube
tui-tion
twice
type
typ-ing
tyr-anny

U

un-able
unani-mous
under
un-der-gradu-ate
un-der-stand
un-der-stand-ing
un-der-stood
un-der-writ-ing
un-doubt-edly
un-fa-vor-able
un-for-tu-nate
un-for-tu-nately
union
unique
unit
uni-ver-sal
uni-ver-sity
un-less
un-mis-tak-able
un-nec-es-sary
un-paid
un-til
un-used
un-usual
up-com-ing
up-date
up-per
urge
us-age
use-ful
user
usual

usu-ally
utili-ties
util-ity
uti-li-za-tion
uti-lize

V

va-cancy
va-ca-tion
vac-cine
vac-uum
valu-able
value
vari-a-tion
va-ri-ety
vari-ous
ve-hi-cle
ven-dor
ven-geance
veri-fi-ca-tion
ver-sa-tile
ver-sion
ver-sus
via
vice
vice-presi-dent
view
vigi-lance
vil-lain
vio-la-tion
visit
vi-sual
vital
vo-ca-tional
vol-ume
vol-un-tary
vot-ing

W

ware-house
war-ranty
waste
wa-ter
wear
wear-ing
weather
week-end

weekly	wife	writ-ing
weight	will-ing	writ-ten
wel-come	win-dow	
weld-ing	wire	**Y**
wel-fare	with-hold	yacht
west-ern	within	yard
what-ever	with-out	yawn
when-ever	women	year
whether	wood	yes-ter-day
which	worker	yield
whis-per	work-ing	young
white	work-shop	your-self
whole	world	
whom	worth	**Z**
whose	would	zone
wide	write	

WORD HYPHENATION

The following are basic rules used to hyphenate words. Refer to a good dictionary when in doubt as to whether to hyphenate.

7.16 Hyphenate a spelled-out compound number from 21 to 99.

twenty-three   eighty-nine   two hundred fifty-nine

7.17 In general, hyphenate spelled-out fractions.

The heirs were each given a one-eighth share of the property.
A two-thirds vote will be required to pass the law.
A little less than one-half of the damaged machines were returned for service.

7.18 Hyphenate a compound adjective that immediately precedes a noun. Do not hyphenate a compound adjective that follows a noun.

hard-to-find parts   parts that are hard to find
stain-resistant fabric   fabric that is stain resistant

7.19 Hyphenate words that are formed with the prefixes *all-*, *ex-*, *great-*, *half-*, and *self-*; with the suffix *-elect*; and all prefixes before a proper noun or proper adjective.

all-encompassing	ex-athlete	self-denial
great-grandfather	half-hearted	mayor-elect
ante-Wilson	non-Asian	pre-Mayan
post-World War II	pro-British	trans-Canadian

7

7.20 Generally, do not hyphenate words formed with the prefixes *anti-*, *bi-*, *circum-*, *fore-*, *inter-*, *mis-*, *mono-*, *over-*, *super-*, *tri-*, *under-*, *uni-*, *up-*, *and where-*.

antibacterial	misconstrued	undergirded
bifocal	monoplane	unidirectional
circumspect	overridden	upcoming
foreboding	superhighway	wherefore
international	trifocal	

7.21 Hyphenate after the prefix to prevent misunderstanding if the prefix ends with a vowel and the root word also begins with a vowel.

re-examine	co-anchor	re-establish

7.22 The prefix *re-* should generally not be followed by a hyphen. Hyphenate a word that might otherwise be misunderstood by the reader except for the hyphen.

re-create (to create again)	recreate (to refresh)
re-collect (to collect again)	recollect (to remember)

7.23 Do not hyphenate titles and official positions.

general contractor	vice chairperson
lieutenant governor	editor in chief

7.24 Do not hyphenate a combination of an adverb ending in *-ly* and an adjective that immediately precedes a noun.

rapidly increasing taxes	accurately stated position
strongly supported action	slowly rising inflation

WORD CHOICE

7.25 The proper selection from groups of easily confused words is important to successful business communication. Use special care with words that look or sound almost alike. Refer to a dictionary for more specific meanings than those shown below.

accede (agree to; comply with)	access (admittance)
exceed (to surpass)	excess (surplus)
accent (to emphasize; give prominence to)	
ascend (to climb)	adapt (to adjust; revise)
ascent (advancement)	adept (highly skilled)
assent (to agree to)	adopt (to take by choice)
accept (to receive; agree)	addition (increase; attachment)
except (to exclude)	edition (publication)

adverse (unfavorable)
averse (opposed)

advice (recommendation;
    guidance)
advise (to give information;
    suggest)

affect (*v.,* to influence)
effect (*n.,* result)
effect (*v.,* to bring about; cause)

aid (*n.,* help; comfort)
aid (*v.,* to help)
aide (assistant)

air (atmosphere)
heir (one who inherits)

aisle (passageway)
isle (island)

allowed (permitted)
aloud (audibly)

all ready (completely prepared)
already (previously)

all right (never *alright* or *allright*)

all together (including all)
altogether (completely)

allude (to refer to)
elude (to escape; avoid)

altar (worship table)
alter (to change)

any one (any person or thing)
anyone (any one person or thing
    in a group)

any more (quantity)
anymore (at present)

are (form of the verb *be*)
hour (60 minutes)
our (possessive form of the
    pronoun *we*)

assistance (help)
assistants (those who help)

assure (to convince)
ensure (to guarantee)
insure (to protect against loss)

attendance (people present)
attendants (assistants)

bases (reasons; foundations)
basis (a reason; a foundation)

biannual (twice a year)
biennial (every two years)
biweekly (every two weeks)
semiweekly (twice a week)

born (given birth)
borne (carried)

brake (stopping device)
break (to separate into parts)

breadth (width)
breath (the air inhaled and exhaled)
breathe (to inhale and exhale)

buy (to purchase)
by (next to; close to)

canvas (heavy cloth)
canvass (to solicit)

capital (material wealth of a business;
    most important; city that is official seat
    of government; punishable by death)
capitol (building for state government)
Capitol (building in which the U.S. Con-
    gress meets)

carton (cardboard box)
cartoon (drawing)

cease (to stop)
seize (to grasp)

ceiling (top; limit)
sealing (closing securely)

cent (penny)
scent (odor)
sent (dispatched)

cite (to quote)
sight (vision)
site (location)

cloths (pieces of fabric)
clothes (apparel)

coarse (rough)
course (plan; path of action)

collision (crash)
collusion (fraudulent; secret agreement)

command (to control)
commend (to compliment)

complement (add to)
compliment (to praise)

conscience (one's moral sense)
conscious (aware of)

consul (foreign representative)
council (governing body)
counsel (*n.*, advice)
counsel (*v.*, to give advice)

costume (dress)
custom (tradition)

datum (information, singular)
data (information, plural)

deceased (dead)
diseased (sick)

decent (having moral qualities)
descend (*v.*, to move downward)
descent (*n.*, a downward step)
dissent (disagreement)

deprecate (to disapprove of)
depreciate (to lessen)

des'ert (*n.*, dry wilderness)
desert' (*v.*, to abandon)
dessert' (*n.*, course in a meal)

device (equipment)
devise (to play)

die (to cease living)
dye (*n.*, color)
dye (*v.*, to color)

disapprove (to have an unfavorable
   opinion)
disprove (to show to be false)

disburse (to pay out)
disperse (to scatter)

elicit (to ask for)
illicit (illegal)

eligible (qualified)
ineligible (not qualified)
illegible (unreadable)

emerge (to come forth)
immerge (to plunge into)

emigrate (to leave a country)
immigrate (to come into a country)

eminent (prominent)
imminent (about to happen)

envelop (*v.*, to surround)
envelope (*n.*, container for a letter)

every day (each day)
everyday (ordinary)

expand (to increase)
expend (to pay out)

farther (at a greater distance)
further (more; in addition)

fiscal (financial)
physical (of material things)

forego (to go before)
forgo (to relinquish; give up)

foreword (preface)
forward (ahead)

formally (ceremoniously)
formerly (at an earlier time)

forth (first; ahead)
fourth (after third)

grate (*n.*, a grill)
grate (*v.*, shred)
great (large; distinguished)

guarantee (to make sure)
guaranty (contract; certificate)

guessed (estimated; supposed)
guest (welcome visitor)

hear (to listen)
here (at this place)

higher (taller; greater)
hire (to employ)

hole (an opening)
whole (entire; complete)

incite (to encourage; arouse)
insight (an understanding of)

instance (example; event)
instants (moments)

intestate (dying without a will)
interstate (between states)
intrastate (within one state)

its (possessive form of *it*)
it's (contraction of *it is*)

knew (was aware of)
new (not old)

later (more recent)
latter (second of two)

lay (to place; sit)
lie (to be situated)
lye (strong chemical solution)

lead (*n.*, metal)
lead (*v.*, to guide; precede; go first)
led (*v.*, taken; escorted)

lean (to bend; rely on)
lien (legal claim)

leased (rented)
least (smallest)

lessen (*v.*, to make smaller)
lesson (*n.*, instruction)

lesser (smaller)
lessor (landlord)

liable (responsible)
libel (written slander)

loan (*n.*, something lent)
loan (*v.*, to lend)
lone (only one)

loose (not tight)
lose (*v.*, to misplace)
loss (*n.*, act of losing; failure
   to keep)

marital (pertaining to marriage)
marshal (legal officer)
martial (military)

may be (can be)
maybe (perhaps)

miner (*n.*, worker in a mine)
minor (*adj.*, smaller amount)
minor (*n.*, under legal age)

moral (legal; ethical)
morale (spirit)

ordinance (law)
ordnance (military supplies)

passed (overtook)
past (over; gone by)

patience (tolerance)
patients (those under medical care)

peace (calmness)
piece (portion)

persecuted (mistreated)
prosecuted (sued in court)

personal (private)
personnel (workers; staff)

perspective (point of view)
prospective (hoped for)

plain (lacking ornament; not fancy; clear)
plane (level; flat surface)

plaintiff (party in lawsuit)
plaintive (mournful)

practicable (possible)
practical (useful)

precede (to go before)
proceed (to continue)

prescribe (to give directions)
proscribe (to forbid; condemn)

presence (attendance)
presents (gifts)

principal (major; main; chief; head)
principle (rule)

profit (to benefit; gain)
prophet (one who predicts)

quiet (still; silent)
quite (completely)

raise (*v.*, to lift something)
raise (*n.*, salary increase)
rays (beams)
raze (to destroy)
rise (to move upward)

real (adjective)
really (adverb)

reality (truth)
realty (real estate)

residence (house)
residents (those living in a house)

seize (to take)
seige (battle)

set (to place; put)
sit (to take a seat)

stationary (in the same place)
stationery (writing paper)

teach (to give knowledge)
learn (to gain knowledge)

than (compared to)
then (at that time)

their (possessive form of *they*)
there (in that place)
they're (contraction of *they are*)

threw (tossed)
through (by way of)
thorough (complete)

to (in the direction of)
too (in addition to; also)
two (one plus one)

waist (middle of the body)
waste (*n.*, unusable material)
waste (*v.*, to squander)

waive (to give up)
wave (to signal)

ware (material goods)
wear (to have on)
where (at what place)

weak (without strength)
week (seven days)

weather (climate)
whether (if)

who's (contraction of *who is*)
whose (possessive form of *who*)

your (possessive form of *you*)
you're (contraction of *you are*)

SELF-CHECK EXERCISE 1, *UNIT 7*

_____
(Name)

Complete the spelling of the following words by supplying the correct prefix or suffix. The meanings of the prefixes and suffixes are shown in parentheses.

1. _____ state (between)

2. _____ angular (three)

3. _____ productive (opposing)

4. market _____ (capable of being)

5. _____ determine (before)

6. _____ standard (below)

7. _____ film (very small)

8. hope _____ (lack of)

9. _____ control (reversal)

10. _____ announced (opposite of)

SELF-CHECK EXERCISE 2, *UNIT 7*

Write the correct plural form in the blank.

1. dollar _____

2. match _____

3. rally _____

4. attorney _____

5. half _____

6. tomato _____

7. deer _____

8. child _____

9. goose _____

10. daughter-in-law _____

Circle the correctly spelled word in the following pairs of words.

1. affidavid
   affidavit

2. bracelet
   bracelette

3. bennefits
   benefits

4. corporate
   corperate

5. information
   infomation

6. anonamous
   anonymous

7. faculities
   facilities

8. financial
   finnancial

9. posible
   possible

10. recieve
    receive

11. embarrassment
    embarassment

12. meterial
    material

13. mantenance
    maintenance

14. custommer
    customer

15. recommendation
    reccommendation

16. advertisement
    advertisment

17. cemetary
    cemetery

18. effect
    efect

19. editorial
    edatorial

20. fassination
    fascination

21. influential
    influintial

22. liesure
    leisure

23. neurotic
    nurotic

24. pamflet
    pamphlet

25. siege
    seige

26. adolesent
    adolescent

27. accompaniment
    acompaniment

28. employee
    employe

29. adition
    addition

30. absense
    absence

31. reciept
    receipt

32. interested
    intrested

33.	immediattely immediately	42.	dispair despair
34.	discriminachion discrimination	43.	dilemma delimma
35.	schedule schdule	44.	espionage espinage
36.	proceedure procedure	45.	heriditary hereditary
37.	comission commission	46.	interrim interim
38.	personnel personel	47.	manuver maneuver
39.	whetther whether	48.	origin origen
40.	mortage mortgage	49.	quietly quitely
41.	blasphemy blasfemy	50.	tyrrany tyranny

SELF-CHECK EXERCISE 4, *UNIT 7*

A definition for one of the words in each of the following pairs is given below. Circle the word that is correctly defined.

Definition	Words	Definition	Words
1. exclude	accept except	6. part of meal	desert dessert
2. people present	attendance attendants	7. financial	physical fiscal
3. inhale/exhale	breath breathe	8. plan	coarse course
4. assistant	aide aid	9. cease living	dye die
5. stop	seize cease	10. large	grate great

Definition	Words	Definition	Words
11. arouse	incite insight	16. listen	hear here
12. smallest	leased least	17. ethical	moral morale
13. mistreated	prosecuted persecuted	18. come forth	emerge immerse
14. visitor	guest guessed	19. misplace	loose lose
15. second of two	latter later	20. contains letter	envelop envelope

Check your answers in the back of the book.

UNIT **8**

THE WRITING PROCESS: PREWRITING AND DRAFTING

Rarely can an individual write a document—essay, letter, report, or memo—in one sitting, from beginning to end. For most people, the writing process involves several stages before arriving at the final version: prewriting, drafting, evaluating, revising, editing, and rewriting. This dynamic process requires continuous thinking, evaluation, and decision making to produce writing that conveys your intended message to a specific audience. This unit examines the first two stages in the writing process: prewriting and drafting.

Prewriting involves establishing the purpose for writing and identifying the audience for which the writing is intended. The prewriting stage answers these questions: Why am I writing (purpose)? For whom am I writing (audience)? What will I write about (topic)? What exactly will I say (supporting information)?

The second stage is *drafting,* the first attempt at writing the document. The goal is to get your thoughts down based on your purpose for writing and the audience for whom you are writing. The first draft represents your first attempt at recording your thoughts. This draft must be evaluated, revised, edited, and rewritten before you arrive at a final document.

PREWRITING

8.1   As part of prewriting, the purpose should be firmly established. The purpose of any writing should be to inform, to describe, to entertain, to narrate, or to persuade.

8.2   The purpose of *expository writing* is to inform or explain.

Possible topics for expository writing:

How to prepare for a successful interview
The laser printer and how it works
How to prepare for the SAT exam
How to conduct a staff meeting

8.3 *Persuasive writing* attempts to convince the reader to accept a point of view or take some action. Persuasive writing uses clear, concise, direct language to express opinions, give reasons, and present evidence.

Possible topics for persuasive writing:

XYZ Company should institute a quality-control program.
Students should investigate the tech prep curriculum.
Every eighteen-year-old should register to vote.
Drug testing should be required in certain occupations.
A year of national service should be required of all.
Driving should be limited to those over eighteen.

8.4 *Writing to entertain* may rely on humor, irony, mystery, sarcasm, and so on.

Possible topics for writing that entertains:

The day I landed the Acme account
The longest day of my life
Taxes—your sacrifice for the nation
The biggest surprise of my life
How not to have a successful interview
What you can do to promote school spirit
The latest fashions for the campus

8.5 *Narrative writing* tells a story or provides the details of a series of events.

Possible topics for narrative writing:

A success story of one tech prep graduate
Climbing Mt. McKinley
The day we lost the state championship
The rescue of motorists in a flash flood
The development of a new product at XYZ Company
Lost in the blizzard of '93

8.6 *Descriptive writing* tells about a person, place, or thing using vivid language and images. Descriptive writing appeals to the senses and tries to catch the imagination of the reader.

Possible topics for descriptive writing:

XYZ Company's new virtual reality game
My grandmother's country kitchen
Paradise Travel Agency's Hawaiian vacation
John Whittier—poet, philosopher, teacher, friend
The miracle of the computer
Fisherman's Wharf in San Francisco

8

8.7 Identifying the audience for whom you are writing is an important part of prewriting. Audiences may vary widely in *gender, education, personal interests, age,* and *socioeconomic background.* To be sure your writing is suitable for your audience, you need to know the following:

1.   What your audience already knows about your topic
2.   How much knowledge your audience has of the topic vocabulary
3.   What kinds of words, sentences, and paragraphs are most appropriate
4.   What opinions or biases are held by your audience about the topic
5.   What background knowledge and experience your audience has about the topic

The following examples show a topic, a purpose, potential audiences, and what might have to be considered to meet the needs of those audiences.

Topic:	COMPUTERS IN THE BUSINESS WORLD
Purpose:	To inform
Audience 1:	Children in elementary school
Considerations:	Their knowledge of and everyday use of computers in school
	Their reading level
	What uses they make of computers
	Whether they might have computers at home
	Whether their parents might work with computers
	Their general knowledge of the business world
Audience 2:	A group of adults
Considerations:	The level of their use and knowledge of computers in their work
	The level of their understanding of computer terms
	Whether they use computers regularly
	Any fear or bias they may have regarding computers
	Their educational background
	Their knowledge of the business world
Audience 3:	A group of computer operators
Considerations:	Depth of training on computers
	Specific needs for information
	Kinds of equipment and software with which they are familiar
	Particular problems or concerns
	New developments in computers

8.8   Choose a subject that can be adequately covered in the form of writing you select. A *subject* covers a broad area of knowledge and may require a lengthy writing to do it justice. A *topic* is a limited subject that might be covered in a paragraph, a short report, or a short essay. The following are examples showing the difference between subjects and topics.

Subjects	Topics
Mathematics	How to Reduce Fractions
The Exploration of Space	What Astronauts Wear
Business Communications	How to Write a Memo
Personal Finance	Balancing Your Checkbook
American Literature	How to Enjoy Poe

8

8.9   The choice of subject should be appropriate to your audience in terms of the readers' general knowledge, maturity level, and interests. Some subjects may simply be too sophisticated for some audiences, uninteresting for some, or too simple for others, unless special precautions are taken. The following examples point out what might or might not be appropriate subjects for various audiences.

Possible Subjects	Audience	Appropriate/ Inappropriate
Conducting a staff meeting	Business executives	Appropriate
Planning for retirement	Mature adults	Appropriate
Theory of relativity	Young children	Inappropriate
Planning a dinner party	Junior high youth	Inappropriate
How to make money	Young adults	Appropriate
Quilt making	High school boys	Inappropriate
Choosing a college	Parents	Appropriate

8.10   Two useful techniques for selecting a topic include *clustering* and *brainstorming*. *Clustering* is an exercise that begins with writing and circling a word, phrase, or topic—something you know you want to write about or just a topic at random to get you started. As you think about related words or ideas, write and circle them and connect them to the original idea or other related ideas. The result is a cluster of related ideas from which you can choose a topic, usually supported by other information in the cluster. The following is an example of clustering beginning with *physical fitness*.

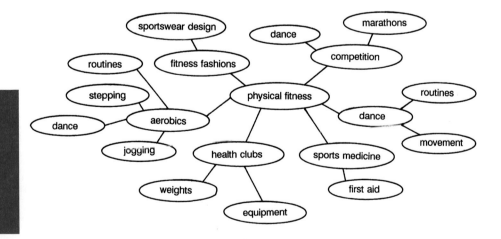

8.11 *Brainstorming* is a technique in which you quickly list ideas that come to mind. You can brainstorm alone with positive results, but brainstorming with a partner or with a group usually creates more ideas. Brainstorming *usually* results in an outpouring of ideas, some usable and some not usable. Record *all* the ideas—regardless of how they sound—since they may help spark other ideas. Brainstorming should be an uninhibited, nonjudgmental flow of ideas. Only at the end of the exercise should you evaluate the ideas to see if a topic has emerged.

Examples of topics produced in brainstorming session around the idea of computers:

software	synthesizers
WYSIWYG	stereo sound
mouse	keyboards
mousepad	hard drives
monitors	hard disks
printers	hard to learn
carpal tunnel syndrome	floppies
bits and bytes	learning systems
modems	word processing
money	spreadsheets
MIDI	desktop publishing
music	

8.12 After deciding on a topic, establishing the purpose, and learning about your potential audience, the next step is to gather information. The kind of information you gather will be influenced by your purpose in writing. Descriptive writing, for example, requires details that enable the audience to share your feelings and experiences with the topic. If your purpose is to inform, you must gather factual information about the topic. These information-gathering techniques may be helpful: *direct* and *indirect observation, personal writings*, and *questioning techniques*.

8.13 *Direct observations* are those made personally, using your senses of touch, sight, sound, smell, and taste. They represent your perceptions of the topic based on your senses and emotions. Such direct observations can help you present a vivid picture with interesting details.

Examples of direct observations that record a visit to a hospital:

The whine of ambulance sirens bringing injured or ill patients
Frequent announcements on the public address system with ominous-sounding codes
The slight suggestion of antiseptic in the air
White-dressed attendants and staff moving with purpose throughout the building
Patients and family members with worried looks in waiting rooms
Frequent encounters with gurneys and wheelchairs
Elevator doors opening with new babies, new mothers, and new fathers spilling out
Sense of relief on leaving, knowing that there is no personal need to stay, yet being grateful for the hospital and its service

8

8.14 *Indirect observations* are those made through the experiences and recollections of others. Indirect observations are made through interviews, listening to others tell about their experiences, or reading about the experiences of others. Much of the information you will use in your writing is likely to come from indirect observations.

Examples of indirect observations:

Interviewing an old man about his experiences in World War I for a report on the use of poisonous gas in wartime

Listening to a group of children talk about what they think about school to learn what motivates children to learn

Reading about the transportation system of a particular city to develop a marketing plan

Using a questionnaire to gain information from teachers about why they chose teaching as a profession

Interviewing employees on an assembly line to gain information about productivity

Listening to elderly relatives at a family reunion talk about growing up in earlier days for a report on how electricity has improved our standard of living

8.15 Personal writings, sometimes known as a *writer's journal,* can be a good source of information to pull from in your writing. A disciplined approach to keeping a journal can be an enjoyable and valuable experience. You can use the journal to record spontaneous feelings, answers to long-standing questions, insights you gain, bits of information you gather in conversations with others, emotions you feel in certain situations and environments, your opinions and those of others, interesting quotations you read or hear, and so on. These writings can often give you ideas, information, or inspiration for something to write about.

Examples of journal entries:

May 16

Visited Grandmother Phillips today—she's 73. She talked about the hard times during the depression, how she sold eggs for ten cents a dozen to get money for school clothes. I learned today that my friend Jan will be moving away. I already miss her. Mom said Granny Phillips was able to go only to the sixth grade because she had to drop out and help at home; they had nine other children in the family. Mr. Jenkins, our counselor, showed us some figures today about how much more money a college graduate will make than a high school dropout. Wow! That made me think.

May 17

We're studying the depression in history. It's hard to believe the suffering that went on. Dad said that his father never believed in banks. (He also didn't believe in girls getting a college education.) I asked Dad for an increase in my allowance. He said only if I made the honor roll. Imagine not having enough money to buy food for your family. It must have been very hard for families during the depression. Makes you more thankful for what you have.

The writer of these journal entries might be inspired to write about friendships, the depression, the value of an education, and so on.

8.16 Using *questioning techniques* can help gather important information. Whether you are seeking information through direct or indirect observations, asking the questions who? what? where? when? why? and how? can provide answers and details that make your writing more credible, more interesting, and more informational. Whether you need to ask each type of question depends on the nature of the topic.

Example topic: The Invention of Television

Who?	Who is given credit for inventing television?
What?	What technological events led up to the invention of television? What impact has television had on our society?
Where?	Where did most of the experimentation with television take place?
When?	When was the first commercial television presentation? When was color television introduced?
Why?	Why did the government impose certain controls on television programming?
How?	How can society benefit from television? How can we protect children from the negative effects of violence on television?

8.17 Once you have selected a topic and gathered information using various techniques, the next step is to *organize your ideas and information.* The first step in organizing is to examine the information you have gathered and classify it into related groups under major headings. By classifying the information, you should be able to determine the major divisions of an outline as well as the supporting items. You may also discover missing details that are necessary for proper coverage and that may require additional research. On the other hand, classifying may indicate too much detail for the type and length of the writing and may require elimination of some of the detail. The following is an example of the type of information that might have been gathered to write a report on tech prep.

Selection of information gathered:

Career skills needed
Technical careers
Local demand for technical graduates
Need for technical training in today's world
Definition of tech prep
Academic/technical integration
Income levels of technical careers
Types of diplomas and degrees
Job opportunities in technical careers
What an articulation agreement is
General education requirements
Curriculum in high school
Meeting the needs of a wider range of students

8

The information might be classified as follows:

What is tech prep?
   definition of tech prep
   articulation agreement
   academic/technical integration
   general education requirements
   types of diplomas and degrees

Why is it needed?
   local demand for technical graduates
   need for technical training in today's world
   meeting needs for wider range of students

What should be considered?
   career skills needed
   job opportunities available
   income levels
   curriculum in high school

8.18 An *outline*, the "road map" for the first draft, can be developed on the basis of the classification of ideas. The organization of ideas in the outline should reflect your purpose in writing the paper. The following is an example of how the order of presentation may reflect your purpose in writing.

Order	Manner of Presentation	Purpose
Chronological	Order of occurrence	To explain a process or give step-by-step information
Spatial	Position of items	To describe relationships
Order of importance	Information in rank order	To persuade, describe, or explain reasons
Cause and effect	Reasons and results	To explain or persuade
Compare and contrast	Similarities and differences	To persuade by showing pros and cons, similarities and differences

The following skeletal outline uses the classification of ideas in paragraph 8.17 with the purpose of explaining the Tech Prep program to persuade students to consider it in their education plans.

```
          TECH PREP—PREPARING FOR THE FUTURE

    I. The Tech Prep Program
       A. What it is
       B. General education requirements
          1. Academic/technical integration
          2. Types of diplomas
       C. Articulation agreements
```

    II. Why Tech Prep is needed
        A. Student need
            1. Continuation of education
            2. Job skills
        B. Technical skills needed for career success
        C. Local demand for technical graduates

   III. Why consider Tech Prep
        A. Job and career considerations
            1. Local job opportunities
            2. Future of technology
            3. Income potential in technology
        B. Opportunities for further training
        C. College credit while in high school

DRAFTING

The second stage in the writing process is writing the first draft. Keeping your purpose and audience in mind at all times and referring frequently to your outline, you should write the first draft freely with the knowledge that you will have an opportunity to make needed changes and improvements at a later stage. The purpose of a first draft is not perfection; rather, it is an opportunity to get your ideas down for further consideration and revision.

8.19 The *introductory paragraphs* generally contain the main idea or purpose of the writing. They should capture the reader's attention and then ensure that the main idea is perfectly clear.

Example of introductory paragraphs:

    Tech Prep is an exciting program that promises to
    build bridges between secondary education and postsec-
    ondary education to help prepare students for careers in
    technology. Students will be taught the technical skills
    that they will need for job success today and in the
    future. While students can begin to study a chosen tech-
    nical field in high school, they continue their path of
    study in a postsecondary institution—a community col-
    lege, vocational-technical school, or university.

    Tech Prep programs require students in middle school
    and high school to take rigorous applied academic pro-
    grams with heavy emphasis on mathematics, science, and
    language arts. These academic studies are integrated with
    vocational skills, laying a firm foundation for further
    education, increased job responsibilities, and additional
    learning on the job.

8

8.20 The *body* of the writing provides support for the main idea with detailed information. Present details in a definite order that helps lead the reader to the desired conclusion, response, or action.

Example of a paragraph in the body:

A solid Tech Prep curriculum is desperately needed when one considers that only 30% of high school students go on to college. By the year 1995, 70% of all jobs will require technical skills beyond the level of high school; however, only 20% of all jobs will require a baccalaureate degree. Adding to the problem is the fact that technology changes approximately every seven years, requiring well-prepared graduates to have the ability to unlearn and relearn and develop transferable skills.

8.21 The *conclusion* should reinforce the main ideas presented in the body and help convince the reader to agree with the intended message. It may include a restatement of the purpose, a summary of the most important points, or a statement that makes a lasting impression.

Example of a paragraph in the conclusion:

Today's world of work, jolted by ever-increasing, ever-changing technology, requires a new kind of worker. That new worker must have a high level of academic knowledge, a firm grasp of specific technical skills, and excellent social skills. In addition, that worker must have the ability to learn new skills, incorporate new ideas, and transfer knowledge from one task to another. Tech Prep will provide the necessary preparation for tomorrow's workers in the highly skilled, competitive careers in technology of the twenty-first century.

8

SELF-CHECK EXERCISE 1, *UNIT 8*

_____
(Name)

In the blanks at the right, write the letter(s) of the item(s) needed to properly complete these statements.

1. (A) Drafting, (B) Revising, (C) Prewriting involves establishing the purpose and identifying the audience. _____

2. The primary purpose of expository writing is to (A) entertain, (B) inform, (C) explain. _____

3. Descriptive writing typically (A) uses vivid language and images, (B) uses humor, irony, and sarcasm, (C) tells about a person, place,or thing. _____

4. Audiences may vary in (A) gender, (B) age, (C) personal interests. _____

5. A subject (A) covers a limited area, (B) covers a broad area, (C) could be covered in a paragraph. _____

6. Two useful techniques for selecting a topic are (A) prewriting and revising, (B) clustering and brainstorming, (C) brainstorming and revising. _____

7. Indirect observations are those made (A) personally, (B) by others, (C) through interviews. _____

8. Using a questionnaire to gain information is an example of (A) direct observation, (B) indirect observation, (C) clustering. _____

9. The manner of presentation using chronological order is (A) reasons and results, (B) relationships of items, (C) in order of occurrence. _____

10. (A) Revising, (B) Drafting, (C) Outlining is the second major stage in the writing process. _____

SELF-CHECK EXERCISE 2, *UNIT 8*

Using the questioning technique to gather information, write two questions that answer who? what? where? when? why? and how? about the topic shown.

Topic: The United States Supreme Court

Who?   1. _____

       2. _____

What?	1.
	2.
Where?	1.
	2.
When?	1.
	2.
Why?	1.
	2.
How?	1.
	2.

SELF-CHECK EXERCISE 3, *UNIT 8*

Using the clustering technique for selecting a topic and beginning with the broad idea, THE WEATHER, think of at least ten related words or ideas. In the space below, write, circle, and join the ideas to the central idea or other related ideas.

THE WEATHER

Check your answers in the back of the book.

UNIT 9

THE WRITING PROCESS: REVISING, EDITING, AND FINAL DRAFTING

The first attempt at writing a document rarely results in the final version. Rather, writing requires evaluation, revision, editing, and rewriting before the document is ready for presentation. Carefully following these steps will help ensure that the final document serves its intended purpose.

EVALUATING THE FIRST DRAFT

9.1 Evaluation should occur after you have written the first draft. Evaluating what you have written is an important stage in producing an acceptable document. Evaluation helps determine whether your document effectively presents your message to your intended audience. You should evaluate your writing for content, organization, tone, and style.

Content refers to the information presented in writing. *Organization* indicates how you arranged and presented your ideas. *Tone* conveys your attitude toward what you are writing about and toward your audience just as your tone of voice shows your attitude in conversation. Writing *style* involves how you used words, sentences, and paragraphs to present your message.

9.2 As you evaluate your writing, seek answers to the following questions.

Content
1. Is the *purpose* for writing set forth clearly in the beginning and kept in focus for the reader throughout?
2. Is enough supporting information provided to ensure that the reader can understand the message?
3. Does all information contribute directly to supporting the intended message?

Organization
1. Is the information presented clearly, logically, and sequentially?
2. Does the writing flow smoothly with appropriate transitions from one idea to another?
3. Does the writing clearly lead the reader toward the desired conclusion?

Tone
1. Is your attitude appropriately conveyed in the writing depending on the purpose of the writing?
2. Do the details provided and the language used express the intended attitude for the writing?

Style
1. Is the writing appropriate for the audience in its vocabulary, sentence construction, and presentation?
2. Does the writing promote a high level of interest through variety in sentence structure, vivid language, and precise wording?

REVISING

9.3 *Revision* refers to correcting weaknesses determined through evaluation. Revision may mean rewriting words, sentences, or paragraphs to achieve clarity, continuity, or interest. Revising may also involve restructuring the organization for clarity and comprehension. Revision may mean adding or deleting ideas or detail to ensure understanding, agreement with the writer's purpose, and adequate coverage. Revision certainly means removing unwanted clichés, jargon, and biased language that may be distracting or offensive.

9.4 Good writing will contain an introduction that clearly sets forth either the main idea or the purpose in writing. It will also contain a body of information in a form and style that will move the reader toward understanding and accepting the writer's point of view. Finally, good writing will provide a conclusion that will restate the main idea and assure acceptance by the reader of that idea. The following may help improve the organization of the writing.

1. Reorder sentences or paragraphs to improve sequencing of ideas or steps and to clarify relationships between ideas.
2. Provide better transitions to help the reader to move smoothly between ideas.
3. Combine paragraphs to join closely related ideas, or divide paragraphs that contain distinctly different ideas.
4. Rewrite the introduction and conclusion to ensure that the main idea is clearly presented and confirmed.

9.5 The following is a list of typical challenges in revising content with suggested revisions.

Challenge	Suggested Revision
1. Insufficient information is provided to support either the main idea or the purpose	Provide more examples, reasons, explanation, and detail.
2. Main idea is difficult to grasp.	Delete extraneous information; check sequence of ideas; replace poor examples; use effective transitions between ideas.
3. Content is too technical.	Clearly define all terms; provide examples and explanations.
4. Reading level or content is too difficult or inappropriate for intended audience.	Shorten sentence length; use simpler vocabulary; break down explanations into smaller segments; check language and tone.
5. Content is uninteresting.	Use livelier, more vivid language; add interesting examples; eliminate unneeded detail that slows the reading.
6. Language is stale, biased, or offensive.	Remove or replace clichés and jargon; rewrite to remove biased language.

9.6 An important part of evaluating and revising is the removal of clichés, jargon, and biased language. A *cliché* is an expression that has been so overused that it has become tired, dull, and almost meaningless. Replace clichés with fresh, vivid, and more interesting expressions. Avoid the following (and similar) clichés:

busy as a bee	plain as the nose on your face
root of all evil	easy as one-two-three
hot as a firecracker	mad as a hornet
few and far between	fresh as a daisy
bottomless pit	dead as a doornail
sad but true	fit as a fiddle
old as the hills	straight as an arrow
green with envy	ugly as sin
hard as a brick	white as a sheet

9.7 *Jargon* is the language of people who share special interests, skill, or knowledge. For example, the vocabulary of those involved in sports, computers, education, government, medicine, or any other specialized activity includes words or phrases those individuals frequently use. Such words or phrases may have little or no meaning to those not directly involved in the areas of activity. Jargon generally tends to make language cumbersome and confusing. Avoid jargon in general writing. Some examples of technical jargon follow.

Jargon	More Appropriate Term
revenue enhancement	increase in taxes
input	question, complaint, suggestion
evaluation	grade
hard copy	printed copy
downsizing	reducing

9.8 *Sexist language* is biased language that perpetuates male or female stereotypes or that may be perceived as limiting or offensive. Replace such language. Terms such as *mailman, chairman,* and *stewardess* are routinely being replaced with *mail carrier, chairperson,* and *flight attendant.*

A more difficult problem has been the use of the pronouns *he, him,* and *his* to refer to such unknown gender antecedents as *doctor, pilot,* and *student.* Although the use of *he or she, him or her,* and *his or hers* may help with the problem, such usage tends to be cumbersome, particularly if it is overused. Another solution may be to reconstruct sentences to avoid the problem entirely. Some examples of rewriting problem sentences are suggested below.

Sexist: A doctor takes *his* work seriously.
Improved: Doctors take *their* work seriously.

Sexist: Any good pilot always checks out *his* plane before *he* takes off.
Improved: Good pilots always check out *their* planes before *they* take off.

Sexist: The rules require every *stewardess* to pass a safety test before *she* can fly.
Improved: The rules require every *flight attendant* to pass a safety test before *he or she* can fly.
Improved: The rules require all *flight attendants* to pass a safety test before *they* can fly.

Another example of biased language that should be avoided relates to race. Such biased language tends to depict individuals unfavorably, unfairly, or unjustly because of their race and should be eliminated from any writing.

EDITING

9.9 The next stage in the writing process is editing. *Editing* is a judgmental evaluation of the material and refers to checking for errors in grammar, mechanics, and usage. Editing also attempts to ensure accuracy, clarity, coherence, consistency, and effectiveness in content.

9.10   As you edit your writing, use the following checklist.

1. Are all sentences complete?
2. Do subjects and verbs agree in all sentences?
3. Is the overall organization of ideas clear and easy to follow?
4. Is the general tone of the writing acceptable?
5. Is correct punctuation used with every sentence?
6. Do pronouns agree with their antecedents?
7. Is parallel structure used throughout?
8. Is correct capitalization used throughout?
9. Are all words spelled correctly?
10. Are all modifiers correctly placed?

9.11   Check your writing for conciseness of expression—making every word count. Check for "big" words that may not be clear to the reader or that may make the writing sound pompous. Some examples follow.

"Big" Words	Better Words or Phrases
endeavor	try
contemplate	think about
prioritize	put in order
ascertain	determine, find out
utilize	use

9.12   Wordy phrases may also take away from the clarity and ease of reading. Use care to eliminate wordy phrases. Some examples follow.

Wordy Phrases	Simplified Terms
comes in conflict with	conflicts
at this point	now
in view of the fact that	because
in order to	to
in the event that	if
owing to the fact that	since

Proofreading

9.13   *Proofreading* as a stage of the writing process involves making sure the final copy reproduces the original material properly. It includes checking such things as capitalization, spelling, punctuation, spacing, transpositions, and so on. Proofreading may be thought of as a more mechanical evaluation of the material.

9

9.14 To ensure effective proofreading, have a dictionary and grammar handbook close at hand to check accuracy in spelling, capitalization, punctuation, and grammar usage. As you proofread, pay special attention to the following types of errors commonly found in writing.

1. Repeated words, particularly at the end of one line and the beginning of another

   conclusion was reached. It was inevitable that a misunderstanding would be the the result.

2. Transposition of words or letters in words

   soon resulted from hte accident. There sudden were lapses of memory, severe headaches, and frequent periods of coughing.

3. Incorrect word usage

   One of the most important scientific principals demonstrated in the experiment was the relationship of volume to density.

4. Incorrect capitalization

   while a student at center High School, marie often selected courses that contributed to her long-term goals.

5. Incorrect or omitted punctuation

   came only after great effort Wilson, a clear choice of the members soon raised his voice to urge the acceptance of the new contract.

6. Typographical errors

   managers of the company. It was apparent that only those who lied in the community would kno about the situation.

7. Inaccurate figures

   about the voyage of Columbus in 1392. It was the long journey on the rough water that caused dissension among the crew.

8. Spacing errors

   went abouthis business.In the meantime,there were too many computer businesses for the limited demand in the area.

9.15 Using proofreaders' marks when editing can make final keying of the copy easier. Commonly used proofreaders' marks are shown in the following table.

Symbol	Meaning	Example	Corrected Copy
ℒ	delete, take out	equip̸ment	equipment
≡	use capital letter	Adam wilson	Adam Wilson
/	use lowercase letter	the Man in the	the man in the
∧	insert here	apearance	appearance
⌃	insert comma	Rob, Ron and I	Rob, Ron, and I
⌄	insert apostrophe	Maries picture	Marie's picture
⌄⌄	use quotation marks	the goal"	the "goal"
⊙	use period	Rand Co	Rand Co.
⌃	use colon	947 p.m.	9:47 p.m.
⌃	use semicolon	each day we	each day; we
⌒	close up	in to the wall	into the wall
#	insert space	betweenthe	between the
¶	new paragraph	¶ Myra saw the car coming.	Myra saw the car coming.
no ¶	no paragraph	no¶ Ron became	Ron became the
∼	transpose	in rain the and	in the rain and
⊏	move to the left	⊏ land of the	land of the
⊐	move to right	⊐ sudden turn to the	sudden turn to
sp	spell out in full	sp Geo. Jones	George Jones
stet	let stand as is	stet very hot day	very hot day

FINAL DRAFTING

9.16   Once you have revised your writing and have proofread it carefully using proofreaders' marks to indicate needed changes, you should reread it to look for any final needed changes and improvements. This careful rereading should reveal any additional usage mistakes, misspellings, lack of appropriate capitalization and punctuation, and typographical errors. In addition, check carefully the accuracy and completeness of the documentation to be sure that appropriate credit is given.

9.17   The next step is to prepare the final draft, working from your revised draft and being careful to interpret all markings for corrections. Follow the format guidelines for the final draft for all writings, including paragraphs, memos, letters, essays, reports, and so on. (See Unit 12, Research Papers and Reports, for suggested guidelines for preparing the final draft of those kinds of documents.)

9.18 After you have prepared the final draft, proofread this version several times to ensure a perfect document. Look for the following:

1. Any keyboarding errors
2. Capitalization and punctuation errors
3. Missing or unneeded words
4. Transposed words
5. Inaccurate figures
6. Grammatical errors
7. Proper use of abbreviations
8. Correct word division and hyphenation
9. Proper documentation
10. Correct format for preparing document

9

_____

(Name)

Indicate whether the following statements are true or false by writing *T* or *F* in the blanks.

1. In writing, organization refers to the way in which ideas are arranged and presented. _____

2. A good introduction clearly sets forth the main idea or the purpose in writing. _____

3. A cliché is a fresh, vivid expression that makes reading more interesting. _____

4. An example of jargon is "ugly as sin." _____

5. Sexist language may be seen by the reader as limiting or offensive. _____

6. Clichés are tired, dull, and almost meaningless. _____

7. Jargon is usually associated with technical or specialized vocabulary. _____

8. Proofreading is generally more mechanical in nature, but editing is more judgmental. _____

9. One way to clarify the main idea when it may be difficult to grasp is to delete unneeded information. _____

10. Revision refers to checking for spelling, spacing, and keyboarding errors. _____

11. The use of the phrase "he or she" is an excellent way to overcome the problem of unknown gender antecedents. _____

12. Transposition refers to letters or words that have been incorrectly reversed. _____

13. Use proofreaders' marks to indicate needed changes in writing. _____

14. One way to improve organization is to combine closely related paragraphs. _____

15. The use of jargon tends to make writing more interesting and clear to the reader. _____

16. The term *astronaut* may appear as an antecedent with unknown gender. _____

17. One way to simplify the reading level is to use longer sentences. _____

18. The phrase *bottomless pit* is an example of a cliché. _____

19. Check documentation carefully to be sure you give proper credit to sources of information. _____

20. The term *repairman* could be perceived by some as a sexist term. _____

SELF-CHECK EXERCISE 2, *UNIT 9*

Indicate whether the following sentences include examples of clichés (C), jargon (J), or sexist language (S) by writing *C, J,* or *S* in the blanks.

1. The chairman of any committee should clearly know his responsibilities before the meeting begins. _____

2. It is sad but true, but not a single department reached its quota. _____

3. Every student turned white as a sheet as his or her score was announced. _____

4. The software required that the hard drive have a minimum of 30K bytes of memory. _____

5. The driver of the car was mad as a hornet when he was struck from behind. _____

SELF-CHECK EXERCISE 3, *UNIT 9*

Indicate the needed corrections in the following paragraph by using the appropriate proofreaders' marks.

On february 13, 1983, Ronald became an employee of the local newspaper, the Daily Tribune. he began first at by handling routnie assignments. For example he was required to call the local Funeral homes each morning to seee who had died died during the night. He wold then compose obituaries for each of the deceased following a precribed format. This assignment did not require a llot of imagination as a result he began to devise ways in which to express his creetivity. He sometimes added a lone of copy listing fictitious accomplishments of the deceased. On one occasion hee even made up a complete obituary for someone who did not even exist. Needless to say, his "creativity led to a lotof trouble for him

Check your answers in the back of the book.

UNIT 10

REFERENCE SOURCES

Writers frequently need to refer to authoritative sources of information when preparing written communications. Some reference sources are quite well known and widely used. Some sources, such as almanacs, cover a broad range of topics and give summary information. Other sources, such as a manual on banking practices, provide detailed information covering a specialized area. Some, such as style books, may relate only to acceptable practices in preparing written communications.

Knowing where to find needed information is a critical skill in effective communication. The following represents a sample of the kind of reference sources that are available. A good library will have these and many other resources.

ALMANACS

10.1 Almanacs, usually published annually, contain a wide range of facts and general information on important events of the year, politics, sports, geography, history, statistics, and so on.

Information Please Almanac. Boston: Houghton Mifflin Co. [Covers politics, sports, taxes, geography, vital statistics, and social and political conditions.]

World Almanac and Book of Facts. New York: Pharos Books. [Contains a wide variety of information on education, events, sports, population, U.S. government organizations, and political activities.]

Statistical Abstract of the United States. Washington, D.C.: U.S. Government Printing Office. [Revised annually; provides summary of statistics on the social, political, and economic organizations of the United States.]

ATLASES
....

10.2 Atlases contain an array of maps, charts, and tables relating to the geography of cities, states, countries, continents, and the world.

Hammond Citation World Atlas. Maplewood, N.J.: Hammond Inc., 1992.

National Geographic Atlas of the World, 6th ed. Washington, D.C.: National Geographic Society, 1990.

New York Times Atlas of the World, 3rd ed. New York: Random House, 1992.

BIOGRAPHICAL BOOKS
....

10.3 Biographical publications supply general information about notable individuals including personal background, education, occupation or profession, accomplishments, and honors. Many are regularly revised and updated.

Dictionary of American Biography. 17 vols. New York: Charles Scribner's Sons, 1981. [Information about notable nonliving Americans. Updated periodically.]

Who's Who. New York: St. Martin's Press, Inc., 1992. [Directory of eminent British people.]

Who's Who in America, 47th ed. 2 vols. Chicago: Marquis Who's Who Books, Inc., 1992–1993. [Information about prominent living Americans.]

Other *Who's Who* publications include *Who's Who of American Women, Who's Who in Finance and Industry, Who's Who in American Law, Who's Who in Commerce and Industry, Who's Who in the World,* and others covering particular geographical areas.

DICTIONARIES
....

10.4 Dictionaries are an essential part of any good reference library. Dictionaries range in size from small pocket editions to large, unabridged volumes. Dictionaries generally provide the following: spelling, syllabication, pronunciation, part of speech, word origin, definitions, uses, capitalization, synonyms, and irregular word forms. Specialized dictionaries contain the specific vocabulary of certain professions (legal, medical, engineering, and so on), synonyms, and special word lists.

The American Heritage Dictionary. 2nd college ed. Boston: Houghton Mifflin Co., 1993. [Clear, understandable definitions for over 155,000 entries.]

Funk & Wagnalls Standard Dictionary. Rev. ed. Scranton, Pa: Funk & Wagnalls Co., dist. by Harper & Row Publishers, 1991. [Desk-sized reference book for correct spelling, syllabication, definitions, and so on.]

Zoubek, C. E. and Hosler, Mary Margaret, *20,000+ Words.* 9th ed. Columbus, Oh.: Glencoe, 1991. [(A pocket-sized book for checking spelling and word division.]

The Random House College Dictionary. Rev. ed. New York: Random House Inc., 1989. [Special college edition of the *Random House Dictionary.*]

Roget, Peter M. *Roget's International Thesaurus.* 5th ed. Scranton, Pa.: Thomas Y. Crowell Co., dist. by Harper & Row Publishers, 1992. [A guide to the right word choice.]

Webster's College Dictionary. Glencoe edition. New York. Random House, 1991. [Up-to-date guide to the English language.]

Webster's Collegiate Thesaurus. Springfield, Mass.: Merriam-Webster, Inc., 1976. [A desk-sized guide to choosing the right word.]

Webster's Ninth New World Dictionary. Springfield, Mass.: Merriam-Webster, Inc., 1988. [Desk-sized spelling guide.]

Webster's Third New International Dictionary. Springfield, Mass.: Merriam-Webster, Inc., 1981. [Unabridged form.]

Webster's Tenth New Collegiate Dictionary. Springfield, Mass.: Merriam-Webster, Inc., 1993.

10

DIRECTORIES
....

10.5 Directories provide alphabetical listings of the names and addresses of people in a particular business, industry, or profession in a given geographical area. Directories provide assistance in finding the names, addresses, and telephone numbers of persons or companies and also may give information about company officers and products. These publications are updated annually.

City directories. [These directories generally list names, addresses, and occupations of city residents.]

Congressional Directory. Washington, D.C.: Superintendent of Documents, U.S. Government Printing Office. [Lists members of Congress and Executive Department personnel.]

Dun & Bradstreet Ratings and Reports. New York: Dun & Bradstreet, Inc. [Lists credit ratings of firms.]

Fortune Directory. New York: Fortune Magazine. [Lists major firms in the United States by sales, assets, and net profits.]

Moody's Manuals. New York: Moody's Investors Service, Inc. [Gives financial information on investment companies including transportation, public utilities, banks and financial institutions, and government.]

Rand McNally Bankers Directory. Chicago: Rand McNally & Co. [Provides names of bank officers and directors for all banks, foreign and domestic.]

Standard & Poor's Register of Directors and Executives. New York: Standard & Poor's Corp. [Gives information on directors of corporations in the United States and Canada.]

Telephone directories. [Lists telephone subscribers by name and address.]

United States Government Manual. Washington, D.C.: National Archives and Records Service, General Services Administration, annual. [Describes the purposes and programs of most government agencies and lists key officials.]

ENCYCLOPEDIAS

10.6 Encyclopedias provide information on a wide variety of subjects. General encyclopedias provide brief coverage of many topics; specialized encyclopedias provide broader coverage of fewer topics in a specific area.

Collier's Encyclopedia. 24 vols. New York: Collier, Macmillan Educational Corp., 1991. [A useful, readable encyclopedia.]

Encyclopedia Americana. 30 vols. New York: Grolier Educational Corp., 1989. [Standard, 30-volume encyclopedia.]

The Encyclopedia of Banking and Finance. 9th ed. New York: Bankers Publishing Co., 1990. [Defines and explains banking terms.]

Encyclopaedia Britannica. 15th ed., rev. 32 vols. Chicago: Encyclopaedia Britannica, Inc., 1992. [Standard 32-volume encyclopedia with yearly updating supplement.]

World Book Encyclopedia. 22 vols. Chicago: World Book, 1992. [Standard 22-volume encyclopedia.]

GENERAL REFERENCE SOURCES

10.7 A number of publications give information regarding shipping rates, hotel and motel rates, geographical locations, postal information, and so on. These publications are updated regularly.

Directory of Business and Financial Services. 8th ed. New York: Special Libraries Association, 1984. [Lists business and financial services by scope, type, frequency of publication, format, and price.]

Encyclopedia of Business Information Sources. 7th ed. Detroit: Gale Research, Inc., 1992. [Record of sourcebooks, periodicals, organizations, directories, handbooks, bibliographies, and other sources of information.]

Hoover's Handbook of American Business. Austin: The Reference Press, Inc., 1993. [Profiles of 500 major U.S. companies.]

Hotel and Motel Red Book. New York: American Hotel Association Directory Corp. [Lists hotels and motels geographically giving address, room information, and room rates.]

Lovejoy's College Guide, 22nd. ed. New York: Prentice Hall, 1993. [Comprehensive directory of colleges.]

National ZIP Code Directory. Washington, D.C.: Superintendent of Documents, U.S. Government Printing Office. [Lists post offices and ZIP Codes.]

Official Airline Guide. Oak Brook, Ill.: Official Airline Guides, Inc. [Comprehensive listing of all commercial flight information.]

Postal Manual. Washington, D.C.: Superintendent of Documents, U.S. Government Printing Office. [Provides comprehensive postal information.]

Rand McNally Commercial Atlas and Marketing Guide. Chicago: Rand McNally & Co. [Provides general geographical and statistical information.]

GRAMMAR AND STYLE BOOKS

10.8 It is often necessary to determine correct grammar or writing style. However, because some rules and styles vary from one reference source to another, you should select a style manual that you consistently use in the office and elsewhere.

Fowler, Henry W. *Dictionary of Modern English Usage.* 2nd ed. New York: Oxford University Press, Inc., 1987. [Includes definitions of terms and essays on the use and misuse of words and expressions, parts of speech, etc.]

MLA Handbook for Writers of Research Papers. 3rd ed. New York: The Modern Language Association of America, 1988. [A detailed manual on the mechanics of preparing research papers and business reports.]

The Chicago Manual of Style. 14th ed., rev. Chicago: University of Chicago Press, 1993. [A standard handbook for those preparing typewritten manuscript for printers.]

United States Government Printing Office Style Manual. Rev. ed. Washington, D.C.: U.S. Government Printing Office, 1984. [Typographical rules followed in government printing.]

Words into Type. 3rd ed. Englewood Cliffs, N.J.: Prentice-Hall, Inc., 1986. [A comprehensive style manual for writers, editors, and the print media.]

INDEXES

10.9 Indexes list the contents of books and periodicals and are used to locate information on particular subjects. Indexes generally list titles of books and articles, periodicals, date of publication, and publishers. Most of these indexes are published at least annually.

Biography Index. 15 vols. Bronx, N.Y.: Wilson Publishing. [Information about authors of books and articles.]

Books in Print. New York: R. R. Bowker Co. [Provides information about books, including author, title, price, publisher, and year of publication.]

Business Periodicals Index. New York: The H.W. Wilson Co. [Index to periodicals in a number of specialized areas including accounting, advertising, and banking.]

Cumulative Book Index. New York: The H.W. Wilson Co. [Information on books, scholarly pamphlets, proceedings and selected periodicals in the English language published by trade publishers, university presses, and so on.]

Education Index. New York: The H.W. Wilson Co. [Provides listings of publications in education.]

Gale Directory of Publications and Broadcast Media. Detroit: Gale Research, Inc. [Contains information on newspapers and periodicals, radio stations, television stations, and cable systems in the United States, its territories, and Canada.]

The New York Times Index. New York: The New York Times Co. [Listings by subject, title, person, and organization of all articles appearing in the *New York Times.*]

Readers' Guide to Periodical Literature. New York: The H.W. Wilson Co. [Provides listings of articles appearing in a wide range of general periodicals by subject and author.]

HANDBOOKS AND TEXTS

10.10 Information on office procedures and practices can be found in a number of handbooks and textbooks.

Clark, James L., and Clark, Lyn R. *A Handbook for Office Workers.* Boston: PWS-Kent Publishing Company, 1991. [Office workers' guide.]

Doris, Lillian, and Miller, Bessie May. *Complete Secretary's Handbook.* 5th ed. Englewood Cliffs, N.J.: Prentice-Hall, Inc., 1987. [Outlines the tasks and responsibilities of the secretary.]

Harris, Muriel. *Prentice-Hall Reference Guide to Grammar and Usage.* Englewood Cliffs, N.J., Prentice-Hall, Inc. [Summary rules of grammar.]

House, Clifford R., and Sigler, K. *Reference Manual for the Office.* 7th ed. Cincinnati: South-Western Publishing Co., 1989. [Reference sourcebook.]

McCauley, Rosemarie. *Professional Reference for the Office.* Columbus, Oh.: Glencoe, 1987. [Practical handbook for the office worker.]

Sabin, William A. *The Gregg Reference Manual.* 7th ed. New York: Glencoe Division, McGraw-Hill Book Co., 1992. [Reference source for written communication.]

QUOTATIONS SOURCEBOOKS

10.11 Quotations sourcebooks are handy references to the authors of both familiar and not-so-familiar quotations. These books may list quotations by author, by the subject of the quotation, or by the first or other important word in the quotation.

Bartlett, John. *Bartlett's Familiar Quotations.* Boston: Little, Brown, and Co., 1992. [A collection of passages, phrases, and proverbs traced to their sources in ancient and modern literature.]

The Macmillan Book of Proverbs, Maxims, and Famous Phrases. New York: Macmillan, 1976.   [Sources, development, variations, and perversions of proverbs, maxims, and familiar phrases.]

The New York Public Library Book of 20th-Century American Quotations. New York: Warner Books, 1992.   [A collection of truly popular American quotes from the twentieth century.]

Oxford Dictionary of Quotations. 3rd ed. New York: Oxford University Press, 1992. [A collection of quotations from ancient and modern literature.]

LOCATING MATERIALS IN THE LIBRARY

10

10.12 Libraries generally use either the Library of Congress classification system (the most popular system) or the Dewey decimal system. The following chart shows the 20 categories of the Library of Congress classification system.

Library of Congress Classification System

Letters	Category	Letters	Category
A	General Works	N	Fine Arts
B	Philosophy and religion	P	Language and literature
C–F	History	Q	Science
G	Geography and anthropology	R	Medicine
		S	Agriculture
H	Social science	T	Technology
J	Political science	U	Military science
K	Law	V	Naval science
L	Education	Z	Biography and library science
M	Music		

The following chart shows the ten categories of the Dewey decimal system.

Dewey Decimal System

Numbers	Category	Examples
000–009	General works	Encyclopedias
100–199	Philosophy	Psychology
200–299	Religion	Theology
300–399	Social sciences	Law, education
400–499	Language	Dictionaries
500–599	Sciences	Chemistry, mathematics
600–699	Technology	Medicine, engineering
700–799	Arts	Music, theater, sports
800–899	Literature	Poetry, essays
900–999	History and geography	Medieval history, biography

10 **10.13**   You can locate library information by using either the card catalog or a computer catalog. Most card catalogs contain three cards for each book in the library. *Author cards* are used when you know the name of the author but do not know the name of the book. *Title cards* are used when you know the title of a book but not necessarily the author. *Subject cards* are used when you want to find information about a subject but do not know specific authors or titles of books. In addition, *cross-reference cards* refer you to other headings in the card catalog where you may find more information.

10.14   Articles in newspapers, magazines, and journals usually provide the latest available information on current events or in specialized fields of continuous change. Special indexes are usually available in the library for locating information in periodicals.

The most widely used index for periodicals is the *Readers' Guide to Periodical Literature*. It lists articles from over 175 journals by author and by subject.

10.15   Most libraries today use computers to store information about their materials as well as materials in other libraries. By keying in certain words, you can access the database of the system and get listings of information. The use of computerized systems is growing rapidly. Many systems are linked to networks that provide even greater access to information.

SELF-CHECK EXERCISE 1, *UNIT 10*

....

_____
(Name)

Write the name of the specific publication described in the following statements.

1. Provides complete information on all commercial flights _____

2. Lists major firms in the United States by sales, assets, and net profits _____

3. Describes the purposes and programs of most government agencies and lists key officials _____

4. Provides comprehensive postal information _____

5. Provides names of hotels and motels and gives room information and rates _____

SELF-CHECK EXERCISE 2, *UNIT 10*

....

Identify the type of reference publication described in the following statements.

1. Provides spelling, syllabication, part of speech, pronunciation, origin, definitions, synonyms, and irregular forms of words _____

2. Provides a wide range of facts and general information on important events; published annually _____

3. Provides general information on a wide variety of subjects; usually in a series of books; not published annually _____

4. Provides alphabetical listings of the names and addresses of people in a particular business _____

5. Provides general information about notable individuals _____

SELF-CHECK EXERCISE 3, *UNIT 10*

Indicate whether each of the following statements is true or false by writing *T* or *F* in the blank.

1. Almanacs are usually updated every five years. _____
2. *Who's Who* is a directory of eminent British people. _____
3. An unabridged dictionary can fit in one's pocket. _____
4. Encyclopedias usually provide very complete information on a narrow selection of topics. _____
5. Most indexes are published at least annually. _____
6. The Library of Congress classification system is the most popular classification system in use in libraries. _____
7. In using the card catalog, if you do not know the name of the writer, you would refer to the author card. _____
8. The title card in the card catalog is used if you know the title of the book but not necessarily the author. _____
9. The *Readers' Guide to Periodical Literature* is used to locate information in hard-bound books. _____
10. The Dewey decimal system includes ten major categories. _____

SELF-CHECK EXERCISE 4, *UNIT 10*

From the list below, select the term that best matches each description. Place the letter of the term on the blank line.

A. *Books in Print, U.S.A.*   C. *Who's Who*   E. *20,000 Words*
B. City directories   D. *Fortune Directory*   F. *U.S. Government Manual*

1. Pocket-size book for checking spelling and word division _____
2. Contains information about a notable British person _____
3. Lists names, addresses, and occupations of city residents _____
4. Lists major firms in the United States by sales, assets, and net profits _____
5. Contains information about books, authors, titles, prices, and publishers _____

Check your answers in the back of the book.

UNIT

11

LETTERS AND MEMOS

Millions of business letters are sent and received every day. They are the means of contact between individuals and the lifeblood of business. Letters introduce people, sell products and ideas, order goods and services, inform associates and customers, make inquiries, provide answers, and perform many other functions.

Business letters represent the writer and/or the company; therefore, it is critical that a letter make the very best impression. The letter should be pleasing in appearance; accurate in content; contain all the correct letter parts in the proper order; be free of spelling, capitalization, grammatical, and punctuation errors; and be clean and free of smudges and fingerprints.

The cost of producing business letters continues to rise rapidly. To contain this expense, quick and accurate production of letters is important.

Interoffice memos are widely used within companies to exchange information, provide instruction, communicate project status, announce meetings, and so on. While they are generally informal in style, interoffice memos must, nevertheless, be produced accurately, rapidly, and completely if they are to meet the demands of high productivity.

LETTER STYLE

11.1 Several letter styles are used in business. Most business firms use only one style for all business letters. The most common letter styles are *block, modified block* (with and without indented paragraphs), and *simplified*.

11.2 With the *block style* (Figure 11–1), all lines in the letter begin at the left margin with the exception of tables, quotations, or other similar items in the body of the letter. This letter style is very popular and easy to key since all lines begin at the left margin, requiring no tabular stops.

niversal
Computer
Center

800 Overlook Trail
Bayside, TX 78340
713-555-3300

April 15, 19—

Mr. Anthony Watson
3701 Wisteria Drive
Bayside, TX 78340

Dear Mr. Watson

Thank you for inquiring about our summer schedule of computer application classes at Universal Computer Center. We do indeed have a full
lineup of classes for those who want to learn the basics, brush up on
their skills, or examine some of the latest software packages.

We are a fully accredited school, having affiliations with the National
Computer Accrediting Society and the Southwest Computer Schools
Association. Our faculty is composed of individuals with degrees in
computer science and years of practical experience in large corporations.

Our summer school brochures are currently being printed and will be
available for distribution within the next week or so. You can be sure
we will send you one as soon as they are received. In the meantime,
thanks again for your interest in our program.

Sincerely

Tammy MacFarland

Tammy MacFarland
Program Manager

bjh

Figure 11–1   Block-style business letter, open punctuation

11.3   With the *modified-block* style (Figures 11–2 and 11–3), all lines in the letter begin at the left margin except the date and closing lines (complimentary
close, company name, name and title of the originator), which begin at the center.
The paragraphs in the body may or may not be indented, according to preference.

RAINBOW
LANDSCAPING COMPANY
One River Bank Road
West Palm Beach, FL 33401
407-555-7246

May 5, 19—

Attention: Ms. Cynthia Small
Wilson Motors, Inc.
1700 Shoreline Boulevard
West Palm Beach, FL 33402

Ladies/Gentlemen

Congratulations on your wonderful new facility on Shoreline
Boulevard! It is certainly a beautiful addition to the neighborhood and
no doubt will be pointed to with pride by those who are interested in
making our city more attractive.

At Rainbow Landscaping we are committed to keeping facilities like
yours beautiful. Our certified landscaping and grounds maintenance
department can do exactly that. We have the latest equipment, a
well-trained team of groundskeepers, and the technical knowledge to
handle any landscaping maintenance problem. Our reputation is well
established, based on over half a century right here in West Palm
Beach.

We should welcome the opportunity to discuss our service with you at
your convenience. Please call today to set up an appointment.

Sincerely

Joyce Lamb

Joyce Lamb
Landscape Director

djb

**Figure 11–2   Modified-block style business letter, blocked paragraphs,
open punctuation**

11.4   With the *simplified style* (Figure 11–4), open punctuation is used. All
lines in the letter begin at the left margin. A subject line in capital letters replaces
the salutation. The originator's identification is keyed in capital letters on one
line in place of the complimentary close. This style is said to be the easiest to
key, resulting in higher productivity.

BREAKTIME
Hospitality Service

June 1, 19—

Mr. Frank Diaz
Diamond Distributing Company
3278 Hilltop Avenue
Columbus, GA 31903

Dear Mr. Diaz:

    Your employees, like others everywhere, look forward to a few minutes away from the job each morning and afternoon. Their break time should be a time of relaxation and refreshment, allowing employees to renew their energy and commitment to their work. Our mission is to see that this happens in companies all over the Columbus area.

    We can take charge, providing wholesome snacks, delicious cold beverages, and satisfying hot drinks to all your employees at their designated break times. Not only that, we can do so at a very reasonable cost.

    Our reputation as a supplier of good service is well established here in Columbus. After all, we've been providing in-house hospitality service to Columbus-area businesses since 1953. We'd like to be on your team too. We'll be in touch with you to see if we can help.

Sincerely,

James Ogle

James Ogle
Service Manager

clh

1699 HISTORIC DRIVE • COLUMBUS, GA 31902 • 706-555-7433

Figure 11–3 Modified-block style business letter, indented paragraphs, mixed punctuation

LETTER PUNCTUATION

11.5 Two basic punctuation styles are used in business letters—open and mixed. In *open punctuation,* no punctuation is used after the salutation or the complimentary close. In *mixed punctuation,* sometimes called *standard punctuation,* a colon is used after the salutation and a comma after the complimentary close. (See Figures 11–1, 11–2, and 11–3).

WILLIAMSBURG
SPECIALTY
f u r n i t u r e
800 CENTER BOULEVARD
LINCOLN, NE 68502
402-555-2874

September 13, 19—

Mrs. Aileen Buchanan
1449 Redding Knight
Lincoln, NE 68504

HERITAGE FURNITURE DISPLAY

As owner of a beautiful new home, you are no doubt interested in
furnishing it with quality pieces that reflect your good taste and that
add to the beauty of your residence. Williamsburg Specialty
Furniture has been making quality furniture for the residents of
Lincoln and the surrounding area for over fifty years.

You can see examples of our fine furniture at the Heritage Furniture
Display every day next month at the new Lincoln Center Mall in
Westwood. Beautiful handcrafted pieces that fit the decor and budget
of every fine home will be shown.

We know you'll find something that will fit right in with your decorat-
ing plan and that will add to the beauty of your home. Please stop
by to see us at our display and receive an attractive door stop for
your home. We look forward to meeting you.

Herman Weinstein
HERMAN WEINSTEIN, DIRECTOR OF MARKETING SERVICES

se

Figure 11–4 Simplified-style business letter

LETTER PLACEMENT

Use the following information to place letters properly on the page.

Top Margin

11.6 Key the date on the third line below the letterhead, or, if you are using
plain paper, on line 13 (2 inches from the top of the page).

Side Margins

11.7 Most computer software packages automatically provide for 1-inch default side margins. The result is a $6\frac{1}{2}$-inch writing line for all materials keyed on $8\frac{1}{2}$- by 11-inch stationery. These margins are recommended whether you are using a computer or a typewriter to produce a letter.

Bottom Margin

11.8 Leave a bottom margin of at least 1 inch (6 lines). If the letter requires more than one page, the bottom margin on the first page may be increased to as much as 2 inches.

Lengthening a Letter

11.9 To "lengthen" a short letter (one that has fewer than 8 lines of text in the body) and give it a better appearance on the page, you may do one or more of the following as needed:

1. Key the date as low as line 18.
2. Leave up to 8 blank lines between the date and inside address.
3. Leave $1\frac{1}{2}$ blank lines (if your equipment will permit) between the paragraphs.
4. Leave 4 to 6 blank lines for the signature.
5. Key the originator's name and title on separate lines.
6. Leave an additional line before the reference initials.
7. Key the body using double-spacing, and indent the first line of each paragraph.

LETTER PARTS

11.10 A business letter may contain as many as 19 parts, but most letters do not include them all. In the list that follows, an asterisk denotes the letter parts that are optional in most business letters. These letter parts are shown in Figure 11–5.

1.	Letterhead	8. Body
2.	Date	9. Complimentary close
*3.	Personal or Confidential notation	*10. Company name
*4.	Attention line	11. Signature
5.	Inside address	12. Originator's keyed name
6.	Salutation	13. Originator's title
*7.	Subject line	14. Reference initials
		*15. Enclosure notation

11

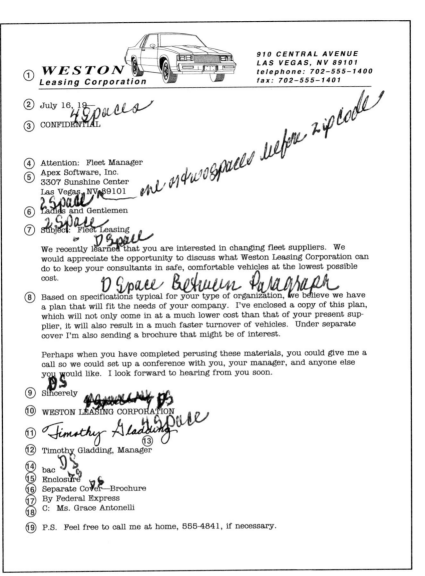

① *WESTON*
Leasing Corporation

910 CENTRAL AVENUE
LAS VEGAS, NV 89101
telephone: 702-555-1400
fax: 702-555-1401

② July 16, 19—   *4 Spaces*

③ CONFIDENTIAL

one or two spaces before zipcode

④ Attention: Fleet Manager
⑤ Apex Software, Inc.
3307 Sunshine Center
Las Vegas, NV 89101

2 Space

⑥ Ladies and Gentlemen

2 Space

⑦ Subject: Fleet Leasing

D Space

We recently learned that you are interested in changing fleet suppliers. We would appreciate the opportunity to discuss what Weston Leasing Corporation can do to keep your consultants in safe, comfortable vehicles at the lowest possible cost.

D Space Between Paragraph

⑧ Based on specifications typical for your type of organization, we believe we have a plan that will fit the needs of your company. I've enclosed a copy of this plan, which will not only come in at a much lower cost than that of your present supplier, it will also result in a much faster turnover of vehicles. Under separate cover I'm also sending a brochure that might be of interest.

Perhaps when you have completed perusing these materials, you could give me a call so we could set up a conference with you, your manager, and anyone else you would like. I look forward to hearing from you soon.

DS

⑨ Sincerely

⑩ WESTON LEASING CORPORATION

⑪ Timothy Gladding   ⑬

⑫ Timothy Gladding, Manager

⑭ bac
⑮ Enclosure
⑯ Separate Cover—Brochure
⑰ By Federal Express
⑱ C: Ms. Grace Antonelli

⑲ P.S. Feel free to call me at home, 555-4841, if necessary.

Figure 11–5   Business letter

*16. Separate cover notation	*18. Copy notation
*17. Delivery notation	*19. Postscript

Letterhead

11.11   The letterhead (see Part 1, Figure 11–5) usually contains the complete name and address of the originator's company. It may also contain a telephone number, company insignia or logo, slogan, or other information such as a special cable address or fax number. The letterhead tells the reader where to address replies to the letter.

If a personal business letter is written on plain paper, the address of the originator should be shown. This address, known as the *return address,* includes the originator's street address, city, state, and ZIP Code.

An increasingly common practice is to show the return address for a personal business letter as part of the signature block (see Figure 11–6). The return address begins at the same point as the closing lines: at the left margin for the block and simplified styles and at the center for the modified-block style.

Date

11.12 The *date* (see Part 2, Figure 11–5) shows when the letter was prepared and serves as a reference if several letters have been sent to or received from the same person or company. When keying the date, keep the following points in mind:

Always show the date in full, never abbreviated or expressed in figures alone.

    April 13, 1995

In military correspondence (and instances where this style has been adopted), the day of the month precedes the month and the year. Use no punctuation between the month and the year in military style.

    13 April 1995

Depending on the letter style, placement of the letterhead, or personal preference, the date may appear at the center of the page, at the right margin, balanced with the letterhead, or at the left margin. The most common procedure is to center the date.

Leave 5 blank lines between the date and the inside address.

Personal or Confidential Notation

11.13 The *personal* or *confidential notation,* when used (see Part 3, Figure 11–5), should be keyed on the second line below the date at the left margin. Key the notation in capital letters or with an initial capital letter. The notation may be underlined or in boldface.

Attention Line

11.14 An *attention line* (see Part 4, Figure 11–5) directs the letter to a specific person or department. It indicates that the letter is business-related and that someone other than the person named in the attention line may handle the letter. It also directs a letter to a specific department when the writer does

October 21, 19—

Ms. Shannon DuVall
Human Services Director
Belou Cosmetics, Inc.
4999 Middle Street
Canton, OH 44707

Dear Ms. DuVall

While in Cincinnati last week, I received a demonstration treatment
using your new product, Vitamour. The person demonstrating was
certainly an excellent representative of your company, and that is
the reason I am writing you.

Miss Kristi Parker White introduced herself to me as I was shopping
in Murphy's in Riverfront Mall. Her sparkling personality and bright
smile made me feel comfortable immediately, and her charming manner enticed me to listen to her and examine her product. Miss
White's demonstration was obviously well prepared and practiced,
and she was very careful to explain the procedure every step of the
way. Needless to say, I bought the product and have been very satisfied with it.

It occurred to me that employees like Miss White should be recognized for their good work, and I should like to do so. If she is a typical representative of your company, you are fortunate indeed.

Sincerely

Lucille Wagoner

Lucille Wagoner
7023 Paddison Road
Dayton, OH 45420

11

Figure 11–6 Personal business letter in block style, open punctuation

not have a particular name to which to address the letter. If you are using electronic equipment and expect to generate the envelope address by repeating the
inside address, key the attention line as the first line in the inside address.

```
Attention: Mr. Rodney McNair
Denison Industries
1317 Commercial Drive
Asheville, NC 27801
```

The attention line may also be keyed in all capital letters or initial capitals on the second line below the inside address beginning at the left margin.

```
Denison Industries              Star Photographic Services
1317 Commercial Drive           801 Main Street
Asheville, NC 27801             Pittsford, MI 49271


Attention: Mr. Rodney McNair    ATTENTION: SALES MANAGER
```

Inside Address

11.15 The *inside address* (see Part 5, Figure 11–5) provides the complete name, title, company name, and address of the addressee (the person or firm to whom the letter is written). The following points should be observed.

1. Place the inside address on the sixth line below the date (or on the fourth line below the personal or confidential notation if one is used).
2. Key the name of the person or company receiving the letter.
3. When an inside address includes a person's official title, place the title (capitalized) on the same line as the name (separated by a comma) or on the line following (to maintain balance of the lines).

```
Ms. Sally Anderson, President   Mr. Edward A. Parker
Perceptive Communications       Development Director
936 Westwind Circle             Museum of Popular Science
Houston, TX 77070               77 South High Street
                                Columbus, OH 43215
```

4. Spell out street names using numbers up to and including ten. Use ordinal figures for numbered streets over ten. Always spell out a compass point (north, south, east, west) that is part of the street name.

```
1336 Seventh Street             69 East 42nd Street
```

5. Use figures for building numbers, with the exception of "One."

```
One Market Center               1993 77th Street
```

6. Show the complete name of the city, state, and ZIP Code. Use the two-letter state abbreviations recommended by the Postal Service or spell the state name in full. (See Section 4.5 for a list of these two-letter state abbreviations.) One space is left between the two-letter state abbreviation and the ZIP Code. (When a nine-digit ZIP Code is used, a hyphen and four additional figures follow the basic ZIP Code.)

11

```
Vicki Matthews              Mr. Arturo Lopes
123 Acme Street             2600 West 32nd Street
Meridian, MS 39301          Danville, IL 61323-1788

Mrs. Nelda O'Connor, Director
Record Clubs of America
200 Eastline Drive
Los Angeles, CA 90010-2276
```

For a Canadian address, the Canadian Postal Code number must be the last item of the address. For other foreign addresses, the name of the country, in all capital letters, must be the last item of the address.

```
Ms. Amy Fox                 Mr. Andrew M. Helms
123 King Street             Centre for Medical Research
Ottawa, Ontario             Private Bag A51
CANADA                      London 100 F8F
KIA OB3                     ENGLAND
```

For mail addressed to military post offices, use the following examples as models.

```
PVT SC WINSTON              JANE E WHITE QMSN USN
COMPANY G, PSC 1630         USS TOLEDO (DD 729)
120TH INFANTRY REGT         MPO SAN FRANCISCO 96601
MPO, NY 09801
```

11

Salutation

11.16 Place the *salutation* (see Part 6, Figure 11–5) a double-space below the inside address (or attention line) at the left margin. The salutation usually begins with *Dear* and contains a courtesy title (Mr., Miss, Ms.) and the addressee's last name. In open punctuation, use no punctuation following the salutation. In mixed punctuation, use a colon following the salutation.

```
Ms. Marlo West              Mr. Daniel Barnes, President
3900 Cedar Point Drive      Technical Products
Hamilton, MT 59840-7388     1600 Cypress Drive
                            Winchester, OH 45697
Dear Ms. West
                            Dear Mr. Barnes
```

[Note: When using an attention line, make the salutation agree with the first line of the address, not with the attention line.]

```
Ridley Manufacturing Company
ATTENTION Mr. Ray Black
1640 First Street
Detroit, Michigan 48130


Dear Sir or Madam (not Dear Mr. Black)
```

11.17 The tone of the salutation may range from informal to formal depending on the relationship of the originator and receiver. The following salutations are arranged from informal to formal.

Dear Rex	Dear Lucille
My dear Rex	My dear Lucille
Dear Professor Knight	Dear Miss Wright
My dear Mr. Knight	My dear Miss Wright
Dear Sir	Dear Madam
Sir	Madam

11.18 The following salutations are commonly used for business letters. (See Section 11.34 for other forms of address.)

To a business firm:	Ladies and Gentlemen Ladies/Gentlemen Gentlemen
To an individual:	Dear Sir, Dear Madam Dear Miss, Mr., Mrs., Ms. Chung
To a husband and wife:	Dear Mr. and Mrs. Hanson
To two men:	Dear Mr. Lee and Mr. Long Dear Messrs. Greene and Lamb
To two married women:	Dear Mrs. Drake and Mrs. Ruiz Dear Mmes. Queen and Winston
To two single women:	Dear Miss Jackson and Miss Lambert Dear Misses Sessions and Carley
To two women, regardless of marital status:	Dear Ms. Wunche and Ms. Gonzales

[Note: In the simplified style, omit the salutation. (See Figure 11–4.)]

11.19 If the name of a specific person is not known when writing to a company, you may use the salutations *Ladies and Gentlemen, Dear Sir,* or *Dear Madam,* whichever is appropriate. It is also permissible to use the department name or a title when you don't know the name of a particular person; for example, *Dear Credit Department* or *Dear Credit Manager.*

Subject Line

11.20 The purpose of a letter may be emphasized by a *subject line* (see Part 7, Figure 11–5). Key the subject line at the left margin a double-space below the salutation. The word *Subject* may be shown in all caps or initial caps followed by a colon, two spaces, and the topic of the subject line in initial caps. Double-space to the beginning of the body of the letter. (For special emphasis or to match the style of the letter, the subject line may be centered or begun at the paragraph indention).

```
Dear Ms. Daly

SUBJECT: Company Benefits


Dear Mr. Andrews

              SUBJECT: Company Benefits


Dear Dr. Fox

   SUBJECT: Company Benefits
```

In the simplified style, the subject line is keyed on the third line below the inside address at the left margin in all capital letters. The word *subject* is not used in the subject line.

Body

11.21 The *body* (see Part 8, Figure 11–5) is the message. Begin the body a double-space below the salutation or subject line.

Except for very short letters, use single-spacing for the body. Double-space between paragraphs to ensure ease of reading and proper division of the message. Try to keep the right margin as even as possible to display a pleasing appearance. This is automatically accomplished with "word wrap" or "right justification" on electronic equipment. The first line of each paragraph may or may not be indented depending on the letter style used. Indentions are usually a uniform five spaces.

11.22 When the body of a letter contains more than about 300 words, prepare the letter as a multiple-page letter. Use letterhead stationery for the first page. For the second and subsequent pages (called *continuation* sheets), use plain paper of the same size, color, and quality as the letterhead. Use the same margin settings as on the first page. Leave a 1-inch top margin on the continuation pages, and place a heading containing the name of the addressee, the page number, and the date. Use either block or spread format. Triple-space (two blank lines) between the heading and the continuation of the body.

11

The block format is the most efficient heading format to key because the lines are single-spaced at the left margin. Always use this format with *block-style* letters. When using the spread format, place the addressee's name beginning at the left margin and the page number at the center. Backspace from the right margin to begin the date. Triple-space between the heading and the body of the letter. Begin each additional page of a letter with a heading.

Block Format

```
Ms. Elaine Murphy
Page 2
October 14, 1995
```

Spread Format

```
Ms. Elaine Murphy              2              October 14, 1995
```

Complimentary Close

11.23 Key the *complimentary close* (see Part 9, Figure 11–5) a double-space below the last line of the body. It should align vertically with the date. Capitalize only the first word of the complimentary close.

If mixed punctuation is used, the complimentary close is followed by a comma; if open punctuation is used, no punctuation follows it.

11.24 The tone of the complimentary close should match that of the salutation. Typical complimentary closes, arranged from informal to formal, are as follows.

Cordially	Yours cordially
Cordially yours	Sincerely
Yours sincerely	Very truly yours
Sincerely yours	Yours respectfully
Yours truly	Respectfully

Company Name

11.25 Some companies follow the practice of showing the *company name* (see Part 10, Figure 11–5) in all capital letters a double-space below the complimentary close.

```
Sincerely

APEX ELECTRONICS, INC.
```

Since the company name already appears on the letterhead, this practice is used infrequently; however, it may be used to indicate that the content of the letter represents the company and not the originator.

11

Originator's Name and Title

11.26 Key the *originator's name* a quadruple-space (leaving 3 blank lines) below the complimentary close. The name as keyed should represent the person's preference. The originator's *official title* may be shown on the same line as the name, separated by a comma. The title may also be shown on a separate line below the name (see Parts 12 and 13, Figure 11–5).

Sincerely,

Nan Austin   *OR*   Sincerely

Nan Austin

Nan Austin, Manager   Nan Austin
Manager

11.27 The personal title of a man (*Mr.*) or the professional title of a man or a woman (*Dr., Professor,* and so on) should not appear before the originator's name in the name and title section.

The personal title of a woman (*Miss, Mrs., Ms.*) may be shown in parentheses before the name.

Sincerely

Judy Pastor   *OR*   Sincerely

Judy Pastor

(Miss) Judy Pastor   Judy Pastor

The signature of a married woman or widow may appear as follows.

Sincerely

Nola Nunez   *OR*   Sincerely

Nola Nunez

(Mrs.) Nola Nunez   Nola Nunez

Some women prefer not to indicate their marital status and prefer to use *Ms.* as their title whether they are married or unmarried. The title *Ms.*, however, is never used with a husband's first name.

Ms. Sandy Clark or Ms. Clark (not Ms. Jim Clark)

Sincerely

Diane Williams   *OR*   Sincerely

Diane Williams

(Ms.) Diane Williams   Diane Williams

11

A married woman may prefer to sign her first name followed by her husband's surname in the signature line.

Sincerely

Rachel Whitmore

(Mrs.) Rachel Whitmore

Sometimes a letter is signed by someone other than the originator. When this happens, the person actually signing the letter should write his or her initials below the signature.

Sincerely

James R. Folsom

James R. Folsom

Reference Initials

11.28 *Reference initials* (see Part 14, Figure 11–5) indicate who keyed the letter. Key the reference initials at the left margin, a double-space below the last line of the signature line. The reference initials may include only those of the person keying the letter or both those of the originator and the one keying the letter. The reference initials may be in either capital letters or lowercase letters.

Sincerely	Sincerely
Mindy Fong	*Mindy Fong*
Mindy Fong Editor in Chief	Mindy Fong Editor in Chief
apd (*or*) APD	MF:APD (*or*) mf/apd

Enclosure Notation

11.29 When there is a reference in the body of the letter to other items enclosed in the envelope in addition to the letter itself, key an *enclosure nota-tion* (see Part 15, Figure 11–5) a double-space below the reference initials. (Single-spacing may be used to conserve space in a lengthy letter.) The enclo-sure notation is a reminder to the one preparing the letter to be mailed to insert the item in the envelope before sealing. It also reminds the addressee to check to see that the item was received.

When only one item is enclosed, key the word *Enclosure.*

When more than one item is enclosed, the number of enclosed items may be indicated or listed separately. A variety of acceptable styles is shown here.

Enclosure	2 ENC.
Enc.	ENC. 2
1 ENC.	Check Enclosed
1 Enclosure	Enclosures 2
Enclosures	Catalog
Enclosures 2	Order Blank

Separate Cover Notation

11.30 When a letter refers to something sent in another envelope or package, key a *separate cover notation* (see Part 16, Figure 11–5) a double-space below the reference initials or the enclosure notation. (Single-spacing may be used in lengthy letters.)

When only one item is sent under separate cover, use the words *Separate Cover.* When more than one item is sent under separate cover, show the number of items or a list of the items following the separate cover notation. The delivery method may also be indicated.

Separate Cover	Separate Cover 2
Separate Cover-Air Express	Separate Cover-Catalog Price List

Delivery Notation

11

11.31 If correspondence is to be sent via a special postal service such as Certified Mail, Registered Mail, or Special Delivery, key a *delivery notation* (see Part 17, Figure 11–5) at the left margin below the enclosure notations (if used) or below the reference initials.

By certified mail	By Federal Express
By messenger	By special delivery

If a letter is first faxed and then delivered through the mail as a confirmation copy, type a confirmation notation a double-space below the date line or a double-space below any other notation that follows the date.

January 16, 1995

Confirmation of fax sent on January 16, 1995

Copy Notation

11.32 When copies of a letter are to be sent to persons other than the addressee, the *copy notation, c,* (meaning copy) is typed a double-space below the last items (see Part 18, Figure 11–5) followed by a space and the name of the individual(s) to receive the copy. Use the person's title and full name.

If the copies are to be sent to individuals without the knowledge of the addressee, the notation *bc* (meaning blind copy) is shown only on the copies, not on the original.

```
c Mr. Dan Mayfield          bc Ms. Gretel Wascomb
  Dr. Lou Ann Miller
```

Postscript

11.33 A *postscript* (see Part 19, Figure 11–5) is a brief addition to a letter generally emphasizing a special message by setting it apart from the body of the letter. Key the postscript at the left margin, a double-space below the last item. *PS* is keyed in all caps with no space before the *S* followed by a colon. Leave two spaces between the colon and the first word of the message. The second and any other lines of the message are aligned beneath the first word of the message.

```
PS: If you'll send your order by June 10, we'll include a
    free travel video.
```

FORMS OF ADDRESS

11.34 The correct forms of address for various officials are shown next.

Official and Address	Salutation	Complimentary Close
President of the United States		
The President	Sir *or* Madam	Very respectfully
The White House	Mr. President	yours
Washington, DC 20500	Madam President	Respectfully yours
	Dear Mr. President	Respectfully
	Dear Madam President	
Former President		
The Honorable (*full name*)	Dear President (*last name*)	Sincerely yours
(*full address*)	Dear Mr. (*last name*)	Respectfully
	Dear Mr. President	Very truly yours

11

Official and Address	Salutation	Complimentary Close
Vice President of the United States		

The Vice President
The United States Senate
Washington, DC 20510
	Sir *or* Madam
	Dear Sir *or* Dear
	   Madam
	Mr. Vice President
	Madam Vice
	   President
	Dear Mr. Vice
	   President
	Dear Madam
	   Vice President
		Respectfully yours
		Very truly yours
		Sincerely yours

Chief Justice of the U.S. Supreme Court		

The Chief Justice of the
   United States
The Supreme Court
Washington, DC 20543
	Sir *or* Madam
	Mr. Chief Justice
	Madam Chief
	   Justice
	Dear Mr. Chief
	   Justice
	Dear Madam
	   Chief Justice
		Respectfully
		Very truly yours
		Sincerely yours

Associate Justice of the U.S. Supreme Court		

Mr., Mrs., Miss, Ms.
   Justice (*last name*)
The Supreme Court of
   the United States
Washington, DC 20543
	Sir *or* Madam
	Mr. Justice
	Madam Justice
	Dear Mr. Justice
	Dear Madam Justice
		Very truly yours
		Sincerely yours

Cabinet Member		

The Honorable (*full name*)
Secretary of
   (*department*)
Washington, DC 20515
	Sir *or* Madam
	Dear Sir *or* Dear
	   Madam
	Dear Mr. Secretary
	Dear Madam
	   Secretary
		Very truly yours
		Sincerely yours

United States Senator		

The Honorable (*full name*)
The United States
   Senate
Washington, DC 20515
	Sir *or* Madam
	Dear Sir *or* Dear
	   Madam
	Dear Senator (*last name*)
		Very truly yours
		Sincerely yours

11

Official and Address	Salutation	Complimentary Close
Congressional Representative		
The Honorable (*full name*) House of Representatives Washington, DC 20515	Sir *or* Madam Dear Sir *or* Dear Madam Dear Representative (*last name*) Dear Congressman (*last name*) Dear Congress- woman (*last name*)	Very truly yours Sincerely yours
Governor of a State		
The Honorable (*full name*) Governor of (*state*) (State capital, State, ZIP Code)	Sir *or* Madam Dear Sir *or* Dear Madam Dear Governor (*last name*)	Respectfully yours Very truly yours Sincerely yours
State Legislator		
The Honorable (*full name*) The House of Represen- tatives (*or* The State Assembly) (State capital, State, ZIP Code)	Sir *or* Madam Dear Sir *or* Dear Madam Dear Representative (*last name*) Dear Mr., Miss, Mrs., Ms. (*last name*)	Very truly yours Sincerely yours
State Senator		
The Honorable (*full name*) The State Senate (State capital, State, ZIP Code)	Sir *or* Madam Dear Sir *or* Dear Madam Dear Senator (*last name*)	Very truly yours Sincerely yours
State Official		
The Honorable (*last name*) (Position) (State capital, State, ZIP Code)	Sir *or* Madam Dear Sir *or* Dear Madam Dear Mr., Miss, Mrs., Ms. (*last name*)	Very truly yours Sincerely yours
Mayor		
The Honorable (*full name*) Mayor of the City of (*City*) City Hall (City, State, ZIP Code)	Sir *or* Madam Dear Sir *or* Dear Madam Dear Mr. Mayor Dear Madam Mayor Dear Mayor (*last name*)	Respectfully yours Very truly yours Sincerely yours

11

ENVELOPES

11.35 Two standard sizes of envelopes are used most frequently. The No. 10 envelope (9½ by 4⅛ inches) is used for one- and multiple-page letters and for letters with enclosures.

The No. 6¾ envelope (6½ by 3⅝ inches) is most often used for baronial-size (small letterheads) stationery. It may also be used for one-page letters on full-size letterheads, although the preferred size is the No. 10 envelope.

Envelopes should, of course, be the same quality, weight, finish, and color as the letterhead stationery.

11.36 Observe the following guidelines when preparing envelopes.

1. Be certain that the mailing address on the envelope is the same as the inside address of the letter and that names and addresses are accurate.
2. The U.S. Postal Service recommends the use of the Optical Character Recognition (OCR) format for addresses on envelopes. (See Figures 11–7 to 11–9.) The Postal Service has established this format as the preferred method for preparing envelopes so that they can be processed quickly. Because OCR equipment reads and sorts mail nearly eight times faster than a human, correspondence reaches its final destination more quickly. (Although the Postal Service recommends this procedure, many people still use the traditional styles of capitals and small letters with punctuation.)

   No. 10 Envelope (Business Size)
   Begin the mailing address approximately 2½ inches down from the top edge and 4 inches in from the left edge. (See Figure 11–7.)
   a. Single-space all lines, blocking each line at the left.
   b. Use all capital letters.
   c. Omit all punctuation.
   d. Place the city, state, and ZIP Code on the same line.
   e. Leave 1 space between the two-letter state abbreviation and the ZIP Code.

   No. 6¾ Envelope
   Begin the mailing address about 2 inches down from the top edge and 2½ inches in from the left edge. (See Figures 11–8 and 11–9.)
   a. Single-space all lines.
   b. Use all capital letters.
   c. Omit all punctuation.
   d. Place the city, state, and ZIP Code on the same line.
   e. Leave 1 space between the two-letter state abbreviation and the ZIP Code.

3. Never use the word *City* in place of the actual name of the city.

11

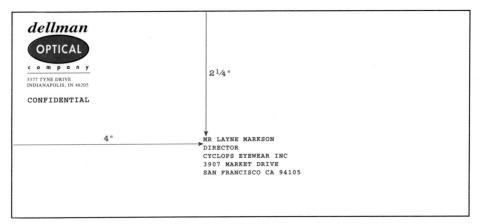

Figure 11–7   No. 10 envelope

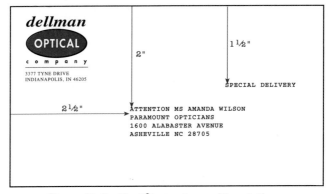

Figure 11–8   No. 6¾ envelope with notations

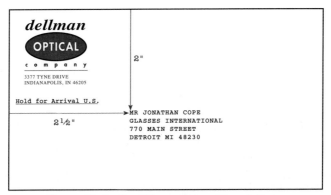

Figure 11–9   No. 6¾ envelope with notations

11

4. If an attention line appears in the letter, it should also be shown on the envelope. It may be shown on the first line of the address or in the same position as a personal or confidential notation. (See Figure 11–7.)
5. Place other special notations (such as "Please Forward," "Personal," and "Hold for Arrival") in capital letters or lowercase with underlining a double-space below the return address. (See Figure 11–9.)
6. Place mailing notations (such as "SPECIAL DELIVERY" and "REGISTERED") in all capital letters below the position for the stamp. (See Figure 11–8.)
7. Some firms follow the practice of showing the name of the originator immediately above the printed company name in the return address.
8. If a plain envelope is used, begin the return address in the upper left corner two lines down from the top and three spaces in from the left edge of the envelope.

FOLDING AND INSERTING LETTERS

11.37   To fold and insert a letter in a No. 10 envelope, follow these steps:

1. Place the letter on the desk face up.

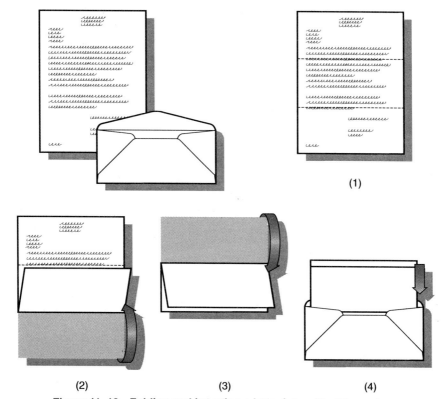

Figure 11–10   Folding and inserting a letter into a No. 10 envelope

2. Fold the lower third of the letter up toward the top and crease.
3. Fold the top third of the letter down to within ⅜ inch of the first fold and crease.
4. Put the letter in the envelope, inserting the last crease first.

11.38 To fold and insert a letter into a No. 6 ¾ envelope, follow these steps:

1. Place the letter on the desk face up.
2. Fold the bottom of the letter up to within ⅜ inch of the top edge of the letter and crease it.

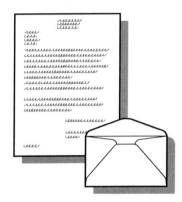

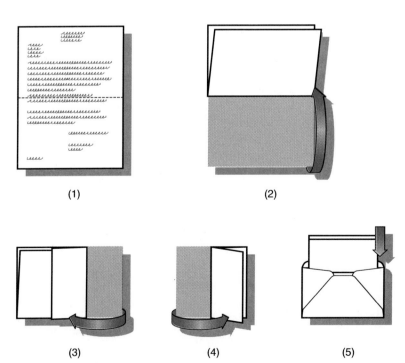

(1)   (2)

(3)   (4)   (5)

Figure 11–11   Folding and inserting letter into No. 6 ¾ envelope

3. Fold the right third of the letter toward the left and crease it.
4. Fold the left third of the letter to the right within ⅜ inch of the last fold and crease it.
5. Turn the letter and insert it with the last crease first.

11.39 To fold and insert a letter into a window envelope, follow these steps:

1. Place the letter on the desk face down, with the letterhead toward you.
2. Fold the top down slightly less than a third of the way and crease.
3. Fold the bottom to within ½ inch of the first fold and crease. Make sure that the address is visible at this point.
4. Put the letter in the envelope, inserting the last crease first. Make sure that the address is clearly visible through the window.

To fold and insert a statement into a window envelope, follow these steps:

1. Place the statement on the desk face down.
2. Fold the bottom half of the form up toward the top and crease.
3. Put the statement into the envelope, inserting the crease first. Make sure that the address is clearly visible through the window.

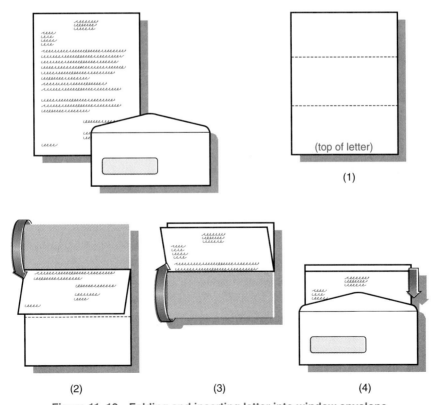

(top of letter)

(1)

(2)   (3)   (4)

Figure 11–12 Folding and inserting letter into window envelope

11

INTEROFFICE MEMORANDUMS

11.40 Much business correspondence never leaves the company. This correspondence, sent from one employee of the company to another, is called an *interoffice memorandum* or an *interoffice memo*.

dellman
OPTICAL
c o m p a n y

I N T E R O F F I C E
M E M O R A N D U M

TO: Lynnette Williams

FROM: Terry Brockmeier

DATE: September 30, 19—

SUBJECT: Research Group Findings

As you know, for quite some time our research group has been engaged in a study of the comfort level and durability index of all our frames and glasses. This group has made exhaustive tests, conducted numerous surveys and interviews, and field tested every model that we produce and sell. The purposes of this memo are (1) to summarize the results of the study of the research group and (2) to make several recommendations for consideration by the product development group.

Among the findings of the research group are these: (1) many customers complain that the nose guards on our frames do not consistently hold the glasses firmly enough without discomfort; (2) many customers feel that the quality of the tinting on our tinted eyewear leaves much to be desired; and (3) many customers would like us to implement an automatic repair and service feature when they purchase our eyewear.

Incidentally, the group also found that our glasses generally held up well in ordinary use and that our patented bifocal imaging was "outstanding."

Based on the findings of the research group, I recommend the following: (1) we immediately develop a new model using the new coated padding to ease the problem of slippage; (2) we immediately initiate a no-questions-asked policy of repair and servicing for our customers; and (3) we investigate the tinting problem and engage some quality control experts to improve this situation.

I'll be in the office all next week if you would like to schedule a conference with the product development staff and with others.

ns

Figure 11–13   Full-page memo

dellman

(OPTICAL)

c o m p a n y

INTEROFFICE
MEMORANDUM

TO: Pansy Greer

FROM: Angie Worley

DATE: November 3, 19—

SUBJECT: Advertising Campaign

As we discussed in the monthly staff meeting, I have been
developing an advertising campaign that will focus on good
vision. Several interesting ideas have emerged as I have con-
sulted departments throughout the company. I should like to
run these ideas by you and your staff as soon as possible to be
sure that I am on the right path. Could you arrange a meeting
next Tuesday at 2 p.m. to go over my proposals.

gdw

Figure 11–14   Half-page memo

Because memos are intended for circulation only within the company, the inside address, salutation, complimentary close, signature, and formal titles are generally omitted. The company name may or may not appear on the form. Even though the message is not formally signed, the sender usually initials the memo.

The memos may be printed on half-page forms for short messages or on full-page forms for longer messages. The headings *To, From, Date,* and *Subject* are generally printed on the memos in a variety of formats. The spacing should allow for the use of a macro or a document format saved as a computer file.

A well-designed interoffice memo form allows for double-spacing between lines in the heading and does not require tabulation to fill in the heading information. Such a block heading saves preparation time.

If a printed interoffice memo form is not available, use a plain sheet of paper and key the headings in all capital letters in block format.

The first line of the body begins a double- or triple-space after the heading. To save time, all lines in the body are usually blocked at the left margin and single-spaced, with a double-space between paragraphs. If the body is short (five lines or less), it can be double-spaced. The reference initials are keyed at the left margin a double-space below the last line in the body. Any additional notations (such as attachment, copy, or postscript) are keyed according to the format used in business letters.

11

11.41 Interoffice memos are often sent to more than one person. When this occurs, the names of all recipients should be shown on the *To* line. Some firms prefer to indicate a "distribution list" for multiple-address memos.

dellman OPTICAL company

INTEROFFICE MEMORANDUM

TO: Timothy MacFarland, Amber Harwood, Pauline Wilson

FROM: Lloyd Buchanan

DATE: April 16, 19—

SUBJECT: First Quarter Sales Reports

Figure 11–15 Multiple-address memo

TO: Distribution List*

Distribution: Ruby Ortega
Warren Reece
Everett Hyde
Glenn Andrews
Marie Galvez

Figure 11–16 Distribution list memo

SELF-CHECK EXERCISE 1, *UNIT 11*

_____
(Name)

From the list of terms in the box, select the letter of the term that best matches the description at the left. Place the letter of the term on the blank line.

1. The second and subsequent pages of letters   _____

2. Indicates something sent with a letter   _____

3. Another name for the message in a letter   _____

4. Number of creases in a letter for a No. 10 envelope   _____

5. A colon follows the salutation and a comma follows the complimentary close

6. Number of creases in a letter for a 6 3/4 envelope   _____

7. An added statement at the bottom of a letter   _____

8. All lines begin at the left margin   _____

9. Used to indicate that a copy was sent to another without the knowledge of the receiver of the letter   _____

10. No punctuation after salutation or complimentary close   _____

A. bc
B. block style
C. body
D. enclosure
E. simplified style
F. multiple pages
G. mixed punctuation
H. open punctuation
I. postscript
J. salutation
K. continuation sheets
L. three
M. two

SELF-CHECK EXERCISE 2, *UNIT 11*

Using the numbers 1 through 19, arrange the following parts a business letter in the order in which they would be found.

Reference initials	_____	Delivery notation	_____	Subject line	_____
Complimentary close	_____	Inside address	_____	Letterhead	_____
Originator's keyed name	_____	Originator's title	_____	Salutation	_____
Separate cover notation	_____	Attention line	_____	Postscript	_____
Enclosure notation	_____	Company name	_____	Body	_____
Personal or	_____	Copy notation	_____	Date	_____
Confidential notation	_____	Signature	_____		

Indicate whether each of the following statements is true or false by writing *T* for true or *F* for false on the blank line.

1. In the Optical Character Recognition format for addresses on envelopes, all capital letters should be used. _____

2. Second and subsequent pages of letters are called continuation pages. _____

3. If a personal business letter is written on plain paper, the return address may be shown as part of the signature block. _____

4. The day of the month precedes the month and the year in dates using the military style correspondence. _____

5. On the envelope address, leave two spaces between the two-letter state abbreviation and the ZIP Code. _____

6. In a modified-block format letter, all lines begin at the left margin. _____

7. Double-spacing may be used in the body of very short letters. _____

8. To triple-space means to leave three blank lines. _____

9. Interoffice memos are never sent to more than one person. _____

10. In a block-style letter, all lines begin at the left margin except the date. _____

11. Delivery notations are placed at the left margin a double-space below the subject line. _____

12. In the inside address, spell out street names using numbers ten and under. _____

13. Mixed punctuation is sometimes called standard punctuation. _____

14. A ZIP Code can have as many as nine digits. _____

15. Reference initials are always used to determine the originator of the letter. _____

16. The Postal Service will not accept letters unless the OCR format is used on the envelope. _____

17. If an attention line appears in a letter, it should also be shown on the envelope. _____

18. Interoffice memos generally do not contain an inside address. _____

19. Interoffice memos may be keyed on plain paper if a printed form is not available. _____

20. Interoffice memos are always single-spaced with a double-space between paragraphs. _____

Check your answers in the back of the book.

RESEARCH PAPERS AND BUSINESS REPORTS

Research papers and business reports are based on information gathered from a variety of sources. The information is used to support ideas and opinions or to explain or inform about plans, proposals, or business decisions. Such communications should be presented in a form that is easy to read and understand, that follows the accepted or prescribed style and format, and that appropriately indicates the source of the information provided.

Many similarities exist in the ways *research papers* and *business reports* are developed and prepared. Procedures, format, and style may vary somewhat from one classroom or office environment to another, but some generally established rules apply in most situations.

RESEARCH PAPERS

A *research paper* is a composition developed from information gathered from a variety of sources. Research papers are commonly developed in classrooms or other academic or scholarly environments. They generally attempt to present information, state and support the writer's point of view, make recommendations for action, and so on. Among the steps commonly used in developing a research paper are the following.

1. Select the topic.
2. Identify sources of information.
3. Prepare a working bibliography.
4. Prepare a thesis statement.
5. Prepare the outline.
6. Gather information.
7. Write the first draft.
8. Document sources of information.
9. Key the report.

10. Revise and proofread the report.
11. Prepare the final draft for presentation.

Select the Topic

12.1 The choice of a topic for a research paper may be prescribed by someone else or selected by the writer. Choosing a topic requires preliminary reading or reviewing materials to get an overview or general understanding of the subject. The topic should not be so broad that it cannot be covered in the length of the proposed report, nor should it be so narrow that there are not enough research materials to support it. Finally, the topic should be evaluated in terms of its purpose and of the audience for which it is intended.

Identify Sources of Information

12.2 Gather information for a research paper from a variety of sources. Libraries will provide printed resources such as magazines, books, newspapers, journals, and pamphlets as well as specialized publications. Other resources such as videos, recordings, and electronic databases may also be available.

The computerized reference systems, microfiche listings, or card catalog found in most libraries will provide listings of resources. In addition, special references such as the *Readers' Guide to Periodical Literature* and the *New York Times Index* provide listings of current periodicals and information arranged by title and author. (See Unit 10 for a more complete listing of reference sources.)

Prepare a Working Bibliography

12.3 As information is examined from various sources, prepare a 3-inch by 5-inch *bibliography card* for each source containing useful information. Include the source's title, author, publisher, city of publication, date, and other information that will clearly identify that source. Number each card consecutively in the upper left corner. (It may also be useful to include the call numbers of books in the upper right corner.)

12.4 Bibliography cards identifying books should include the following information. (See Figure 12–1.)

1. Author's or editor's full name in inverted order—last name first. (If the book has two or more authors, write only the name of the first author in inverted order. Write the other authors' names in regular order.)
2. Title of the book (underlined or in italics if that capability is available), edition number (if there is one), the volume number (if there is one), or the number of the series (if there is one)
3. City of publication
4. Publisher's name
5. Most recent copyright year or date

12

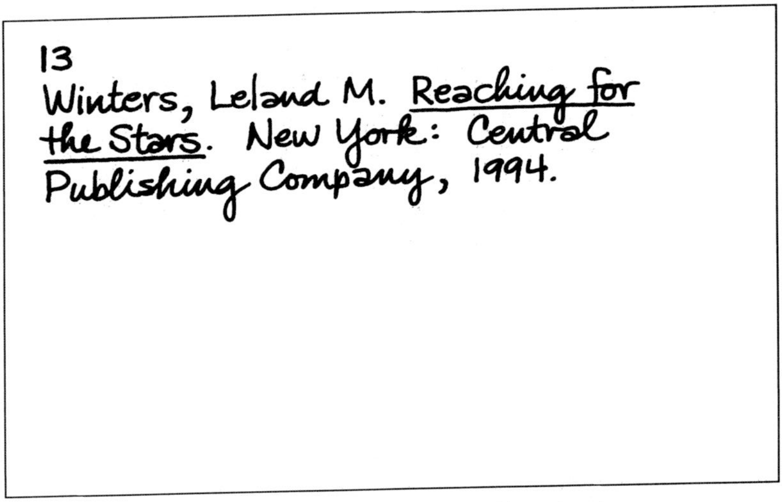

13
Winters, Leland M. Reaching for
the Stars. New York: Central
Publishing Company, 1994.

Figure 12–1   Bibliography card for a book

12.5   Bibliography cards identifying articles in periodicals should include the following information. (See Figure 12–2.)

1. Author's full name (in inverted order)
2. Title of the article in quotation marks
3. Name of the magazine, journal, newspaper, encyclopedia, or other periodical (underlined or in italics if that capability is available)
4. For magazines, the date and page numbers; for newspapers, the date, edition, section, and page numbers; for professional journals, the volume, year, and page numbers; for encyclopedias, the edition and year of publication

17
Lyman, Linda Marie. "The Saturn
Bands." Astronomy Today, October
1994: pages 34-37.

Figure 12–2   Bibliography card for a magazine article

12

Prepare a Thesis Statement

12.6 A *thesis statement* is a clear, concise sentence stating the idea or point of view that you will present in the paper or report. The thesis statement should help to bring into focus the main idea of the paper. Preparing the thesis statement helps define and limit the topic and provide a guide for the research.

Examples of Thesis Statements

According to recent educational research, a strong Tech Prep program will improve students' chances for academic and occupational success.

Recent medical research by noted authorities has clearly indicated and confirmed the dangers of secondhand smoke to those who are exposed to it.

Stricter billboard laws will not only enhance the growth of tourism but can also positively affect the financial growth of the advertising industry.

Prepare the Outline

12.7 An *outline* is a skeletal organization. An outline helps the writer decide on the organization and content. Some writers prefer to develop the outline before gathering information. Others prefer to gather preliminary information before preparing the outline. The outline should indicate the major divisions, secondary topics, and supporting data. As you gather information and prepare notecards, you may discover that the outline needs to be revised to eliminate headings that are not relevant and to add headings for additional information.

12.8 Outlines use roman numerals to identify the major divisions, capital letters to identify secondary topics, and arabic numerals to identify major points. If still other divisions are needed, lowercase letters and arabic numerals in parentheses can be used. Since an outline represents the division of material, there should logically be at least two entries for each level of heading. For example, if there is a *I*, there should also be a *II*; if there is an *A*, there should also be a *B*; if there is a *1*, there should also be a *2*, and so on. Some outline styles include the thesis statement following the title. Some utilize double spacing throughout the entire outline. One example showing the appropriate divisions and suggested spacing for an outline follows.

TITLE

I. Major Division   (Triple-space)

    A. Secondary topic   (Double-space)
    B. Secondary topic
       1. Major point
       2. Major point
    C. Secondary topic

12

(Double-space)

II. Major Division

(Double-space)

    A. Secondary topic
        1. Major point
        2. Major point
            a. Minor point
            b. Minor point
                (1) Supporting data
                (2) Supporting data
    B. Secondary topic

(Double-space)

III. Major Division

Set tabs so that the number or letter of each new level begins under the first word of the previous entry. Align the periods following the various headings. Two spaces follow the periods at each division level.

Gather Information

12.9 Record useful information gathered from the resources used on 4-inch by 6-inch cards. Identify carefully the source (using the number of the bibliography card that matches the source of the information) and the page number on which you found the information. The card should include the central idea of the information. This central idea should be a division of the outline for the paper.

12.10 Prepare the content of the notes in one of three forms: a paraphrase, a summary, or a direct quotation. A *paraphrase* is a restatement of the author's ideas in your own words. A *summary* is a listing of key points and concepts. A *direct quotation* is an exact copy of the passage. Each card should indicate whether the content is a paraphrase, a summary, or a direct quotation. Each card should also indicate the page of the source from which the information was taken. (See Figure 12–3.)

12.11 *Plagiarism* is the inclusion of the ideas or words of another person without giving credit to that person. Plagiarism, even if unintentional, is a serious offense. Plagiarism can, at the very least, lead to lack of credibility.

Plagiarism occurs when a writer quotes directly without using quotation marks or paraphrases a source without giving credit. It can even occur when a writer summarizes the ideas of someone else without giving credit to the source.

12.12 Careful note taking and documentation can help avoid plagiarism. Be sure to note on each card whether you have directly quoted, paraphrased, or summarized a source of information, and then give appropriate credit.

12

13

History of Astronomy

"There can be no doubt that Copernicus, in his great wisdom, changed the world's thinking about astronomy."

Quote, page 39.

Figure 12–3a Example of direct quotation notecard

13

History of Astronomy

Winters's opinion:

—— Even prehistoric man wondered about the heavens.

—— Early "technology" enabled man to see greater distances.

Summary, page 393.

Figure 12–3b Example of summary notecard

13

History of Astronomy

Throughout the ages such great minds as
Copernicus, Ptolemy, and even
Michelangelo changed forever the views
about the heavens.

Paraphrase, page 41

Figure 12–3c   Example of paraphrase notecard

Write the First Draft

12.13   Before you write the first draft, organize your notecards. Ordering your notecards to follow the order of your outline can help determine whether you need to revise or refine the outline itself. Organizing your notecards may also indicate the need for additional research in certain areas or the elimination of areas that seem to be irrelevant.

12.14   Once you have organized your notecards and are satisfied you have enough material on which to base your report, begin to develop the first draft. The first draft should not be looked upon as a final copy; in fact, you may go through several revisions before you arrive at a final draft. The first draft should simply be an attempt to record your ideas in a somewhat organized form.

12.15   As you write the first draft, keep in mind your purpose as reflected by your thesis statement. In addition, keep in mind the audience for whom you are writing.

12.16   Use the content of your notecards to support your thesis statement. Indicate the number of the notecard (the same number as on the related bibliography card) immediately after recording the information. Use the number later to document the source of the information.

12.17   Every paper should have an introduction, a body of supporting information, and a conclusion.

12

12.18 The introduction should capture and keep the attention of the reader. It should also indicate your purpose in writing the paper and tell how you will approach the topic. Finally, the introduction may include some interesting background information, fact, or statistic to entice the reader to continue reading.

12.19 The body of the report should be organized to lead the reader through the information you have gathered toward the conclusion you have reached. It should contain facts, quotations, and general knowledge about your topic. It should be arranged logically, following the outline you developed.

12.20 The conclusion should restate the purpose of the paper and review your main points. It should also state your conclusion or recommendation for action.

Document Sources of Information

12.21 *Documentation* is giving credit to the sources of information used in a report. Documentation is necessary to avoid plagiarism. It also provides more credibility to your writing by showing that you are fair-minded enough to seek and to acknowledge the use of outside sources.

12.22 In general, the following should always be documented.

1. The source of direct quotations
2. The source of researched information such as studies, statistics, surveys, experiments, polls, charts, tables, maps, and so on
3. The source of a paraphrase of the conclusion reached by another writer

12.23 Various methods are used to document sources of information. Research papers generally use footnotes, endnotes, or textnotes to identify the sources of quotations or references in the body of the report. A bibliography is generally included to list all the resources to which the paper referred.

Before you begin preparing the paper or report, find out the preferred or required format for documentation placement and style. Authoritative style guides should be used if there is no preference. (See Section 10.8 for the names of several style guides.)

The following rules provide an overall style and placement guide. Remember that consistency is necessary for the greatest readability.

Footnotes

12.24 Footnotes have traditionally been used to indicate the source of information in research papers and reports. As the name implies, footnotes are placed at the bottom of the page on which the reference appears. Because the manual keying of footnotes requires careful planning and generally reduces the level of productivity, there is a tendency today to use endnotes or textnote references unless electronic equipment is available.

12

Electronic equipment makes the handling of footnotes and endnotes much easier. Computers with appropriate software eliminate the difficulty associated with manually keyed reports of placing footnotes precisely on the page.

When footnotes are used, they are indicated in the text by a superior (raised) figure at the point of reference. Footnotes are generally numbered consecutively throughout the report.

12.25 Footnotes generally contain the following information.

1. Author's name (in first-name-first order)
2. Title of author's work (underlined or in italics if that capability is available)
3. Publication information: city of publication, name of publisher, latest copyright date
4. Volume and page references, if available

After you document a source the first time, you may show a shortened form of the footnote using the author's last name only and the page reference. Note that in a footnote entry a comma is used to separate the parts. If the item referred to is from a periodical, enclose the title of the article in quotation marks and underline the name of the periodical.

12.26 Some word processing software packages provide for automatic placement of footnotes. The footnote feature of the software will automatically place the footnote in the proper position on the page with the related text. If there are additions or deletions of text, the footnote will automatically shift positions as necessary. Automatic numbering of footnotes is also provided. This feature relieves much of the difficulty associated with the counting of lines and spaces and planning for the proper placement of footnotes as described in Section 12.27. If you have access to this kind of software, refer to the user's manual for specific instructions for handling footnotes.

12.27 If you are manually keying footnotes follow these general guidelines. (See Figure 12–4.)

in the early 1700s.[1] His theory later was accepted by all but a hand

ful of noted astronomers; however, there were exceptions and these

exceptions proved troublesome.

[1]Leland M. Winters, Reaching for the Stars (New York: Central Publishing Company, 1994), p. 36.

12

Figure 12–4 Footnote

1. Place a 2-inch dividing line a single space below the last line of the text at the left margin. Double-space after the line.
2. Indent the first line of each footnote the same number of spaces as the paragraph indentations.
3. Be sure to use the same superior number for the footnote as for its reference in the text.
4. Single-space each footnote with a double-space between footnotes.
5. Leave a 1-inch bottom margin below the last line of the footnote.

12.28 To determine the point on the page at which to place the dividing line, follow these steps.

1. Count 6 lines for the 1-inch bottom margin.
2. Count 1 line for each line of each footnote.
3. Count 1 line for each blank line between footnotes.
4. Count 2 lines for the divider line (1 line for the divider line itself and 1 line for the blank line between the divider line and the footnotes).
5. Subtract the total of the lines in Steps 1 through 4 from 66 (the number of lines on a full sheet). The answer will tell you the number of lines from the top of the page at which you should place the dividing line.

Endnotes

12.29 Endnotes are gaining in popularity because of their ease of use and the elimination of a cluttered look on pages with footnotes. Endnotes are used in place of footnotes, keyed on a separate page, and placed at the end of a report rather than at the bottom of pages. Endnotes provide the same information in nearly the same style as footnotes.

12.30 Electronic equipment and software automatically place endnotes in the proper position. To prepare the endnotes page manually, center the word *Notes* in all capital letters 2 inches from the top of the page. Triple-space after

NOTES

1. Leland M. Winters, Reaching for the Stars (New York: Central Publishing Company, 1994), p. 36.

2. Linda Marie Lyman, "The Saturn Bands," Astronomy Today, October 1994, p. 34.

Figure 12–5 Endnotes

the heading, indent 5 spaces, and type the number of the note and a period. Unlike footnotes, which are identified by superior numbers, endnote numbers are placed evenly on the line. Single-space within the note and double-space between the individual notes. (See Figure 12–5.) Note that in an endnote entry a comma is used to separate the parts.

Textnotes

12.31 The textnote format is also growing in popularity because of ease of use. Textnote references, sometimes called *parenthetical citation* or *parenthetical documentation,* may be used in place of footnotes or endnotes. In this format the writer prepares the bibliography *before* keying the report.

To prepare textnotes, number the bibliography entries in alphabetical order (preferred format) or list them in the order cited in the report. Then, in the body of the report, key the reference number using an opening parenthesis, the number of the entry, a colon, the page number being cited, and a closing parenthesis. If the entry is located within a sentence, leave one space before and after the parentheses. If the entry comes at the end of a sentence, key the entry two spaces *after* the period. List each source only once in the bibliography, but cite each as many times as necessary in the body of the report. (See Figure 12–6.)

Bibliography

12.32 The *bibliography* (also known as *works cited*) is a complete listing of all sources referred to, quoted from, or used by the writer in preparing the report. The bibliography may include books, periodicals, government publications, and articles. References in the bibliography should be listed in alphabet-

in the early 1700s. (2:36) His theory was later accepted by all but a

handful of noted astronomers; however, there were exceptions (1:37)

and these exceptions proved troublesome.

BIBLIOGRAPHY

1. Lyman, Linda Marie. "The Saturn Bands," <u>Astronomy Today</u>, October 1994: 34-37.

2. Winters, Leland M. <u>Reaching for the Stars</u>. New York: Central Publishing Company, 1994.

3. Woffield, Timothy; Jones, C. H. <u>The Mystique of the Stars</u>. Boston: Apex Press, 1994.

12

Figure 12–6 Textnotes

ical order by author or, if the authors' names are not given, by titles or editors. The bibliography is generally shown on a separate page at the end of a report. (See Figure 12–7.)

12.33 Center the word *Bibliography* in all capital letters 2 inches from the top of the page. The first entry begins a triple-space below this heading. The bibliography is single-spaced with a double-space between entries. The first line of each entry in the bibliography begins at the left margin, with second and succeeding lines in each entry indented 5 spaces.

BIBLIOGRAPHY

Lyman, Linda Marie. "The Saturn Bands," <u>Astronomy Today</u>, October 1994: 34-37.

Winters, Leland, M. <u>Reaching for the Stars</u>. New York: Central Publishing Company, 1994.

Woffield, Timothy; Jones, C. H. <u>The Mystique of the Stars</u>. Boston: Apex Press, 1994.

Yancy, Pauline R. "The Copernican Theory: Revelations and Revolutions." Master's thesis. Keystone State College, 1992.

Figure 12–7   Bibliography

12.34   The entries in the bibliography are arranged in alphabetical order by author, or by title if there is no author. There is no need to number alphabetical entries in a bibliography unless you intend to use the textnote format described in Section 12.31. Each entry should contain the following information.

1. Author's name, last name first. If there is more than one author, transpose all names.
2. Title of the source. Underline or use italic type for the title of a book or periodical; enclose the title of a magazine article in quotation marks.
3. Publication information. For a book, list the city of publication, the name of the publisher, and date of publication. For an article, list the name of the publication, the volume number, and the date of publication. Show page numbers only if the material referred to is part of a larger work.

Note that in a bibliography entry a period is used to separate the parts.

Key the Report

12.35   Reports may be unbound; that is, in loose sheets placed in a folder. They may also be bound (stapled or otherwise secured) at the top or at the left. The following margins are generally used for each of these situations, although there are other variations.

12.36   Unbound

1. A top margin of 2 inches on the first page, 1 inch on succeeding pages
2. Left, right, and bottom margins of 1 inch

12.37   Bound at the Top

1. A top margin of $2\frac{1}{2}$ inches on the first page, $1\frac{1}{2}$ inches on succeeding pages
2. Left, right, and bottom margins of 1 inch

12.38   Bound at the Left

1. A top margin of 2 inches on the first page, 1 inch on succeeding pages
2. A left margin of $1\frac{1}{2}$ inches
3. Bottom and right margins of 1 inch

12.39   Introductory pages such as the outline, preface, and table of contents (if used) are generally numbered with small roman numerals. Although a number does not actually appear on the title page, the title page is considered to be *i*. Beginning with *ii*, the page numbers of introductory pages are typed at the center, $\frac{1}{2}$ inch from the bottom of the page.

12

12.40 Header features of some software automatically provide for page numbering. If you are not using such software, number all pages within the body and supplementary sections with arabic numerals, beginning with page 1 and running consecutively throughout the rest of the report. Some writers prefer to omit the page number on the first page; in this case, page numbers will then begin with page 2.

If the paper is unbound or bound at the left, center the page number for the first page ½ inch from the bottom of the page. Place succeeding page numbers aligned on the right margin ½ inch from the top of the page. Two blank line spaces should be left between the page number and the text at the top or bottom. (Header features on software generally leave only one blank line space.)

If the report is bound at the top, center all page numbers ½ inch from the bottom of the page.

12.41 Center the title of the paper, in all capital letters, 2 inches from the top of the first page of an unbound or left-bound report; 2½ inches from the top of the first page for a top-bound report. If the report is to be bound at the left, center the title over the report, not the center of the paper.

If the title is followed by a centered heading, double-space after the title and triple-space after the centered heading. If the title is followed by the text of the report, triple-space.

Note: Because some word processing software may have spacing limitations, some flexibility in spacing rules is permissible. For example, triple-spacing after headings may be difficult with some software; in that case, double-spacing may be acceptable.

12.42 The body of the paper is always double-spaced, with 5-space paragraph indentations. If quotations of 4 or more lines appear, single-space them and indent 5 spaces from both the left and right margins (see Figure 12–8). Quotations of 3 lines or less may be double-spaced and run into the text. If numbered lists of items appear, single-space them and use a double-space to separate the items. (See Figure 12–9.)

after years of speculation. In his research, Winters summarized the

thinking of the general population of those times as follows:

> It was a time of great superstition and ignorance about
> the universe. People generally believed that the earth
> was the center of the universe. Such phenomena as
> eclipses sometimes ignited mass hysteria, people fearing
> that the end of time had arrived.[9]

It was quite obvious to Winters that dark times had fallen upon the

Figure 12–8   Quotation of more than four lines

Winters concluded that "Only a few great minds of the times kept alive a glimmer of hope for the resurrection of knowledge."[10] He listed three reasons for the maintenance of that hope during those bleak periods of history:

1. Communication between the great thinkers of the time, even though such communication was limited.

2. The invention of the printing press, the spread of information through books, and the development of great libraries as depositories of information.

3. The sponsorship of research by wealthy and influential individuals.[11]

Knowledge continued to spread, changing the ideas of the masses about the heavens. Centuries passed, however, before evidence of advances in

Figure 12–9   Run-in quotation and numbered list

12.43   Centered headings, if used, relate to the major divisions of an outline as indicated by the roman numerals. Triple-space before these headings and double-space after them. Spacing above and below headings may have to be changed if you are using word processing equipment. The headings are usually keyed in all capital letters, but they may be shown in capitals and lowercase and underlined or boldfaced if this capability is available. (See Figure 12–10.)

12.44   Side headings, sometimes known as secondary headings, may be used within the body of the report to relate to the divisions of the outline represented by capital letters. Leave a triple-space before them and a double-space after. Key these headings in capitals and lowercase letters, underlined, at the left margin. Capitalize only the first and important words.

12.45   Paragraph headings may be used to relate to the division of the outline represented by arabic numerals. They begin at the paragraph indentation point and "run into" the paragraph itself. Leave a double-space above these headings. Capitalize only the first word, and underline the entire heading. The heading is usually followed by a period.

Revise and Proofread the Report

12.46   Once the first draft of the paper has been prepared, revising and proofreading are necessary. In revising the paper, consider the following.

1. Does the introductory paragraph include the purpose and intent of the writer? Does it truly invite and encourage the reader to continue?

2. Does the body contain ideas that support the thesis statement in a clear and logical fashion?

3. Is the language appropriate for the intended audience? Are technical terms clearly defined?

4. Does the conclusion reinforce the thesis statement in a convincing manner?

12

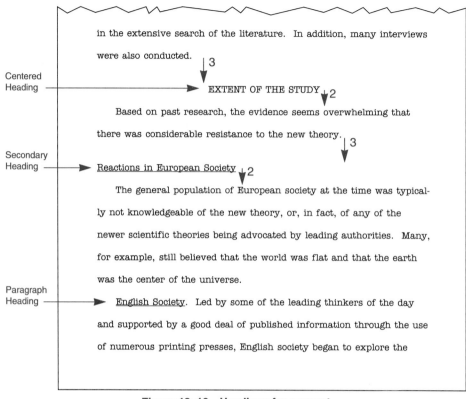

Figure 12–10 Headings for a report

5. Are accepted conventions of style and format followed throughout?
6. Is the paper free of typographical and grammatical errors?
7. Is the documentation complete and accurate, giving credit to sources of information where necessary?

12.47 In proofreading your paper, check the following.

1. Are any words omitted, or are there extra words?
2. Is every sentence grammatically correct?
3. Are spelling, capitalization, and punctuation correct throughout?
4. Are there any typographical errors?
5. Is there correct spacing throughout?

Prepare the Final Draft for Presentation

12.48 Prepare the cover, if one is used, on paper of the same quality as that used for the paper itself. The cover generally contains only the title of the report, in all capital letters, centered vertically and horizontally. If the

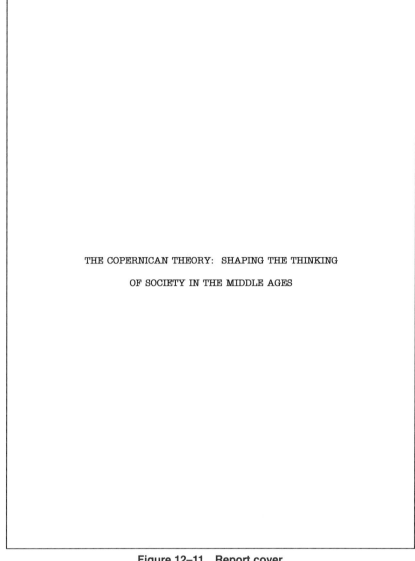

THE COPERNICAN THEORY: SHAPING THE THINKING

OF SOCIETY IN THE MIDDLE AGES

Figure 12–11   Report cover

title is longer than one line, double-space between each centered line. (See Figure 12–11.)

12.49   The title page, if one is used, may follow any one of several arrangements. The title page generally contains the title of the paper, the writer's name, for whom the paper was prepared, the name of the class, and the date. (See Figure 12–12.)

12.50   Assemble the parts of the paper in the following order: cover (if used), title page (if used), final outline, the report, and documentation.

12

THE COPERNICAN THEORY: SHAPING THE THINKING
OF SOCIETY IN THE MIDDLE AGES

Submitted by

Franco Ruiz

Prepared for

Mr. John Wilson
English IV

April 16, 19—

Figure 12–12   Title page for academic research paper

12 BUSINESS REPORTS

Business reports are much like research papers in that they report information, present points of view or opinions, make recommendations for action,
and so on. Business reports are prepared in a business environment for the
benefit of a business operation. Research papers, on the other hand, are generally prepared in an academic environment. Business reports, like research
papers, can be long or short, formal or informal. They may or may not include

tables and illustrations. Business reports generally contain introductory pages, the body of the report, and supplementary pages.

Procedures for report preparation vary from office to office, but the rules generally established for any kind of report or paper are appropriate for business reports.

12.51 Brief, informal reports may be prepared in a business letter format or an interoffice memorandum format. (See Figures 12–13 and 12–14.)

12.52 Formal reports in manuscript format are generally intended to be published, either for distribution to individuals within an organization or in

---

PINNACLE CONSULTING SERVICE
3600 Skyline Drive
Asheville, NC 28701

(Voice) 704-555-9366
(Fax) 704-555-9300

March 16, 19—

Mr. John Baker
Pinewood Products Company
1260 Industrial Place
Asheville, NC 28703

Dear Mr. Baker

After several months of an intensive survey study of your advertising needs, we have concluded that some new directions must be taken.

Extent of the Survey

Every customer on the current customer list was contacted and asked to complete the survey. Some 93 percent of these customers responded with information that could be classified as useful. Furthermore, some 867 potential new customers in the surrounding five-county area were also surveyed.

Results of the Survey

Based on the interpretation of the survey, 78 percent of current customers surveyed had little or no knowledge of your long-term service agreements. While an overwhelming 93 percent of current customers felt "general satisfaction" with your products, most felt a need for better service.

Conclusions and Recommendations

Based on the results of the survey, we recommend an entirely new approach. The approach should center heavily on service aspects, including service after installation of your products. We recommend that a new agency be retained.

The entire report is available for you and your staff.

Sincerely

Lynette Kwai

Lynette Kwai
Chief Consultant

Figure 12–13   Business letter report

12

INTEROFFICE MEMORANDUM

TO: John Baker
FROM: Lynette Kwai
DATE: May 16, 19—
SUBJECT: Results of Advertising Survey

After several months of an intensive survey study of your advertising needs, we have concluded that some new directions must be taken.

Extent of the Survey

Every customer on our current customer list was contacted and asked to complete the survey. Some 93 percent of these customers responded with information that could be classified as useful. Furthermore, some 867 potential new customers in the surrounding five-county area were also surveyed.

Results of the Survey

Based on the interpretation of the survey, 78 percent of current customers had little or no knowledge of your long-term service agreements. While an overwhelming 93 percent of current customers felt "general satisfaction" with your products, most felt a need for better service.

Conclusions and Recommendations

Based on the results of the survey, we recommend an entirely new approach. The approach should center heavily on service aspects, including service after installation of your products. We recommend that a new agency be retained.

The entire report is available for you and your staff.

Figure 12–14   Interoffice memorandum report

the form of a newsletter or bulletin. Formal reports may be rather lengthy and detailed and will likely contain most or all of the following parts.

1. Cover
2. Title page
3. Letter of transmittal
4. Preface   }—Introductory Pages
5. Table of contents
6. List of tables and charts
7. Summary

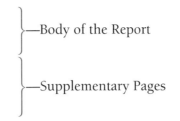

8. Introduction
9. Text of the report }—Body of the Report
10. Conclusions
11. Notes
12. Appendix }—Supplementary Pages
13. Bibliography
14. Index

Cover and Title Page

12.53 The cover and title page are generally prepared in much the same way as those for a research paper. The title page may differ as to the kind of information provided. (See Figure 12–15.)

Letter of Transmittal

12.54 The letter of transmittal, which may take the place of a preface, is addressed to the readers of the report. It usually contains information regarding the purpose of the report, the scope of the report, methods of gathering information, findings, and conclusions. Prepare the letter on letterhead stationery, using the customary letter style.

   If a preface is also prepared for the report, the letter of transmittal serves only as a cover letter to indicate what is enclosed.

Preface

12.55 The preface may take the place of an introduction to the report. It provides information regarding the report's purpose, scope, general findings, and conclusions.

Table of Contents

12.56 The table of contents lists the page numbers of the parts of the report and the major headings in the body of the report (as shown in the outline). Prepare it after the report is completed so that the page numbers will be accurate. A table of contents is needed only for lengthy reports or if there are many divisions within the report.

   The table of contents should be attractively placed on the page. Center the word *Contents* in all capital letters 2 inches from the top of the page. Use a triple-space between *Contents* and the first entry. Use a double-space between the individual entries. "Leaders," made by alternately striking the period and the space bar (. . . .), may or may not be used. (See Figure 12–16.)

12

List of Tables and Charts

12.57 If the report includes many tables and charts, prepare a separate page listing those items, using the same format as the table of contents. (See Figure 12–16.)

REPORT ON THE ADVERTISING NEEDS

OF THE PINEWOOD PRODUCTS COMPANY

by

Lynette Kwai
Chief Consultant
Pinnacle Consulting Service

May 16, 19—

Figure 12–15   Title page for a business report

12

Summary

12.58   The summary (sometimes called "an executive summary"), prepared after the text has been written, presents major points, significant findings, conclusions, recommendations, and suggested actions. The summary gives the reader a quick overview of the report.

CONTENTS

Figure 12–16   Table of contents for business report

Introduction

12.59   The introduction provides the reader with the reasons for and purposes of the report, sources of information, methods of gathering the information, scope of the report, and format of presentation. A preface may replace the introduction.

Text of the Report

12.60 The text is the main body of the report including the discussion, proposals, findings, and so on. It should follow the divisions reflected in the report outline.

Conclusions

12.61 The writer's conclusions, based on the information provided in the report itself, may be presented in a list or in strict narrative form. Recommendations or suggested actions may also be a part of this section.

Notes

12.62 Follow the same procedures for documenting sources in business reports as in a research paper. (See Document Sources of Information, pages 204–209.)

Appendix

12.63 An appendix presents additional information or illustrations that expand or interpret the information provided in the text of the report. The appendix may contain tables, surveys, supporting statements, or technical data.

Bibliography

12.64 Follow the same procedures for preparing a bibliography for a business report as for a research paper. (See Bibliography, pages 207–209.)

Index

12.65 The index is an alphabetical guide to the contents of a report. An index is compiled after the text of the report has been completed and lists all topics, subtopics, tables, and charts in the report and the pages on which they are found. An index assists the reader in locating specific information in the text of the report. An index should be prepared only if the report is especially lengthy and detailed.

12

_____

(Name)

Indicate whether the following statements are true (T) or false (F) by writing
T or *F* in the blank following each statement.

1. *Readers' Guide to Periodical Literature* provides listings of books and   _____
   encyclopedias.
2. A thesis statement presents the idea or point of view to be presented in the   _____
   research paper.
3. A paraphrase is a restatement of another's ideas in your own words.   _____
4. It is not necessary to document a source giving another person's   _____
   conclusions if you put the information in your own words.
5. Plagiarism can lead to a lack of credibility.   _____
6. The content of note cards need not support the thesis statement.   _____
7. Direct quotations should always be documented.   _____
8. Textnotes have traditionally been used to indicate the source of   _____
   information used in research papers.
9. Endnotes are prepared on a separate page and placed at the beginning of a   _____
   research paper for easy reference.
10. A bibliography is a complete listing of all sources referred to, quoted from,   _____
    or used by the writer in preparing a report.
11. Reports must always be bound by stapling or otherwise securing in some way.   _____
12. The introductory pages of a report, such as the outline and table of contents,   _____
    are usually numbered with small arabic numbers.
13. The cover of a research paper, if one is used, generally contains the title,   _____
    writer's name, date, class, and name of school.
14. Brief, informal business reports may be prepared in the form of a letter or   _____
    interoffice memo.
15. In a business report, the letter of transmittal may take the place of the   _____
    summary.
16. Documenting sources of information for a formal business report is similar   _____
    to that of documenting sources for an academic research paper.
17. The index, if one is used in a business report, is generally prepared before   _____
    the report is completely written.
18. The text of a business report may include discussion, proposals, and findings.   _____
19. Textnote referencing is sometimes referred to as parenthetical documentation.   _____
20. The body of a research paper or business report is generally single-spaced.   _____

Arrange in order the steps to develop a research paper by numbering the steps (1 through 11) in the blanks.

a. Write the first draft.   1. _____

b. Prepare the outline.   2. _____

c. Select a topic.   3. _____

d. Prepare the final draft for presentation.   4. _____

e. Prepare a working bibliography.   5. _____

f. Identify sources of information.   6. _____

g. Revise and proofread.   7. _____

h. Prepare a thesis statement.   8. _____

i. Gather information.   9. _____

j. Key the report.   10. _____

k. Document sources of information.   11. _____

Using the following information, prepare a bibliography card in the box.

Copyright year: 1994
Title of book: The Art of Revision
Author's name: Elizabeth C. Stein

Publisher: Center Publishing Co.
City of publisher: Boston
Bibliography card #6

UNIT 13

EMPLOYMENT COMMUNICATION

According to recent employment statistics, total employment is expected to increase by 20 percent in the next five years, even though this rate is less than in other recent periods. The shift from goods-producing to service-producing employment is projected to continue.

Service jobs are expected to be the largest and fastest growing division within the services-producing sector, accounting for about one-half of all new jobs. Health services and business services are expected to lead the growth.

While the service sector will produce many new clerical, sales, and service jobs, it will also create many new jobs in management, electrical and electronic technology, finance, engineering, nursing, and technical areas. The fastest growing occupations will require the most formal education and training.

A look in the Help Wanted ads in most newspapers will verify that there are job openings. If you have the necessary qualifications, finding employment should not be difficult.

ORGANIZING YOUR PLAN OF ACTION

13.1 If you are to be successful in your search for just the right job, you should have a plan of action that includes these steps:

1. Investigate career demands and opportunities.
2. Locate job openings.
3. Develop your résumé.
4. Prepare your letter of application.
5. Complete the application form and possibly take an employment test.
6. Interview for the job opening.
7. Write a follow-up letter.

Investigate Career Demands and Opportunities

13.2 To help you make wise choices about the job you are looking for, you should gather as much information about career opportunities as possible.

13

Good sources of information and assistance include your placement director or guidance counselor, employment agencies, professional organizations, and your local library. Publications such as *The Occupational Outlook Handbook* can be especially helpful in discovering those job/career areas that have growth potential. Find out as much as you can about working conditions, the nature of the work, salary and employment benefits, and opportunities for advancement. Making a self-assessment can help you determine the types of jobs for which you are prepared. A self-assessment helps you look at your personal characteristics, education, experiences, aptitudes, likes, and dislikes.

Locate Job Openings

13.3 There are many sources of job information and leads for specific job openings, including the following:

1. Friends and relatives
2. Newspaper classified sections
3. Private employment agencies
4. Public employment service agencies
5. Temporary employment agencies
6. School placement services
7. Social agencies
8. Teachers and counselors
9. Direct inquiries
10. Specialized publications
11. Company recruiters
12. Job fairs
13. Civil Service announcements
14. Labor unions
15. Professional associations
16. Women's counseling and employment programs
17. Youth programs

Develop Your Résumé

13.4 A résumé—sometimes referred to as a personal data sheet (see Figure 13-1)—is a picture of your background as you want to present it to a prospective employer. Its purpose is to convey, in as positive and concise a manner as possible, your qualifications for the position you are seeking. In addition to personal information, résumés may include information about the position sought or your career objectives, a summary of your educational background and special training, your previous work experience, and any activities or accomplishments that might be pertinent to the position you are seeking.

13.5 The following guidelines should be remembered in developing your résumé:

1. Try to hold your résumé to one page. Most corporate personnel directors and prospective employers do not have the time to consider lengthy résumés and are not particularly impressed by them. Résumés prepared for a job in the education field may be longer than one page. Most other résumés should be limited to one page.

2. Be sure the appearance of your résumé is impeccable. It should be typewritten or prepared on a word processor. Use good quality bond paper, and be sure that the typewriter or printer produces clear, black type. While a perfect original copy of a résumé is likely to make the best impression, a clear, clean photocopy is generally acceptable.

   Your résumé should be absolutely free of grammatical and spelling errors, easy to read, and eye-catching in appearance.

   Although white paper is always safe, an off-white or light pastel may help your résumé to stand out from others. Avoid large blocks of type. Separate the parts of the résumé with section headings for easier reading.

3. Be direct and to the point regarding your past work experience. If you have had no previous paid work experience, list any volunteer experience that can indicate your abilities and willingness to work. Indicate the month and year you worked for each employer, and include the employer's complete mailing address.

4. List awards, honors, and promotions, especially those that emphasize qualities of leadership and scholarship.

5. Include specific educational experiences and travel that furthered your occupational goals or that made you a well-rounded individual.

6. Be honest about your accomplishments and experiences.

Prepare Your Letter of Application

13.6 A letter of application (see Figure 13–2) should always be typewritten or prepared on a word processor. It should usually include the following:

1. Your complete address and your telephone number so that you can be notified of an interview

2. If possible, the name of a particular person in the company instead of just a position (such as Personnel Director)

3. Three paragraphs that do the following:
   a. Indicate the specific position for which you are applying and how you learned of the position
   b. Present your basic qualifications and express the belief that you can make a contribution to the organization
   c. Request an interview

LYNETTA A. DEVORE
1339 Delhaven Drive
Covington, Kentucky 41017
Telephone 606-555-3636

CAREER OBJECTIVE   A responsible marketing position utilizing strong computer, organizational, and writing skills.

EDUCATION

September 1994
to present
Wilson College, Covington, KY 41019. Will receive associate of arts degree in marketing in May 1996, with 3.4 average in all course work.

September 1990
to June 1994
Highland Central High School, Covington, KY to 41017. Advanced placement classes in English and mathematics. Graduated with honor.

EXPERIENCE

December 1994
to April 1995
Computer Services, Inc., 1667 Lucien Avenue, Covington, KY 41022. Served as marketing assistant in intern program.

September 1993
to November 1994
Apex Advertising Agency, 3000 Plaza Court, Covington, KY 41018. Served as part-time copy editor and proofreader.

June 1992 to
August 1993
Kentucky Medical Center, 3636 Riverfront Drive, Covington, KY 41026. Part-time receptionist.

ACTIVITIES   President, Wilson College Writers Club.

Member (elected) of Wilson College Student Senate.

Treasurer Interdenominational Fellowship, Wilson College.

Recognized as Outstanding Marketing Student at Wilson College.

Figure 13–1   Résumé

Naturally, the letter of application should represent your very best effort. It should be attractive and absolutely free of grammatical, spelling, and punctuation errors. Revise the letter as many times as necessary. Proofread it carefully to make sure that it contains no errors. Although a good grade of white bond paper is generally preferred, an attractive off-white or light pastel color may separate your letter from others. Be sure to use the same quality and color of paper as for your résumé. Also be sure that the typewriter or printer produces clean, clear, black type.

May 16, 19—

Ms. Janna Chambers
Human Services Director
Gateway Computer Corporation
10037 Research Park
Lexington, KY 40508-1123

Dear Ms. Chambers

Mr. William Turnage, Placement Services Director at Wilson College, recently told me of your need for a marketing assistant in the product division of your company. I know that Gateway has developed a reputation for quality products and innovative marketing practices, and I should welcome the opportunity to be part of your organization. I believe that my education and experience make me an excellent candidate for the marketing position.

On May 29, I will be awarded the associate of arts degree in marketing from Wilson College in Covington. In addition to the emphasis in marketing, I have considerable strength and experience with computers and writing that I think will be valuable to your company. As indicated by the enclosed résumé, I have the work experience to make an immediate and lasting contribution to your firm. To further my education and expand my potential, I plan to enroll in the evening marketing program at the University of Kentucky in the fall.

May I have the opportunity to discuss further my qualifications and the extent to which I might contribute to the success of Gateway Computer Corporation. You may write me or phone me at 606-401-3636. I look forward to hearing from you.

Sincerely

Lynetta A. DeVore

Lynetta A. DeVore
1339 Delhaven Drive
Covington, KY 41017

Enclosure

Figure 13–2   Letter of application

13.7   Remember these tips about writing a letter of application:

1. The letter should not repeat the facts contained in the résumé. Instead, the letter should highlight or interpret those facts that relate to the specific job for which you are applying.
2. Show that you know something about the company.
3. Be positive in your approach. Use statements of fact. Show confidence in your ability to perform without being overly bold.

4. If you have a contact within the company, consider adding that person's name as a special reference.
5. Never send a résumé without a letter of application. The letter and résumé are your introduction to a prospective employer.

Complete the Application Form

13.8 After the prospective employer receives your letter of application and résumé, you may receive an application form (see Figure 13-3) or be invited to the company office to complete the form. Here are some points to remember in completing an application form:

1. If you will be completing the form at the office of the employer, be sure to take with you:
   a. Two dependable pens, preferably with black ink
   b. Your social security number and your driver's license number
   c. Your résumé or a listing of your education and work experience
   d. A listing of your references, including addresses and telephone numbers (Be sure to secure permission from those you list.)
2. Read the application form thoroughly before you begin to complete it. Plan your answers as you are reading the form.
3. Study each blank carefully before you complete it. You may be asked to type or print the information on the form, or you may be told specifically to complete it in your own handwriting. If you complete the form using a pen, print neatly and legibly. Do not use a pencil.
4. Follow the directions exactly, and complete each blank on the form. Where blanks do not apply to you, draw a line through, type hyphens through, or write *NA* (Not Applicable) in the spaces. Answer all questions honestly. Emphasize your strengths and special skills as you did on your résumé.
5. If you are asked to state an expected salary, you may indicate a range or that your salary expectations are "open," meaning that the question of salary is open for discussion. Listing a definite amount almost always means that you agree to accept that amount. If you have done your homework, you will know the range for the position.
6. Proofread the application form carefully. Be sure that you have completed each blank and that you have made no errors.
7. Sign and date the form.

13.9 Here are some tips to remember:

1. Ask whether you can take the application form home. If so, you can make a photocopy for a rough draft, and transfer your answers (by typewriter if possible) to the original form.
2. Judge your space carefully. Judging the space in each blank lets you know how large to print your answers.

3. Carry a small pocket dictionary if spelling is a problem for you. Make absolutely sure that you have no misspelled words.
4. Carry some scratch paper with you to organize your thoughts on open-ended questions that require more than just a word or two.

13.10 While employers were once free to ask almost any question on application forms and during interviews, federal and state laws now prohibit questions relating to the following:

13

1. Age
2. Sex
3. Race
4. Health
5. Height and weight (unless this is important for the job)
6. Marital status
7. Religion
8. Arrest record
9. Whether you have or plan to have children

The employer cannot ask for your age or date of birth, but he or she can ask if you are between 18 and 65 years of age. If you are not between 18 and 65, you must give your age.

Employers cannot require that you attach a photograph to a résumé or application form at any time before you are hired.

Although legally you do not have to answer questions related to sex, age, race, veteran status, or health, some employers ask for this information (which still has to be submitted voluntarily) to help them reach affirmative-action goals.

The Equal Employment Opportunity Commission (EEOC) oversees and enforces fair employment practices. It forbids discrimination based on age, religion, race, or sex.

Take an Employment Test

13.11 Depending on the job you are seeking, you may be required to take an employment test or to provide a "work sample." Employment tests for office support positions, for example, may include a typewriting/keyboarding test, a shorthand test, and/or a computation skills test. Other occupations may require psychological testing, basic skills testing, or manipulative skills testing. A "work sample" may be required to provide evidence of your writing ability, for example.

13.12 If you take an employment test, remember the following:

1. If the test involves working with equipment, ask for some time to warm up on the equipment so that you can familiarize yourself with its features.

13

Computerworks   Date _____
Employment Application
An Equal Opportunity Employer
Computerworks policy and federal law forbid discrimination because of race, religion, age, sex, marital status, disability, or national origin.

Personal Data _____

Applying for position as _____ Salary required _____ Date available _____

Name _____
             (Last)   (First)   (Middle)
Address _____
                  (Street)   (City)   (State)
Telephone number_____ Social Security Number _____

Are you a U.S. citizen? ☐ Yes ☐ No   If non-citizen, give Alien Registration No. _____

Person to be notified in case of emergency:

Name_____ Telephone_____
                                           (Area code)
Address _____

Relatives employed by Computerworks:

Name_____ Department _____

Name_____ Department _____

Have you ever been employed by Computerworks or its subsidiaries? Yes ☐ No ☐

If "Yes," indicate department or subsidiary   Dates _____

Have you previously applied for employment with Computerworks?   If "Yes," when? _____

How were you referred to Computerworks? ☐ Agency ☐ School ☐ Advertisement ☐ Direct contact
                                        ☐ Computerworks employee ☐ Other

Name of referral source above _____

Military Data _____

Have you ever served in the Military Service of the United States? _____

Branch of Service_____ From_____ To_____ Rank _____

Give details of Service duties which might apply to civilian occupations _____

_____

Figure 13–3a   Application form

13

Educational Data

Schools	Print Name, Number and Street, City, State, and ZIP Code for Each School Listing	Dates	Types of Courses or Major	Graduated?	Degree Received
High School		From ___ To			
College		From ___ To			
Trade, Bus., Night, or Corres·		From ___ To			
Other		From ___ To			

Approximate scholastic average: High school _____ College _____ Class rank: High School _____ College_____

Percent of college expenses earned _____ How earned? _____

Skills

List any special skills you may have _____

_____

Business machines you can operate _____

Word processing/data processing: ☐ Yes   Equipment used_____

Employment Data

List all full-time, part-time, temporary, or self-employment. Begin with current or most recent employer.

		Mo-Yr	Mo-Yr
Company name	Employed from	To	
Street address	Salary or earnings Start	Finish	
City State ZIP Code	Telephone (Area code)		
Name and title of immediate supervisor	Your title		
Description of duties			
Reason for terminating or considering a change			

		Mo-Yr	Mo-Yr
Company name	Employed from	To	
Street address	Salary or earnings Start	Finish	
City State ZIP Code	Telephone (Area code)		
Name and title of immediate supervisor	Your title		
Description of duties			
Reason for terminating			

Figure 13–3b   Application form

2. Listen carefully to instructions.
3. Try to remain calm and relaxed during the test.
4. Write clearly and legibly.
5. Use your time effectively, especially if the test is timed.
6. If you complete the test early, review your work.

Interview for the Job Opening

13.13 Once you have completed the application form and the employment test to the employer's satisfaction, you may be invited for an interview. The interview is an opportunity for you to present your qualifications for the job in person and to seek specific information about the company and the job. It is an opportunity for the employer to discuss your qualifications, evaluate you personally, and give you information about the company.

13.14 Prepare yourself for the interview by doing the following:

1. Write down the name and title of the interviewer, the name and address of the company, the name of the department, and the time of the interview.
2. Learn to pronounce the interviewer's name. (A call to his or her secretary might be necessary.)
3. Try to learn something about the interviewer—title, area of responsibility, and so on.
4. Learn something about the organization—products, how it is organized, location of offices, etc.
5. Be prepared to give a few reasons why you want to work for this organization.
6. Try to learn something about the job for which you are applying—title, qualifications, salary, career path, and so on.
7. Review your résumé and be prepared to answer questions about it.
8. Decide on two or three questions you want to ask about working hours, fringe benefits, immediate supervisor, specific responsibilities, and so on.

13.15 Remember the following tips:

1. Go alone to the interview. Never take a friend or relative along.
2. Dress appropriately. Do not overdress or dress too casually. It is best to wear clothes that give you a businesslike appearance.
3. Arrive a few minutes—perhaps 10 to 15 minutes—before the scheduled interview time. Do not arrive too early. Never arrive late for an interview.
4. Be sure you know in advance where to go and to whom to report.
5. Carry two copies of your résumé in case they are requested.
6. Carry two reliable pens with you.

7. Do not carry a lot of belongings with you that will create clutter.
8. Give your name to the receptionist, and indicate with whom you have an appointment. Wait to be told what to do. You may be asked to take a seat until the interviewer is ready for you.
9. Do not chew gum or smoke in the reception area or during the interview even if you are told you may do so.
10. If the interviewer asks your name, give your full name clearly and firmly.
11. Let the interviewer offer the handshake. If you do shake hands, use a firm grip, but don't be overwhelming.
12. Never place your personal items (folders, papers, and so on) on the interviewer's desk. Hold them in your lap or place them by your chair.
13. Let the interviewer take the lead. Answer all questions clearly and fully, but do not elaborate too much. Be sure to answer some questions with more than just a yes or no. The interviewer may be evaluating your ability to respond fully.
14. Use proper grammar. Don't use slang or offensive language.
15. Don't be afraid to ask questions about the job and the company.
16. Don't hesitate to talk about your accomplishments. Sell yourself, but don't oversell.
17. Don't be afraid to smile. A pleasant expression and a good smile indicate self-confidence.
18. If the matter of salary is not brought up by the interviewer, ask what the salary range is. If you are asked what salary you expect, indicate a salary range you have in mind or say you would consider what is generally paid by the company for someone of your qualifications and experience.
19. Be courteous throughout the interview even if you decide you do not want the job. You might change your mind later, or another position may become available with the firm.
20. Don't flatter the interviewer.
21. Watch for an indication that the interview is drawing to a close. Be ready to leave the office as soon as the interview is over.
22. Try to determine what the interviewer's next step will be. Find out if and when you will be notified of the decision.
23. Be sure to thank the interviewer for the opportunity to discuss the job. If you are interested in the position, indicate that you hope you will be considered favorably.
24. Thank the receptionist on your way out.

Write a Follow-Up Letter

13.16 A day or so after the interview, write a brief follow-up letter thanking the interviewer for the opportunity to discuss your qualifications for the position. A follow-up letter indicates a businesslike attitude and may set you apart

13

May 29, 19—

Ms. Janna Chambers
Human Services Director
Gateway Computer Corporation
10037 Research Park
Lexington, KY 40508-1123

Dear Ms. Chambers

Thank you for the opportunity to discuss with you and Mr. Johnston
my qualifications for the marketing assistant position with your firm.
I was certainly impressed with the description of the position and with
the opportunities that exist with your company. I know the work
would be challenging and very fulfilling.

Needless to say, I am very interested in the position and hope that
you feel, as I do, that my education and experience match the requirements of the job. The potential growth of the company and the ways
in which I could make a contribution to that growth appeal to me.

Please call me if you need additional information. I hope to hear from
you soon regarding your decision.

Sincerely

Lynetta A. DeVore

Lynetta A. DeVore
1339 Delhaven Drive
Covington, KY 41007
606-401-3636

Figure 13–4   Follow-up letter

from other applicants. If you have decided that you do not wish to be considered further for the job, indicate this and your reasons—you do not believe
you are suited for the job, you have found another position, your plans have
changed, and so on. If you are still interested in the job, indicate this and the
specific ways that you could make a contribution to the organization. Be courteous, regardless of your decision; you may want to approach the organization
for a different position in the future.

ADVANCEMENT TIPS
• •

13.17 If you have properly evaluated a position, you should have a good idea of advancement opportunities and requirements for that advancement. It might require additional training or courses; the ability to assume additional responsibility; or the ability to organize, plan, and supervise. Many companies provide additional training, or they pay for courses that can help you in your work.

13

13.18 Here are some techniques for helping you get ahead in your job:

1. Always arrive early or on time for work; never leave early without good reason. Always get approval from your supervisor for any change in your schedule.
2. Perform above standard. Those who get promotions generally work longer and harder than those who do not.
3. Be productive. Do not waste time, supplies, or energy.
4. Be persistent. See a job through until it is finished.
5. Meet your schedules. Take care of your responsibilities. Don't let your organization down.
6. Don't make excuses for your failures. Determine what caused you to fail, and resolve not to let it happen again.
7. Don't participate in office gossip.
8. Be loyal to and supportive of your supervisors, management, and the organization.
9. Learn to get along with those with whom you work. Be cooperative, courteous, and considerate.
10. Learn to give and to follow directions. Develop a good memory. Take notes of complicated instructions.
11. Express your ideas and opinions freely and constructively.
12. Never discuss company matters outside the office in the presence of individuals who need not know about company business.
13. Be dependable—all the time.
14. Be cost-conscious.
15. Continue to develop and enlarge your skills.
16. Leave your personal life at home. Do not bring it to the workplace.
17. Represent your company well to customers and to the outside world.
18. Always be businesslike in your dress, attitude, and behavior.
19. Learn as much as you can about the operations in your company.
20. Maintain a positive attitude toward your job. Do not become disgruntled because someone else was selected for a promotion over you.
21. Make every day count. Let your work make a real difference in the success of your company.
22. Set goals for yourself, and try hard to achieve them.
23. Be on the lookout for job advancement possibilities. Check for openings in other departments.

24. Find a mentor—a person who has a higher position than you and who can serve as a guide and professional friend.
25. Be flexible. Be prepared for change in your job.

PERFORMANCE APPRAISALS

13 **13.19** Many employers use a performance appraisal to measure how well employees are doing on the job. A performance appraisal is usually a formal review conducted by the employer. It is generally held once a year, although it can be more frequent, especially for new employees. A performance appraisal can be a time for a frank discussion about the job, its responsibilities, and growth potential. The employee is generally free to discuss problems and ask questions. After the review, both parties sign and date the form, and the original copy becomes a part of the employee's personnel record.

SELF-CHECK EXERCISE 1, *UNIT 13*

....

_____

(Name)

Indicate whether the following statements are true or false by writing *T* (True) or *F* (False) in the blank following each statement.

1. A résumé is sometimes referred to as a personal data sheet. _____

2. If possible, you should address a letter of application to a particular person rather than to a department. _____

3. It is acceptable to take a friend along for a job interview provided the friend waits in the reception area. _____

4. Employers may legally ask questions relating to your marital status and whether you have school-age children. _____

5. If chewing gum helps you relax, you may do so during the interview, especially if the interviewer has given permission. _____

6. During the job application process, you may be required to take an employment test or provide a "work sample." _____

7. During an interview, you should place personal items in your lap or alongside your chair. _____

8. If you decide that you don't want a job for which you were interviewed, there is no need to let the employer know about your decision. _____

9. A clear, clean photocopy of a résumé is generally acceptable. _____

10. If the matter of salary is not brought up by the interviewer, it is proper to ask what the salary range is. _____

SELF-CHECK EXERCISE 2, *UNIT 13*

....

On the blank lines to the right, write the letter of the most appropriate word or phrase needed to complete the following statements.

1. A good letter of application will probably (a) be written in your best handwriting, (b) include a complete address and telephone number, (c) be two pages long. _____

2. Under no circumstances can an employer legally require you to answer questions about your (a) race, (b) height and weight, (c) previous work experience. _____

3. It is recommended that the résumé be limited to (a) 2 to 3 pages, (b) 3 to 4 pages, (c) 1 page. _____

4. When you report for the interview, take with you (a) a list of questions for the interviewer to look at and answer during the interview, (b) a portable typewriter in case you have to take a typing test, (c) two copies of your résumé and two reliable pens. _____

5. To prepare yourself for the interview, you should (a) be ready to give two or three reasons why you want to work for the organization, (b) formulate several questions regarding company benefits and working hours, (c) both a and b. _____

6. In reporting for an interview, you should arrive (a) right on time, (b) several minutes before the scheduled time, (c) very early, just to be sure that you get there. _____

7. An application form generally provides spaces for (a) name, address, age, and sex; (b) name, education, employment record, and references; (c) name, employment record, and race or national origin. _____

8. During the interview, you should (a) flatter the interviewer, (b) let the interviewer offer the handshake, (c) answer questions only with yes or no. _____

9. Where blanks on an application form do not apply to you, (a) leave them blank, (b) make up answers, (c) write *NA* or draw lines in the spaces. _____

10. During the interview, (a) let the interviewer take the lead, (b) be hesitant to talk about your accomplishments, (c) ask about salary early in the interview. _____

Check your answers in the back of the book.

APPENDIX A:
SURVIVAL TIPS

1. Stress is a part of life. Learn to deal with it.
2. Acknowledge that you cannot change everything, that you cannot please everyone, and that things will not always turn out as planned.
3. Keep your priorities straight. Know what is really important to you. Keep things in proper perspective.
4. Realize and accept the fact that you are not perfect; neither is anyone else.
5. Keep yourself in good physical condition. Eat right. Rest well. Exercise regularly.
6. Develop a variety of interests. Don't be "possessed" by any activity.
7. Control your anger. Direct your energy toward more productive outcomes.
8. Plan ahead. Reduce the unexpected. Anticipate change.
9. Don't just "endure" conflict; resolve it as quickly as possible.
10. Learn to compromise; yet, when appropriate, be assertive.
11. Don't constantly make unreasonable demands of yourself or of others.
12. Set schedules; follow them. Set priorities; deal with them in order.
13. Don't put things off. Follow through to completion; things left undone can trouble the mind.
14. Change your environment if necessary for awhile. Get away periodically.
15. Learn to separate your daily, required work from other private aspects of your life.
16. For temporary relief from stress, try the following:
    a. Breathe deeply several times.
    b. Relax totally with eyes closed.
    c. Listen to soothing music.
17. "Talk" to yourself. Assure yourself. Calm down. Things will get better.
18. Get help from others. Talk with a trusted friend or mentor. Get counseling if necessary.
19. Spend time in meditation.
20. Trust that many things change with the passage of time. Be patient.

A

APPENDIX B: GRAMMAR AND WORD DIVISION REFERENCES

GRAMMATICAL TERMS

adjective   A word that describes or modifies a noun or pronoun by telling *which one* (fastest runner), *what kind* (bitter taste), or *how many* (nine questions). A *proper adjective* is derived from a proper noun (Spanish explorer) or is a proper noun used as an adjective (*Canton Daily News*). A *predicate adjective* follows a linking verb and describes the subject (Her life was quite sheltered.).

adjective clause   A clause that modifies a noun or pronoun and is introduced by *whom, whose, that, which, when,* or *where.*

adverb   A word that modifies or changes the meaning of a verb, an adjective, or another adverb. Adverbs tell *when, where, how,* and *to what extent.* Most are formed by adding the suffix *-ly* to an adjective.

adverb clause   A clause that modifies a verb, an adjective, or an adverb and tells *when, where, how, why,* and *to what extent.*

agreement   The manner in which a noun or pronoun relates or refers to its antecedent. Personal pronouns must agree with their antecedents in number and gender.

antecedent   The noun or noun phrase to which a pronoun refers.

appositive   A nonessential element that explains, describes, or renames an immediately preceding noun or pronoun.

article   The most frequently used adjectives; examples are *the, a,* and *an.*

case   The relation of a noun or pronoun to its use in a sentence, including *nominative, objective,* or *possessive* case.

clause   A group of words having a subject and a predicate and that is used as part of a sentence.

comparative degree   The degree used by adjectives and adverbs to compare two persons or things. The comparative degree is usually formed by adding *er* to the positive form.

comparison The manner in which adjectives and adverbs are able to indicate differences. The three degrees of comparison are *positive, comparative,* and *superlative.*

complement A word or group of words in the predicate needed to complete the meaning of the subject and the verb.

complex sentence A sentence having one independent clause and one or more subordinate or dependent clauses.

compound complex sentence A sentence having more than one independent clause and at least one subordinate clause.

compound sentence A sentence having two or more independent clauses joined by a semicolon or by a comma and a coordinating conjunction.

conjunction A word that joins words, phrases, or clauses.

consonants All the letters of the alphabet except the vowels *a, e, i, o,* and *u.*

contraction A shortened form of a word or phrase in which an apostrophe is used to indicate the part that is omitted.

declarative sentence A sentence that makes a statement.

direct address A situation in which the writer or speaker directs a question or statement directly to a person, as in "Will you answer the telephone, Marilyn?"

exclamatory sentence A sentence that expresses strong feeling and emotion.

gender The indication of whether a noun or pronoun is masculine, feminine, or neuter.

gerund A verb form ending in -*ing* used as a noun.

imperative sentence A sentence that makes a request or gives a command.

infinitive A verb form that usually consists of *to* plus a verb.

interjection A word that expresses strong feeling, emotion, or sudden reaction.

interrogative sentence A sentence that asks a question.

modifier A word, phrase, or clause that limits, changes, or qualifies the meaning of a word.

nominative case The case of nouns and pronouns used for the subject or the predicate nominative of a sentence.

noun A word that names a person, place, thing, or idea.

noun clause A clause used as a subject, direct object, object of a preposition, or predicate nominative and that may begin with *how, that, what, whatever, when, where, which, whichever, who, whom, whoever, whose,* or *why.*

number The characteristic of a noun, pronoun, or verb that tells whether a person or thing is singular or plural.

object A person or thing that receives the action of a verb.

objective case The case of nouns and pronouns used as objects of verbs or of prepositions.

participle A verb form used as an adjective to describe nouns or pronouns.

parts of speech The eight categories used to indicate the use of words in a sentence, including *adjective, adverb, conjunction, interjection, noun, preposition, pronoun,* and *verb.*

person The indication of whether a pronoun refers to the speaker (first person), the person or thing spoken to (second person), or person or thing spoken of (third person).

phrase A group of two or more words that does not contain a subject and a verb. Types of phrases include *noun phrases, adjective phrases, adverbial phrases, gerund phrases, participial phrases, infinitive phrases,* and *prepositional phrases.*

positive degree The simplest degree of adjectives and adverbs, used when no comparison is being made.

possessive case The case of nouns and pronouns used to show ownership.

predicate The part of a sentence that shows or tells what the subject is doing or what is done to the subject.

prefix A letter or combination of letters used at the beginning of a word to change the meaning of that word.

preposition A word used to join and show the relation of a noun or pronoun to another part of the sentence.

pronoun A word used to replace or refer to a noun.

quotation Words of a person written exactly as they were spoken.

sentence A group of words containing a subject and a predicate and expressing a complete thought.

sentence fragment A part of a sentence that is missing a subject or a verb or has been punctuated improperly to give the appearance that it is a complete thought.

simple sentence A sentence having only one independent clause.

subject The word or group of words that tells what a sentence is about.

suffix A letter or combination of letters at the end of a word used to change the meaning of that word.

superlative degree The degree of adjectives and adverbs used to compare three or more persons or things.

tense The characteristic of a verb that tells when some action happened or when something existed. Tenses include *present, past, future, present perfect, past perfect, future perfect, present progressive, past progressive, future progressive, present perfect progressive, past perfect progressive, future perfect progressive, present emphatic,* and *past emphatic.*

verb A word that shows action, condition, or state of being.

verbal A word that has the appearance of a verb in its form but which is used as another part of speech.

voice The characteristic of a verb that tells whether the subject performs or directs the action or whether it receives the action.

vowels The letters *a, e, i, o, u,* and sometimes *w* and *y.*

WORD DIVISION RULES

Rules for word division were once strictly defined and closely followed so that right margins of keyed copy ended fairly evenly. With the advent of high-speed computer printing technology, sophisticated software, and increased emphasis on productivity and cost consciousness, the demand and the responsibility for even right margins has lessened.

Preferred Word Division Rules

1. Divide a word only between syllables; never divide a one-syllable word, regardless of its length.

trans-port	earned
trans-for-ma-tion	taught
ac-ci-den-tal-ly	stressed

2. Avoid dividing a word of five or fewer letters.

onto	*not*	on-to
enter	*not*	en-ter
refer	*not*	re-fer
later	*not*	la-ter

3. If there is a single-letter syllable within the body of a word, try to divide the word after that syllable.

regu-late	*not*	reg-ulate
mono-logue	*not*	mon-ologue
reti-cent	*not*	ret-icent

4. Include two or more letters with the first part of a divided word and three or more with the last part.

eter-nal	*not*	e-ternal
about	*not*	a-bout
adver-sity	*not*	adversi-ty

5. Do not divide abbreviations.

UNICEF	*not*	UNI-CEF
approx.	*not*	ap-prox.
r.s.v.p.	*not*	r.s.-v.p.

6. Do not divide contractions.

wouldn't	*not*	would-n't
o'clock	*not*	o'-clock
didn't	*not*	did-n't

Optional Word Division Rules

1. Divide a word between two single-letter syllables that appear together.

situ-ation	*not*	situa-tion
evalu-ation	*not*	evalua-tion
gradu-ation	*not*	gradua-tion

2. Divide words ending in *-ily, -able, -ably, -acle, -icle, -ical,* and the like before these suffixes.

hand-ily	*not*	handi-ly
teach-able	*not*	teacha-ble
remark-ably	*not*	remarka-bly
mir-acle	*not*	mira-cle
log-ical	*not*	logi-cal

3. If a root word ends in a double consonant before a suffix is added, divide after the double consonant.

will-ing	*not*	wil-ling
confess-ing	*not*	confes-sing
pass-ing	*not*	pas-sing

4. If a final letter in a root word is doubled before a suffix is added, divide between the double letters.

rip-ping	*not*	ripp-ing
confer-ring	*not*	conferr-ing
ship-ping	*not*	shipp-ing

5. Divide compound words between the compound elements.

water-front	*not*	wat-erfront
bucket-ful	*not*	buc-ketful
back-water	*not*	backwa-ter

6. Divide hyphenated compound words at the point of the existing hyphen.

self-evaluation	*not*	self-evalu-ation
brother-in-law	*not*	bro-ther-in-law

7. Divide dates, proper nouns, and addresses only if unavoidable. When they must be divided, divide at the point of greatest readability.

Dates

April 16, / 1995	*not*	April / 16, 1995

Proper Nouns

Ms. Winifred / Smith	*not*	Ms. / Winifred Smith

Addresses

1600 Main / Street	*not*	1600 / Main Street
St. Louis, / MO 80112	*not*	St. / Louis, MO 80112

8. Do not divide the last word on a page. Avoid dividing the last word on more than two consecutive lines and the last word of a paragraph.

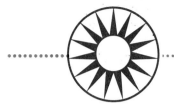

APPENDIX C: COMPUTER REFERENCES

GLOSSARY OF COMPUTER TERMS

address   Number used to indicate a location in memory.

algorithm   Step-by-step set of instructions used to solve a problem.

animation   Computerized design of an object to give it movement.

Arithmetic Logic Unit (ALU)   Electronic circuits in a computer that perform arithmetic and logical operations.

artificial intelligence   Use of the computer in tasks that require imagination and intuition.

ASCII   American Standard Code for Information Interchange.

applications software   Preprogrammed software packages, the most common of which are word processing, database, spreadsheet, graphics, desktop publishing, and communications.

bar code   Standard pattern of vertical lines used to identify products.

binary system   Numbering system based on 0 and 1.

bit   Abbreviated form for binary digit.

boot   To load the operating system into the memory of a computer in order to start it up.

byte   Unit of measure for memory storage of computer—one character or eight bits of data.

cathode ray tube (CRT)   Type of computer screen.

CD-ROM   Compact Disk Read-Only Memory; optical disk that can be read from but not written to.

central processing unit (CPU)   Main component of the computer that performs all the processing of data.

chip   Small silicon wafer containing an integrated circuit.

clone   Type of computer that is compatible with an IBM MS-DOS computer.

COBOL   Common Business Oriented Language; computer language used primarily in business applications.

compatible   Able to run software designed for another kind of personal computer.

computer-aided design (CAD) Use of computers and graphics software in designing various products.

computer-aided design/computer-aided manufacturing (CAD/CAM) Use of computers and software for the design and manufacture of products.

computer virus A program used for unauthorized altering or deleting of data.

copy protection A means of preventing unauthorized copying or manipulation of data.

cursor Flashing indicator that shows where next character can be inserted.

data Facts, figures, or other information to be processed by a computer.

database Collection of related information that can be accessed, processed, or manipulated.

debugging Detecting and eliminating errors in a program.

default A software option automatically used unless otherwise directed.

diskette Magnetic disk used to store data.

documentation Written description of a software program.

drag Pressing and moving the mouse to the desired location.

electronic mail Transmission of messages from one computer terminal to another.

enhancements Visual additions to text, such as boldface or enlarged text.

expansion slots Openings inside computer that permit additional circuit boards to be inserted.

expert systems Technology that enables computers to process and interpret information.

file Unit of stored data.

floppy disk Magnetic disk used to record data.

font An assortment of type of one size and typeface.

formatting Determining the layout of a body of information.

function keys Specially designated keys used to execute common commands.

gigabyte One billion bytes of information.

graphic An illustration created with desktop publishing programs or applications.

hard copy Paper copy of printed information; printout.

hard disk Storage device located inside the CPU of a computer.

header Text placed inside top margin of printout.

icon Graphic image representing a function or object.

index/file List of data files.

ink-jet printer Type of printer that uses a spray of ink in the printing process.

integrated software Applications program that permits a variety of tasks to be performed, including word processing, spreadsheets, database, and graphics.

justification Alignment of text, either right, left, center, or full justification.

kern Adjustment of the space between characters.

kilobyte (KB) 1024 bytes of information.

LAN (local area network) Network of computers covering a small geographic area, such as within an office.

laptop computer Portable computer.

laser printer   Type of printer using a beam of light to transfer images.

mainframe   Large computer used to process large amounts of data quickly.

management information system   An organized way in which information is gathered and presented for use in a business operation.

megabyte (MB)   one million bytes of information.

memory   The means by which information is stored within a computer.

menu   List of commands and keystrokes necessary to access and execute programs.

microcomputer   Small class of computers; also known as personal computers.

microprocessor   Complete processing unit housed in a single tiny microprocessor chip.

modem   A device that converts computer signals so they can be transmitted over telephone lines to other computers.

monitor   The device that displays information processed by the computer.

mouse   Input device used to point, select commands, or direct the operation of the computer.

nanosecond   One billionth of a second.

network   The connection of two or more computers enabling them to use the same resources.

OCR (optical character recognition)   System that uses a light source to read special characters and convert them to electrical signals.

operating system   Set of programs used by a computer to manage information.

output   Data that have been processed into useful information.

pagination   Breaking text into pages.

picosecond   One trillionth of a second.

pitch   Measurement of the number of characters in an inch.

pixel   The elements that make up a picture on a screen.

printer   Device used to create hard copy.

program   Set of step-by-step instructions used by a computer to process information.

prompt   Set of directions on screen.

quit   Command to stop using a program.

RAM (random access memory)   Memory that provides temporary storage for data and instructions.

record   Collection of related fields of data.

resolution   Degree of clarity of screen.

retrieve   To locate and load a previously stored file of data.

ROM (read-only memory)   Memory that can be read only and is stored permanently in the computer.

save   To store a document for later use.

scanner   Device that converts text on paper into a computer image.

scroll   Word processing feature that displays information in 20-line groups.

security   Safeguards that protect against unauthorized use.

site license   License that permits a purchaser to make multiple copies of a software package.

software   Set of instructions that directs the operation of the computer.

sort   The arrangement of data into appropriate sequences.

source document   Original location of data to be input into the computer.

speech synthesis   Electronic enabling of speech between people and computers.

spreadsheet   Worksheet using rows and columns to organize and process business data.

surge protector   Device used to protect computers from sudden increases of electrical power.

telecommuting   Home use of computers for office work to eliminate need for commuting.

teleconferencing   Holding conferences by electronically linked computers.

terminal   Input, output, and communication device linked to a main computer.

user friendly   Description of easy-to-use software.

word wrap   Word processing feature that automatically returns the cursor to the left margin.

WYSIWYG (What You See Is What You Get)   Display screen that enables you to see how the text will appear on hard copy.

DOS COMMANDS

Because of the variety of DOS versions, some of the following DOS commands may not be appropriate in every situation. Check your DOS manual for special instructions for your own version of DOS.

APPEND	Set a search path for data files.	COMP	Compares the contents of two files.
ASSIGN	Redirects operations from one drive to another.	COPY	Copies the contents of one file into another file.
ATTRIB	Allows you to examine archive and read-only file attributes.	CTTY	Switches the device from which you give commands.
BACKUP	Backs up a fixed disk by copying contents to floppy disks.	DATE	Sets computer clock for time and date.
BREAK	Commands the computer to stop operations.	DEL	Deletes files permanently.
		DIR	Displays the files in a directory.
CALL	Calls a batch file from within another batch file.	DISCOMP	Compares the contents of two disks.
CHDIR	Changes the current directory.	DISKCOPY	Makes a copy of a disk.
CHKDSK	Examines a disk for errors.	ECHO	Writes messages to the screen and controls the echoing of other commands.
CLS	Clears the monitor screen.		

c

ERASE   Erases files from a disk.

FASTOPEN   Decreases the time it takes to open a file.

FDISK   Configures a hard disk.

FIND   Searches for a string of text in a file.

FOR   Repeats a series of commands.

FORMAT   Prepares a disk for use.

GOTO   Directs DOS to execute batch commands at a certain location.

GRAPHICS   Allows you to print graphics.

IF   Batch command based on a condition's results.

JOIN   Joins a disk drive to the directory of another.

LABEL   Creates, changes, or deletes the volume label of a disk.

MKDIR   Creates a subdirectory.

MODE   Sets the way various devices operate.

MORE   Pages through text file 23 lines at a time.

PAUSE   Temporarily stops a batch file.

PRINT   Prints text files.

RECOVER   Recovers information from damaged files.

REM   Embeds a remark in a batch file.

RENAME   Changes the name of a file.

REPLACE   Replaces files with updated versions.

RESTORE   Restores files from disks created using BACKUP.

RMDIR   Removes a subdirectory.

SELECT   Installs DOS on a new disk.

SHARE   Installs file sharing and file locking.

SHIFT   Changes the position of parameters.

SORT   Sorts text files.

SUBST   Allows a different drive specifier to access a drive and directory.

SYS   Copies DOS system files to a disk.

TIME   Sets computer clock.

TREE   Prints a list of directories on a specified disk.

TYPE   Displays the contents of a file.

VER   Displays the DOS version.

VERIFY   Confirms that files were copied correctly.

VOL   Displays the volume label of a disk.

XCOPY   Copies files and entire directories.

WORDPERFECT® COMMANDS

Basic Cursor Movement Commands

Cursor Movement	**Keystrokes**
Up one line	Up arrow
Down one line	Down arrow
Left one character	Left arrow
Right one character	Right arrow
Left one word	Ctrl-left arrow

Right one word	Ctrl-right arrow
Beginning of paragraph	Ctrl-up arrow
Beginning of next paragraph	Ctrl-down arrow
Top of previous page	PgUp
Top of next page	PgDn
End of current line	End
Top of screen	Home, up arrow
Bottom of screen	Home, down arrow
Left end of line	Home, left arrow
Right end of line	Home, right arrow
Beginning of document	Home, Home, up arrow
End of document	Home, Home, down arrow
Next tab setting	Tab
Next indent setting	Indent (F4)
Top of current page	Ctrl-Home, up arrow
Bottom of current page	Ctrl-Home, down arrow
Page number *n*	Ctrl-Home, *n*, Enter

Basic WordPerfect® Editing Commands

Command	Keystrokes
Delete character	Delete
Delete left character	Backspace
Delete word	Ctrl-Backspace
Delete to end of line	Ctrl-End
Delete to end of page	Ctrl-PgDn
Delete to end of word	Home, Delete
Toggle between insert and typeover	Insert
Insert hard return	Enter
Insert hard page break	Ctrl-Enter

Basic WordPerfect® Commands

Command	Keystrokes
Appearance attributes	Ctrl-F8, 2
Backspace (with delete)	Backspace
Backspace (no delete)	Left arrow
Base font	Ctrl-F8, 4
Block mode	Alt-F4
Block protect	Shift-F8
Bold	F6 *or* Ctrl-F8, 2, 1
Cancel	F1
Center line	Shift-F6
Center page vertically	Shift-F8, 2, 1
Columns	Alt-F7, 1

Compose characters	Ctrl-V or Ctrl-2
Copy file	F5, 8
Date code	Shift-F5, 2
Delete character	Delete
Display setup	Shift-F1, 2
Double underline	Ctrl-F8, 2, 3
Exit	F7
Fine print	Ctrl-F8, 1, 3
Flush right	Alt-F6
Footers	Shift-F8, 2, 4
Footnote	Ctrl-F7, 1
Format	Shift-F8
Go to DOS	Ctrl-F1, 1
Graphics	Alt-F9
Graphics print quality	Shift-F7, G
Headers	Shift-F8, 2, 3
Help	F3
Horizontal line (graphics)	Alt-F9, 5, 1
Indent left side	F4
Indent both sides	Shift-F4
Italics	Ctrl-F8, 2, 4
Justification	Shift-F8, 1, 3
Large print	Ctrl-F8, 1, 5
Line draw	Ctrl-F3, 2
Line format	Shift-F8, 1
Line spacing	Shift-F8, 1, 6
List files	F5
Macro	Alt-F10
Macro define	Ctrl-F10
Margins (left and right)	Shift-F8, 1, 7
Margins (top and bottom)	Shift-F8, 2, 5
Merge	Ctrl-F9, 1
Move	Ctrl-F4
Move block (block on)	Ctrl-F4, 1
Move page	Ctrl-F4, 3
Move paragraph	Ctrl-F4, 2
Move sentence	Ctrl-F4, 1
Outline mode	Shift-F5, 4
Outline attribute	Ctrl-F8, 2, 5
Page format	Shift-F8, 2
Page numbering	Shift-F8, 2, 6
Page size/type	Shift-F8, 2, 7
Print	Shift-F7
Print block (block on)	Shift-F7, Y
Print number of copies	Shift-F7, N
Print current page	Shift-F7, 2

C

Print full document	Shift-F7, 1
Print multiple pages	Shift-F7, 5
Printer select	Shift-F7, S
Pull-down menu	Alt-=
Redline attribute	Ctrl-F8, 2, 8
Repeat value	Esc, *number, character*
Replace	Alt-F2, Y/N, *old text*, F2, *new text*, F2
Retrieve block (move)	Ctrl-F4, 4, 1
Retrieve document	Shift-F10
Reveal codes	Alt F3 *or* F11
Save document	F10
Screen	Ctrl-F3
Search backward	Shift-F2
Search forward	F2
Setup	Shift-F1
Shadow attribute	Ctrl-F8, 2, 6
Size attribute	Ctrl-F8, 1
Small caps attribute	Ctrl-F8, 2, 7
Sort	Ctrl-F9, 2
Spell check	Ctrl-F2
Strikeout attribute	Ctrl-F8, 2, 9
Style	Alt-F8
Subscript	Ctrl-F8, 1, 2
Superscript	Ctrl-F8, 1, 1
Switch documents	Shift-F3
Tab settings	Shift-F8, 1, 8
Table	Alt-F7, 2
Table box	Alt-F9, 2
Text box	Alt-F9, 3
Text in/out	Ctrl-F5
Text print quality	Shift-F7, T
Thesaurus	Alt-F1
Undelete	F1
Underline	F8 *or* Ctrl-F8, 2, 2
Vertical line	Alt-F9, 5, 2
View document	Shift-F7, 6
Window (change size)	Ctrl-F3, 1

C

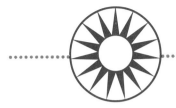

APPENDIX D: BUSINESS REFERENCES

BUSINESS AND LEGAL TERMS

abstract   A summary of the important points of an article or text.

acceptance   Unqualified willingness to go along with an offer.

accrual   Something that increases.

acquisition   Something that is acquired; an addition to a category or group.

act of God   Natural, unforeseeable, unavoidable occurrence.

actuary   One who calculates insurance risks and premiums.

addressee   The person to whom a letter is sent.

adjudication   Hearing and settling a case by judicial procedure.

affidavit   A written statement made under oath before a notary public or other authorized person.

agenda   A list of items to be discussed at a meeting.

agent   One who legally represents another.

amortization   The process of writing off expenditures by prorating the cost over a period of time.

annuity   The annual interest or dividend on an investment.

annul   To make void.

appraisal   The expert or official valuation of something, as for taxation.

arbitration   The process of settling disputes in which the parties agree to abide by the decision of a third party.

arrears   An unpaid, overdue debt.

assessment   An estimate of the value of property for taxation.

asset   Something of value that is owned.

assignment   Transfer of a contractual right.

auditor   One who verifies the financial records of a business or other institution.

beneficiary   One who receives benefits from an insurance policy, will, or other settlement.

bimonthly   Once every two months.

bona fide   Authentic; genuine; in good faith.

breach of contract   Wrongful failure to perform promises of a contract.

broker   One who acts as an agent in the buying and selling of merchandise or securities.

capital   Any form of wealth used or available for use in the accumulation of more wealth; the net worth of a business.

codicil   Amendment to a will.

coinsurance   Insurance held jointly with others.

collateral   Property used as security for a loan or other obligation.

commodity   Something useful that can be turned to advantage; a trade item that can be transported, especially an agricultural or mining product.

comptroller   One who audits accounts and supervises the financial affairs of a corporation or governmental body (also *controller*).

conglomerate   A corporation composed of previously independent companies in unrelated businesses.

consignment   Goods or cargo given to another for sale or custody.

consortium   A group of financial institutions that pool their reserves in a venture requiring extensive financial resources.

contingency   A possibility or future emergency that must be prepared for.

contract   An agreement between two or more parties that is enforceable by law.

convertible   Capable of being exchanged for something else.

conveyance   The transfer of property from one person to another, usually by a deed.

creditor   One to whom a debt is owed.

debenture   A bond backed only by the credit standing of the issuer; no assets are pledged as security.

debtor   One who owes something to another.

decedent   Deceased person.

defendant   Person accused of a crime.

deficit   Financial condition that occurs when expenditures exceed revenue.

denomination   A class of units having specified values.

depreciation   A decrease or loss in value because of wear, age, or other causes.

disbursement   Money paid out; an expenditure.

dividends   Profits distributed to shareholders.

easement   Right to use land belonging to another.

endorse   To sign the back of a check, money order, or stock certificate transferring its ownership, usually in exchange for the cash value stated on its face.

endowment   A donation of funds or property that will serve as a source of income to an institution, individual, or group.

entrepreneur   One who organizes, operates, and assumes the risks for a business venture.

equity   The value of a business or property after any mortgage or other liability has been deducted.

escrow   A document held by a third person until certain conditions are met.

executor   One who is named in a will to carry out the terms of the will.

expenditure   An amount spent; an expense.

felony   Major crime.

fiduciary   One who holds something in trust for another.

forbearance   Not doing something you have a legal right to do.

foreclosure   The legal procedure by which a mortgage is settled or resolved.

franchise   A binding arrangement between a manufacturer and a distributor or dealer to sell the manufacturer's products on an exclusive-territory basis.

grantor   One who transfers property by deed.

grievance   A complaint often arising from misunderstanding.

guaranty   An agreement by which one person agrees to pay or fulfill another's obligation.

heir   One who inherits by right of relationship.

incorporate   To form a corporation.

indebtedness   The state of owing something to another.

indictment   Written accusation of grand jury.

infringement   An encroachment, as of a right.

injunction   A court order forbidding the performance of a certain act.

intangibles   Assets that cannot be seen, precisely defined, or identified.

invalid   Null; legally worthless.

inventory   A detailed list of things in one's possession; a periodic check of all goods and materials on hand.

investment   Property or other possessions purchased for the future income or benefit they provide.

invoice   A bill; a list of goods shipped or services rendered, with a detailed accounting of all costs.

jobber   One who works on a piecework basis; a middleman who buys from a manufacturer and sells to retailers.

judgment   A formal or court decision creating or affirming an obligation.

jurisdiction   Authority or control.

larceny   The theft of another's personal property.

lease   A contract for the use or occupation of property in exchange for rent.

lessee   One who holds a lease; a tenant.

lessor   One who rents property under a lease; a landlord.

levy   To impose or collect a tax.

liability   Something that is owed; a debt.

libel   Any written or visual statement that ridicules or defames one's character.

license   Permission to do or own something; a document that serves as proof of permission.

lien   The right to hold the property of a debtor as security for a debt.

liquidate   To settle a debt; to wind up the affairs of a business by paying off all debts and distributing remaining assets among the owners.

litigation   Legal proceedings; a lawsuit.

lobby   To attempt to influence lawmakers to pass, defeat, or amend pending legislation.

manifest   An itemized list of cargo.

maturity   The date on which a note, bill, or bond is payable.

D

D

merchandise   Goods available for sale or purchase.

merger   The consolidation of two or more business interests or corporations.

micrographics   A method of storing information in reduced form on film.

minor   One who has not reached the age of majority.

misdemeanor   Offense or misdeed or crime less serious than a felony.

monopoly   The exclusive control of an operation that results in lack of competition and control of prices.

mortgage   A claim on property by a creditor as security for the payment of a debt.

mortgagee   One who holds a mortgage.

mutual fund   A fund based on the sale of shares to investors and the use of this capital to invest in other companies.

negligence   Failure to exercise reasonable care.

negotiable   Capable of being transferred from one person to another, usually by endorsement.

notary public   One who is legally authorized to certify documents, take affidavits, and administer oaths.

ordinance   A law or regulation, especially one enacted by a city government.

originator   The person who writes a business document.

partnership   An agreement between two or more persons to co-own a business for profit.

patent   The grant to an inventor for the sole right to make, use, and sell an invention for a period of 17 years.

perjury   Crime of making false statements under oath.

policyholder   One who holds an insurance policy or contract.

portfolio   A detailed list of the investments, securities, and commercial paper owned.

postdated   To date a document as of a later date than the actual one.

premium   The amount paid to obtain a loan or an insurance policy.

principal   A debt, upon which interest is calculated.

probate   The legal process of proving the validity of a will.

proprietor   The owner or owner-manager of a business.

pro rata   In proportion.

prospectus   A formal document summarizing the information about a securities offering.

proxy   A written authorization enabling a stockholder to transfer voting rights.

quarterly   Occurring at regular intervals of three months.

quitclaim   A deed transferring the title, right, or claim to property to another.

realty   Real estate.

receivables   Assets representing the total amounts due from others.

receivership   The office or functions of one who takes custody of property or funds for another.

remedy   Legal means of enforcing a right or correcting a wrong.

remittance   The money or credit sent to another.

renegotiate   To revise the original terms of a contract in order to limit or get back excess profits gained by the contractor.

requisition   A written request for something that is needed.

rescind   To abolish or repeal.

respondent   One who replies to legal claims; a defendant.

retroactive   Applying to a previous time period.

revenue   Income from all sources.

semiannual   Occurring twice a year.

shareholder   One who owns or holds stock.

sinking fund   A plan in which money is periodically deposited with a trustee for the repayment of a bond issue.

solvent   Able to pay debts as they become due.

statute of limitations   State law limiting time within which legal action must be brought.

subpoena   A court order requiring a person to appear in court to give testimony.

subrogation   The substitution of one person for another.

survivorship   The right of a surviving partner or joint owner to the entire assets that were originally jointly owned.

tangibles   Assets that are visible and capable of being touched.

tort   One person's interference with another's rights.

trustee   One who holds legal title to property in order to manage it for another.

underwriter   One who guarantees the purchase of a full issue of stocks or bonds.

violation   Failure to fulfill one's duties or obligations.

voucher   A document that proves that the terms of a transaction were met.

warranty   A legal promise by a seller that the goods or property are as represented or will be as promised.

wholesaler   One who sells goods in large quantities, usually for resale by a retailer.

yield   The profit or return from an investment.

ALPHABETIC FILING RULES

Filing is the process of arranging and storing materials in an orderly manner so they can be located quickly and easily. The most common filing systems used are *alphabetic, geographic, subject,* and *numeric,* although other variations are also found.

The rules given here are adapted from the Simplified Filing Standard Rules recommended by the Association of Records Managers and Administrators (ARMA); other variations of the rules are sometimes followed.

Alphabetizing Names

1. To place names in correct filing order, compare the names unit by unit and letter by letter within the same unit in the following order: surname (last name), first name or initial, middle name or initial.

Delaney, Joyce
Delano, Frances Marie
Delano, Frances P.

Rogers, Elizabeth Ann
Rogers, Elizabeth M.
Roget, Cindy

Nothing Before Something

2. File a surname *without* a first and middle name before the same surname *with* a first name or initial. File a surname with an initial only before the same surname with a full first name beginning with the same letter. In all cases, file single unit names before names with multiple units. In other words, *nothing comes before something.*

Names	Alphabetic Order
Raymond Rodriquez	Rodriquez
Ray Rodriquez	Ray Rodriquez
Rodriquez	Raymond Rodriquez

Names With Prefixes and Hyphens

3. Prefixes in the names of individuals and companies (such as *De* in DeJohn and *Le* in LeBato Trucking Company) are considered to be part of the surname. Some common prefixes are *D', Da, De, Del, Des, Di, Du, Fitz, La, Mac, Mc, O', St., San, Van,* and *Vander.* In filing, *St.* is filed as though it were spelled in full (*Saint*).

4. Hyphenated surnames (such as Langston-Ryan) are filed as one unit.

Names	Alphabetic Order
Lynn Tyne-Lizt	St. James, Lannie
Larry St. James	St. James, Larry
Lannie St. James	Tyne-Lizt, Lynn

Unusual and Foreign Names

5. File unusual or foreign names as all other personal names. When it is impossible to determine which part of the name is the surname, consider the last part of the name to be the surname.

Names	Alphabetic Order
Shere Tsing	Frank, Larry
Larry Frank	Ting, Terry
Terry Ting	Tsing, Shere

Identical Names

6. When two or more personal or business names are identical, use the address given to determine the correct filing order. Compare the parts of the address in the following order: (1) town or city name, (2) state name, (3) street name, and (4) house or building number in numeric order.

Names	Alphabetic Order
Gerald Weiss 497 Peak Road Byford, GA 30455	Weiss, Gerald 967 Peakham Road Byford, AL 35136
Gerald Weiss 967 Peakham Road Byford, AL 35316	Weiss, Gerald 301 Peak Road Byford, GA 30455
Gerald Weiss 301 Peak Road Byford, GA 30455	Weiss, Gerald 497 Peak Road Byford, GA 30455

Titles and Degrees

7. Do not consider professional titles (such as *Dr.* or *Prof.*), personal titles (such as *Mr.* or *Ms.*), academic degrees (such as *Ph.D.* or *B.A.*), or seniority titles (such as *Jr., Sr., II, III*) in filing except when needed to distinguish between two or more identical names.

Names	Alphabetic Order
Roberto Martine, Th.D.	Martine, Robert B., Jr.
Robert B. Martine, Sr.	Martine, Robert B., Sr.
Robert B. Martine, Jr.	Martine, Roberto, Th.D.
Prof. Robin Martine	Martine, Robin, Prof.

8. When a religious, foreign, or royalty title is followed by a first name only, file the name as it is written.

Names	Alphabetic Order
Sister Marie of the Cross	Brother Marin
Brother Marin	Queen Mary
Queen Mary	Sister Marie of the Cross

Company Names

9. File company names as written. (If the word *the* appears as the first word in a name, consider it the last filing unit.)

Names	Alphabetic Order
Tracy W. Royce Antiques	Ranger Trucking Company, The
T. J. Rantz Furniture	T. J. Rantz Furniture
The Ranger Trucking Company	Tracy W. Royce Antiques

Hyphenated Company Names

10. Company names that include hyphenated last names (such as *Acme-Ryan Agency*), coined words (such as *Tite-Fit Company*), and other hyphenated

forms (such as *Trans-State Movers*) are filed with the hyphenated parts considered as one unit.

Names	Alphabetic Order
Big-Sack Supermarket	Bigger-Stein Flowers
Bigger-Stein Flowers	Bigger-Top Coverings
Bigger-Top Coverings	Big-Sack Supermarket

Compass Points in Company Names

11.   Each word or unit in a name containing a compass point (such as *North, South, East*) is considered as a separate filing unit. If the term includes more than one compass point, treat the term as it is written.

Names	Alphabetic Order
Southern Transport, Inc.	South West Truckers
Southwestern Transit	Southern Transport, Inc.
South West Truckers	Southwestern Transit

Numbers in Company Names

12.   Company names starting with numerals (such as *26 Convenience Store* and *3 Corners Garage*) are filed in strict numeric order ahead of the entire alphabetic file. Company names starting with spelled-out numbers (such as *Two Guys Cafe*) are filed alphabetically as usual.

Names	Alphabetic Order
Eighth Wonder Cafe	4 Corners Furniture
Abilene Western Wear	67 Cab Company
67 Cab Company	96 Delights Bakery
96 Delights Bakery	Abilene Western Wear
4 Corners Furniture	Eighth Wonder Cafe

Schools and Colleges

13.   Elementary, middle, and high schools are generally filed as written. Colleges and universities are filed under the most commonly used name.

Names	Alphabetic Order
University of Mississippi	Dallas Elementary School
Dallas Elementary School	Jackson Middle School
Longdale High School	Longdale High School
Jackson Middle School	University of Mississippi

Churches and Organizations

14.   The names of churches, synagogues, clubs, unions, and organizations are filed as written.

Names	Alphabetic Order
State Workers Credit Union	Sacred Church
Sacred Church	Second Order of Panthers
Second Order of Panthers	State Workers Credit Union

Magazines and Newspapers

15. The names of magazines and newspapers are filed as written. If the names are identical, place the city (and state, if needed) as the last filing unit. (If the word *the* appears as the first word in a name, consider it the last filing unit.)

Names	Alphabetic Order
The Anchorage Daily Journal	Americus Weekly Journal
The Daily Herald	Anchorage Daily Journal, The
Americus Weekly Journal	Daily Herald, The

Hotels and Motels

16. Hotel and motel names are filed as written.

Names	Alphabetic Order
Owen Motel	Motel Oxford
Owen Oaks Hotel	Owen Motel
Motel Oxford	Owen Oaks Hotel

Government Agencies

17. When filing the names of federal government agencies, the words *United States Government* are the first three filing units, followed by (1) name of the department, (2) name of the bureau, (3) name of the division or subdivision, and (4) title of the official.

Names	Alphabetic Order
U.S. Department of State	United States Government Coast Guard
U.S. Coast Guard	United States Government Postal Service
U.S. Postal Service	United States Government State

18. When state, county, and city agencies are to be filed, the particular state, county, or city name is the first filing unit, followed by the word *State, County,* or *City*. The department, bureau, and/or title of the official are the next filing units.

Names	Alphabetic Order
Denver Police Department	Akron County Welfare Department
Akron County Welfare Dept.	Denver City Police Department
Illinois Department of Fisheries	Illinois State Fisheries Department

APPENDIX E:
MATH SKILL REVIEW

WORKING WITH NUMBERS

Rounding

Whole Numbers

If the digit to the right of the desired rounding place is 5 or higher, add 1 to the digit in the desired rounding place and replace all succeeding digits with zeros. If the digit to the right of the desired rounding place is 4 or lower, leave the digit in the desired rounding place as it is.

Round to the nearest ten:

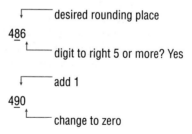

Decimals

If the digit to the right of the desired rounding place is 5 or higher, add 1 to the digit in the desired rounding place and drop all of the succeeding digits. If the digit to the right of the desired rounding place is 4 or lower, leave the digit in the desired rounding place as it is and drop all of the succeeding digits. See the example below. Compare it to the example above.

Round to the nearest hundredth:

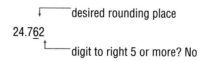

do not change

24.76

drop final digit

Estimating Results

Estimating an answer gives a guide to the correct answer. Round the numbers in the problem and calculate mentally. Compare your estimate with the answer.

$$
\begin{array}{r} 203 \\ + 134 \\ \hline ? \end{array}
\xrightarrow{\text{rounded}}
\begin{array}{r} 200 \\ + 130 \\ \hline 330 \end{array}
\xrightarrow{\text{estimate}}
\begin{array}{r} 203 \\ + 134 \\ \hline 337 \end{array}
\text{answer}
$$

compare

Finding Factors

A factor is any number that can be divided into another number a whole number of times with no remainder.

Find the factors of 12:

    1   $(12 \div 1 = 12)$
    2   $(12 \div 2 = 6)$
    3   $(12 \div 3 = 4)$
    4   $(12 \div 4 = 3)$

Not a factor of 12 → 5 $(12 \div 5 = 2, \text{ with 2 remaining})$
    6   $(12 \div 6 = 2)$
Not a factor of 12 → 7 $(12 \div 7 = 1, \text{ with 5 remaining})$
    12 $(12 \div 12 = 1)$

Factors of 12 are 1, 2, 3, 4, 6, and 12.

WHOLE NUMBERS
· ·

Addition

In addition, two or more numbers are combined into one number called the *sum*. If the sum of the digits in a column total more than 9, carry a digit over to the column to the left.

$$
\begin{array}{r} 1\ 1\ 1 \\ 8\ 6\ 7\ 9 \\ + 9\ 7\ 4\ 8 \\ \hline 18\ 4\ 2\ 7 \end{array}
\leftarrow \text{carry}
$$

sum

$$
\begin{array}{r} 2\quad 1\ 2 \\ 7\ 3\ 5\ 7 \\ 9\ 2\ 8\ 9 \\ + 5\ 3\ 1\ 8 \\ \hline 2\ 1\ 9\ 6\ 4 \end{array}
\quad\text{carry}
$$

Subtraction

Subtraction is the process of finding the *difference* between numbers. When one digit in the column is too large to be subtracted from the other, borrow from the column to the left.

$$
\begin{array}{r}
6 \\
\cancel{7}\,^{1}6 \\
-49 \\
\hline
27
\end{array}
\quad
\begin{array}{l}
\leftarrow \text{borrow} \\
\\
\leftarrow \text{too large} \\
\leftarrow \text{difference}
\end{array}
\qquad
\begin{array}{r}
8^{1}\,2^{1}\,4 \\
\cancel{9}\,\cancel{3}\,\cancel{5}\,^{1}2 \\
-4\ 6\ 9\ \ 4 \\
\hline
4\ 6\ 5\ \ 8
\end{array}
\quad
\begin{array}{l}
\leftarrow \text{borrow} \\
\\
\leftarrow \text{too large} \\
\leftarrow \text{difference}
\end{array}
$$

Multiplication

Multiplication is the process of finding the product of two or more numbers.

$$
\begin{array}{r}
342 \\
\times\,211 \\
\hline
342 \\
3\,420 \\
+\,68\,400 \\
\hline
72{,}162
\end{array}
\begin{array}{l}
\longrightarrow\ 1 \times 342 = 342 \\
\longrightarrow\ 10 \times 342 = 3420 \\
\longrightarrow\ 200 \times 342 = 68{,}400 \\
\longrightarrow\ 342 \times 211 = 72{,}162 \longleftarrow \text{product}
\end{array}
$$

Multiplication by Multiples of 10

When multiplying by 10, simply add a zero to the right of the number being multiplied. When multiplying by 100, add two zeros. When multiplying by 1,000, add three zeros, and so on.

$$
\begin{array}{c}
135 \\
\times\ 10
\end{array} = 1350
\qquad
\begin{array}{c}
265 \\
\times\ 100
\end{array} = 26{,}500
\qquad
\begin{array}{c}
978 \\
\times\ 1000
\end{array} = 978{,}000
$$

Division Without Remainder

In division, one number (a dividend) is divided by another (a divisor) to get the answer (the quotient).

divisor

$$
27\overline{)4941} \longrightarrow
\begin{array}{r}
1 \\
27\overline{)4941} \\
-27 \\
\hline
22
\end{array}
\longrightarrow
\begin{array}{r}
18 \\
27\overline{)4941} \\
-27\downarrow \\
\hline
224 \\
-216 \\
\hline
8
\end{array}
\longrightarrow
\begin{array}{r}
183 \leftarrow \text{quotient} \\
27\overline{)4941} \\
-27\downarrow \\
\hline
224 \\
-216\downarrow \\
\hline
81 \\
-81
\end{array}
$$

dividend

Division With Fractional Remainder

The remainder of a quotient may be shown as a fraction.

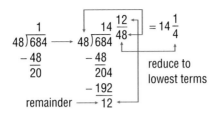

DECIMALS

Addition of Decimals

In addition with decimals, the decimal points must be aligned. If necessary, rewrite the numbers in vertical form. Align decimal points. Supply zeros as placeholders where needed.

$$1.5 + 0.33 + 94$$

```
   1.5          1.50
   0.33         0.33
 + 94.        + 94.00
              95.83   placeholders
```

Subtraction of Decimals

If necessary, rewrite the numbers in vertical form. Align decimals. Supply zeros as placeholders where needed.

```
882.163 − 32.1 → 882.163 → 882.163
              − 32.1     − 32.100
                         850.063   placeholders
```

Multiplication of Decimals

The number of decimal places in the product is equal to the total number of decimal places in the numbers being multiplied.

```
   6.24          6.24 ← 2 decimal places
 × 2.1    →    × 2.1  ← 1 decimal place
              13.104  ← 3 decimal places in product
```

```
   0.06          0.06 ← 2 decimal places
 × 0.03   →    × 0.03 ← 2 decimal places
               .0018  ← 4 decimal places in product
```

Division With Decimals

Division With Whole Number Divisors

When dividing by a whole number, maintain the position of the decimal in the dividend.

$$
\begin{array}{r}
\text{maintain decimal point} \\
\downarrow \\
1.2 \\
46\overline{)55.2} \longrightarrow 46\overline{)55.2} \\
-46 \\
\hline
9 \\
-92
\end{array}
$$

Division With Decimal Divisors

Move the decimal point in the divisor and in the dividend the same number of places to the right.

$$
6.6\overline{)27.72} \longrightarrow 6.6\overline{)27.72} \longrightarrow 66\overline{)277.2}
$$

move one decimal place

$$
\begin{array}{r}
4.2 \\
66\overline{)277.2} \\
-264 \\
\hline
13\ 2 \\
-13\ 2
\end{array}
$$

$$
0.032\overline{)14.4} \longrightarrow 0.032\overline{)14.400} \longrightarrow 32\overline{)14400}
$$

move three decimal places

$$
\begin{array}{r}
450 \\
32\overline{)14400} \\
-128 \\
\hline
160 \\
-160 \\
\hline
00 \\
-00
\end{array}
$$

Division With Remainder

Add zeros to the right of the decimal point in the dividend. Carry the division to one place beyond the desired rounding place in the quotient. Then round to the desired place.

Round to nearest hundredth.

$$
78\overline{)463.} \longrightarrow 78\overline{)463.000}
$$

5.935 → 5.935 rounded to the nearest hundredth is 5.94

$$
\begin{array}{r}
5.935 \\
78\overline{)463.000} \\
-390 \\
\hline
73\ 0 \\
-70\ 2 \\
\hline
2\ 80 \\
-2\ 34 \\
\hline
460 \\
-390 \\
\hline
70
\end{array}
$$

E

FRACTIONS

Changing a Fraction to a Decimal

To change a fraction to a decimal, divide the numerator by the denominator. When needed, round to the desired place.

$$\frac{1}{4} \rightarrow 4\overline{)1.00}^{\,0.25}$$

$$\frac{2}{3} \rightarrow 3\overline{)2.0000}^{\,0.6666} \longleftarrow$$ carry quotient to 4 decimal places

$$\frac{1}{4} = 0.25$$

$$\frac{2}{3} = 0.667 \longleftarrow$$ round to 3 decimal places

Expressing Equivalent Fractions

$$\frac{2}{3} = \frac{?}{15} \quad \frac{6}{9} = \frac{?}{3} \quad \frac{3}{4} = \frac{?}{16}$$

$$\frac{2}{3} \; \frac{10}{15} \qquad \frac{6}{9} \; \frac{2}{3} \qquad \frac{3}{4} \; \frac{12}{16}$$

(× 5) (÷ 3) (× 4)

E

Determining the Least Common Multiple (LCM)

A *common multiple* of two or more whole numbers is any whole number that is a multiple of the given numbers. The *least common multiple* (LCM) of two or more whole numbers is the least nonzero multiple that is common to all of the numbers that are given.

Find the least common multiple of 2 and 3.

Multiples of 2 are: 2, 4, ⑥, 8, 10, ⑫, 14, 16, ⑱, 20, 22, and so on

Multiples of 3 are: 3, ⑥, 9, ⑫, 15, ⑱, 21, and so on

Common multiples are 6, 12, 18. The least common multiple is 6.

Determining the Greatest Common Factor (GCF)

The *greatest common factor* (GCF) of two or more numbers is the largest whole number that can be divided evenly, with no remainder, into each of the numbers. (See also page 263, *Finding Factors*.)

Find the greatest common factor of 6 and 18.

Factors of 6 are: ①, ②, ③, ⑥

Factors of 18 are: ①, ②, ③, ⑥, 9, 18

Common factors are 1, 2, 3, 6. Greatest common factor is 6.

Reducing Fractions to Lowest Terms

To reduce fractions to lowest terms, divide the numerator and the denominator by the greatest common factor.

$$\frac{6}{18} \leftarrow \begin{array}{c} \text{greatest common factor} \\ \text{of 6 and 18 is 6} \end{array} \rightarrow \overset{\div 6}{\underset{\div 6}{\frac{6}{18}}} = \frac{1}{3}$$

Writing Mixed Numbers as Improper Fractions

An *improper fraction* is a fraction in which the numerator is equal to or greater than its denominator.

$$4\frac{3}{4} = 4 \overset{+}{\underset{\times}{\frac{3}{4}}} = \frac{(4 \times 4) + 3}{4} = \frac{16 + 3}{4} = \frac{19}{4}$$

add next

multiply first

improper fraction

PERCENTS

Changing a Decimal to a Percent

To change a decimal to a percent, move the decimal point two places to the right and write a percent sign.

$0.73 = ?\%$ $0.055 = ?\%$

$0.73 \rightarrow 0.73.$ $0.055 \rightarrow 0.05.5$

move decimal point
2 places right

move decimal point
2 places right

$0.73 = 73\%$ $0.055 = 5.5\%$

write
percent sign

write
percent sign

Changing a Percent to a Decimal

To change a percent to a decimal, move the decimal point two places to the left and drop the percent sign.

11.75% → .1 1.7 5   0.75% → .0 0.7 5

     move decimal point 2 places   move decimal point 2 places
     left and drop percent sign   left and drop percent sign

11.75% = 0.1175   0.75% = 0.0075

Finding a Percentage of a Number

To find the percentage of a number, multiply the percent times the base.

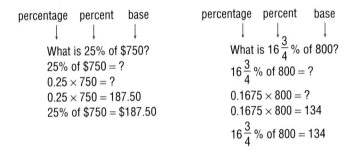

percentage percent base
What is 25% of $750?
25% of $750 = ?
$0.25 \times 750 = ?$
$0.25 \times 750 = 187.50$
25% of $750 = $187.50

percentage percent base
What is $16\frac{3}{4}$% of 800?
$16\frac{3}{4}$% of 800 = ?
$0.1675 \times 800 = ?$
$0.1675 \times 800 = 134$
$16\frac{3}{4}$% of 800 = 134

Finding the Percent One Number Is of Another

To find the percent one number is of another, divide the percentage by the base.

percent base percentage
What % of 10 is 2?

?% of 10 = 2

$?\% = \dfrac{2}{10}$ → $10\overline{)2.0}$ = 0.2   .2 0 = 20%

    move decimal point 2 places
    right and write percent sign

20% of 10 is 2

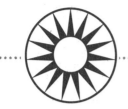

APPENDIX F: ANSWERS TO SELF-CHECK EXERCISES

UNIT 1   PUNCTUATION

Exercise 1, Unit 1

1. John's letter indicated that his doctor's report would be sent to the insurance company.
2. Well, Marie and Daniel's duet won the talent contest; but they didn't accept the award.
3. The instructor asked, "Have you read the article 'Studying Works' by Don Schuller?"
4. "It was the decision of the court [U.S. Supreme Court] on Friday," the speaker said, "to limit representation."
5. Duane said he needed the following items: 3 pencils, 11 folders, and 23 paper clips no later than 8:30 a.m.
6. Charity Hargrove, Ph.D., spoke to the group in clear, positive language, reminding them to "stand tall" in times of trouble.
7. She gave her address as 16 Central Avenue, Apt. 3, Houston, TX 50307.
8. Arthur, did you check to see if that figure of $77,631 was correct in the Wilson Buildings Inc. report?
9. It was a difficult task; nevertheless, it needed to be done.
10. Stop! Your car is on fire!
11. Mr. Anthony, the computer specialist, developed a first-class curriculum for the school.
12. The FTC (Federal Trade Commission) ruled that the J.C. Marlowe Company, Inc. had not acted properly.
13. The amount of $437.21 represented 16.95% of the total.
14. The word "indubitably" is difficult for most people to pronounce.
15. The title of Tony's speech was "How Not To Get It Right."
16. Phyllis left the campus early; she was too ill to continue.
17. On March 17, 1995, Ruth began the task; and she continued until she had completed the final report.

18. Paul gave three reports: one emphasizing employee morale; one centering on employee work habits; and one focusing on stress, time management, and incentives.
19. The title of the book was *Make Room for Me.* [*or Make Room for Me.*]
20. The girls' soccer team, led by Tammy and Lani, scored its goals in the first period.
21. The total pages keyed were 13, 11 of which contained errors.
22. When the order finally arrived, it contained products produced in 1993–1994.
23. Myra requested—perhaps demanded—that we stop talking.
24. One third of the money goes to William, but a one-half share of that goes to Millicent.
25. "It requires a great deal of self-denyal [sic]," wrote Henry, "if you want to develop discipline."

Exercise 2, Unit 1

TO: Ruby McFadden, Data Processing Director

FROM: Tony Whitten, National Sales Manager

DATE: May 16, 1995

SUBJECT: Monthly Sales Reports

At the San Diego meeting of the regional sales managers, I
informed the group that in the future, monthly sales reports
would be provided showing the following information:
(1) equipment sales, (2) service sales, and (3) total sales.
I also indicated that we will accept any suggestions reported
no later than June 30, 1995. Will you design a format, Ruby,
that will readily display specific, concise sales data?

In his address to the group, our president, Mr. Mahoney,
said, "We must have more accurate sales data if we are to
make appropriate projections." As I study this matter, I
will need complete data for all sales representatives--or
perhaps for each sales representative by region. Can you
possibly provide this information?

Would you also provide first-, second-, and third-quarter
sales figures for those representatives with sales of more
than $750,000? According to my recollection, at least seven
representatives have reached this goal.

May I refer you to an article entitled "Making the Most of
Data," which appeared in a recent issue of Data Processing.

F

I believe it presented a good case of providing solid data; however, I am not sure you will agree with the methods advocated.

UNIT 2 CAPITALIZATION

Exercise 1, Unit 2

1. The Democratic Party, Republicans
2. After, Capitol College, Judith, Marine Corps.
3. The, Bible, Koran, India
4. Mr. Childs, The, Thanksgiving, Florida, South, Mississippi River
5. Resolved, That, June
6. It, Veterans' Day
7. Jay's, It's
8. In Miss Quick's
9. The, Winston, Sunshine, Chicopee Rivers
10. Maria, Sunday
11. During, American, West, South
12. Hoyt, U.S.S. Independence, Vietnam Memorial
13. She, The
14. You, Chicago Symphony
15. Larry, Japanese, New England
16. His Majesty, William, April, British Navy
17. After, At, End, Day, Angela Frost, *New York Times*
18. His, Governor, Johnson's
19. My, Harry Jacobs, *Gone, With, Wind,* Flight, Portland
20. The Vietnamese, West

Exercise 2, Unit 2

1. Doctor of Philosophy
   Venus, Earth, Moon
2. Ms. Durkee
   The U.S. Senate
3. Midwest
   town of West Monroe
4. Atlantic Ocean
   Mississippi and Missouri Rivers
5. federal and state governments
   the Vietnam War Monument
6. Catalogue 16, Section 7, page 28
   oriental rugs and china platters
7. Mother
   Ode to the Robins of the South
8. president of the corporation hard work and encouragement from her father
9. Fall Festival
   Friday, September 30
   theater in River City
10. French, drama, Algebra II

UNIT 3 NUMBERS

Exercise 1, Unit 3

1. twelfth
2. $212.02
3. 4 years 2 months and 12 days
4. 11, 400
5. 121
6. Third
7. four, eleven, 20
8. 1.6
9. $38, Fourth
10. One, 4
11. 5; 1/2, 1/4, and 1/4
12. 4, 19, 16, two

13. $223 million
14. 6'3", 183
15. 16, 200, 241
16. 38

17. 22, '62, twenty-fifth
18. 12 o'clock noon
19. Fifty-three percent
20. 28 1/2

Exercise 2, Unit 3

May 23, 1993

Ms. Winnie Malone, Director
XYZ Company
One Center Boulevard
Tampa, FL 33673-1404

Dear Ms. Malone

Seven days ago I wrote you concerning the accident involving
one of your drivers on Eighth Avenue at 3:30 p.m. Seven
minutes after the accident, police officers from the
Eleventh Precinct arrived. They determined the distance
between the initial impact and the actual stopping point to
be 176 feet. A total of three citations were issued to your
driver.

Damage to my car amounted to $750 as determined by estimates
from three repair shops. In addition, I paid $75.65 for a
rental car, which could have cost several hundred dollars
more. I was given a 7 percent discount. I also incurred
other expenses. Because I was out of work for a while, I
did not receive a $25-a-month raise. In addition, my son
Ronnie, 12, missed twenty-one days of school, almost one
third of the marking period.

Most of the twenty-one witnesses to the accident are willing
to testify. Your secretary told me to expect seven 10-page
documents from your office to be returned by May 31. This
will be difficult to do since it will take about five days
just to read the documents.

Please call me after seven o'clock to discuss this matter
further.

Sincerely

Rhonda Wilson
Apartment 10, State Route 9
Tampa, FL 33673

F

UNIT 4   ABBREVIATIONS

Exercise 1, Unit 4

1.	C	6.	Bros.	11.	C	16.	m
2.	General	7.	NNE	12.	FBI	17.	FAN
3.	C	8.	CPU	13.	C	18.	Reverend
4.	P.R. and PR	9.	C	14.	pt	19.	C
5.	C	10.	Sept. or Sep.	15.	C	20.	C

Exercise 2, Unit 4

1. Mr. John White
    1721 First Avenue
    New Orleans, LA 70183
2. Fort Riley is located in Kansas.
3. John works for station WNIT in Boston, MA.
4. Elizabeth Wortham received her Ph.D. last August.
5. Dr. John T. Smith, Jr., lives on West Boulevard.
6. Henrietta White, Ed.D., is from Great Britain.
7. Acme Glass Company
    1900 Center Road
    Jacksonville, FL 45333

Exercise 3, Unit 4

1. Artificial Intelligence
2. Central Processing Unit
3. Disk Operating System
4. Local Area Network
5. Random Access Memory

Exercise 4, Unit 4

1.	Btu	11.	supt.
2.	dc	12.	CPA
3.	ASAP	13.	dept.
4.	Assn.	14.	Esq.
5.	ATM	15.	etc.
6.	copy	16.	vice president
7.	teaspoon	17.	wkly.
8.	horsepower	18.	ETA
9.	miles per hour	19.	w/o
10.	continued	20.	yr.

UNIT 5   GRAMMAR

Exercise 1, Unit 5

1. grew
2. drive, drove
3. chosen
4. hung

5. laid
6. lie
7. ate
8. led, led
9. swim, swum
10. shaken
11. sing, sung
12. told

13. get, got/gotten
14. ran, run
15. lost, lost
16. left
17. begin
18. frozen
19. had, had
20. drink, drunk

Exercise 2, Unit 5

1. n (Sharon); adj (tallest); prep (on)
2. int (Yikes); pro (my); conj (when); n (floor)
3. inf (to win); n (fairness)
4. v (explained); conj (as); adv (patiently)
5. v (completed); v (required); adj (great)

Exercise 3, Unit 5

Correct words: was, it have, louder, his, she, Whom, they, to investigate more thoroughly

UNIT 6   PHRASES, CLAUSES, SENTENCES, AND PARAGRAPHS

Exercise 1, Unit 6

1. V (will give); PR (before the advisory committee)
2. PP (Swimming steadily); PR (in two hours)
3. G (Going home at Thanksgiving); PR (of mine)
4. A (my friend); V (would have been)
5. G (Running laps); I (to do); PR (in my spare time)
6. I (to share)
7. G (setting the record); PR (in the mile)
8. PP (Worn around the edges); V (must be removed)
9. I (To make the highest score)
10. A (the girl in red); G (hiking in the woods)

Exercise 2, Unit 6

(Answers will vary)
1. Tommy was walking to class in a driving rainstorm at the end of the day.
2. He was carrying a bookbag over his shoulder, deep in thought about events of the day.
3. It was seven o'clock in the evening of a very miserable day of his life.
4. He approached the classroom building in a state of complete misery in the cold, damp weather.

5. He stopped in the middle of the street, reminded that the class was to meet in the morning, not in the evening.

Exercise 3, Unit 6

1. expository
2. paragraph
3. cause and effect
4. persuasive
5. narrative
6. topic sentence
7. Supporting sentences
8. descriptive
9. Single sentences
10. evaluated

Exercise 4, Unit 6

1. I
2. IN
3. F
4. E
5. R
6. D
7. IN
8. F
9. I
10. I

Exercise 5, Unit 6

1. S
2. CX
3. CD
4. CCX
5. S
6. CD
7. S
8. CX
9. CX
10. CD

UNIT 7   SPELLING AND WORD CHOICE

Exercise 1, Unit 7

1. inter
2. tri
3. counter
4. able
5. pre
6. sub
7. micro
8. less
9. de
10. un

Exercise 2, Unit 7

1. dollars
2. matches
3. rallies
4. attorneys
5. halves
6. tomatoes
7. deer
8. children
9. geese
10. daughters-in-law

Exercise 3, Unit 7

1. affidavit
2. bracelet
3. benefits
4. corporate
5. information
6. anonymous
7. facilities
8. financial
9. possible
10. receive
11. embarrassment
12. material
13. maintenance
14. customer
15. recommendation

16. advertisement	28. employee	40. mortgage
17. cemetery	29. addition	41. blasphemy
18. effect	30. absence	42. despair
19. editorial	31. receipt	43. dilemma
20. fascination	32. interested	44. espionage
21. influential	33. immediately	45. hereditary
22. leisure	34. discrimination	46. interim
23. neurotic	35. schedule	47. maneuver
24. pamphlet	36. procedure	48. origin
25. siege	37. commission	49. quietly
26. adolescent	38. personnel	50. tyranny
27. accompaniment	39. whether	

Exercise 4, Unit 7

1. except	8. course	15. latter
2. attendance	9. die	16. hear
3. breathe	10. great	17. moral
4. aide	11. incite	18. emerge
5. cease	12. least	19. lose
6. dessert	13. persecuted	20. envelope
7. fiscal	14. guest	

UNIT 8 THE WRITING PROCESS: PREWRITING AND DRAFTING

Exercise 1, Unit 8

1. C	5. B	9. C
2. B, C	6. B	10. B
3. A, C	7. B, C	
4. A, B, C	8. B	

F

Exercise 2, Unit 8

(Answers will vary)

WHO? 1. Who can be on the Court?
      2. Who can argue cases before the Court?

WHAT? 1. What is the purpose of the Court?
       2. What kinds of decisions can the Court make?

WHERE? 1. Where does the Court convene?
        2. Where do most of the cases come from?

WHEN? 1. When does the Court convene?
       2. When does the Court announce decisions?

WHY?   1. Why is it necessary to have a Supreme Court?
        2. Why does the Court sometimes refuse to hear a case?
HOW?   1. How does one get the Court to hear a case?
        2. How do decisions of the Court affect the other branches of government?

Exercise 3, Unit 8

(Answers will vary)

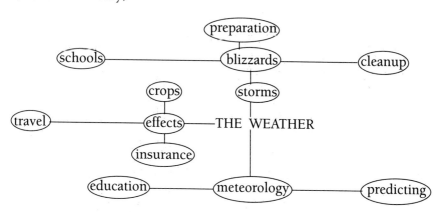

F

UNIT 9   THE WRITING PROCESS: REVISING, EDITING, AND FINAL DRAFTING

Exercise 1, Unit 9

1. T	6. T	11. F	16. T
2. T	7. T	12. T	17. F
3. F	8. T	13. T	18. T
4. F	9. T	14. T	19. T
5. T	10. F	15. F	20. T

Exercise 2, Unit 9

1. S	3. C	4. J	5. C
2. C			

Exercise 3, Unit 9

On february 13, 1983, Ronald became an employee of the local newspaper, the Daily Tribune. he began first at by handling routine assignments. For example he was required to call the local funeral homes each morning to see who had died died during the night. He wold then compose obituaries for each of the deceased following a precribed format. This assignment did not require a lot of imagination as a result he began to devise ways in which to express his creativity. He sometimes added a lne of copy listing fictitious accomplishments of the deceased. On one occasion, he even made up a complete obituary for someone who did not even exist. Needless to say, his "creativity" led to a lot of trouble for him

UNIT 10   REFERENCE SOURCES

Exercise 1, Unit 10

1. Official Airline Guide
2. Fortune Directory
3. United States Government Manual
4. Postal Manual
5. Hotel and Motel Red Book

Exercise 2, Unit 10

1. dictionary
2. almanac
3. encyclopedia
4. directory
5. biographical book

Exercise 3, Unit 10

1. F	4. F	7. F	9. F
2. T	5. T	8. T	10. T
3. F	6. T		

Exercise 4, Unit 10

1. E	3. B	4. D	5. A
2. C			

UNIT 11   LETTERS AND MEMOS

Exercise 1, Unit 11

1. K	6. L
2. D	7. I
3. H	8. B
4. M	9. A
5. G	10. C

Exercise 2, Unit 11

14	17	7
9	5	1
12	13	6
16	4	19
15	10	8
3	18	2
	11	

Exercise 3, Unit 11

1. T	6. F	11. F	16. F
2. T	7. T	12. T	17. T
3. T	8. F	13. T	18. T
4. T	9. F	14. T	19. T
5. F	10. F	15. F	20. F

F

UNIT 12   RESEARCH PAPERS AND BUSINESS REPORTS

Exercise 1, Unit 12

1.	F	6.	F	11.	F	16.	T
2.	T	7.	T	12.	F	17.	F
3.	T	8.	F	13.	T	18.	T
4.	F	9.	F	14.	T	19.	T
5.	T	10.	T	15.	F	20.	F

Exercise 2, Unit 12

C	I
F	A
E	K
H	J
B	G
	D

Exercise 3, Unit 12

6

Stein, Elizabeth C. The Art of Revision.
Boston: Center Publishing Co., 1994.

UNIT 13   SECURING EMPLOYMENT

Exercise 1, Unit 13

1.	T	4.	F	7.	T	9.	T
2.	T	5.	F	8.	F	10.	T
3.	F	6.	T				

Exercise 2, Unit 13

1.	B	4.	C	7.	B	9.	C
2.	A	5.	C	8.	B	10.	A
3.	C	6.	B				

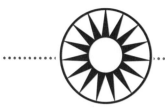

INDEX

Note: In this index, references in decimal form indicate rule sections. References in **boldface** type indicate page numbers.

Dates (*continued*)
  commas in, 1.28
  diagonals in, 1.48
  division rules, **244**
  hyphens with, 1.59
  in letters, 3.21, 11.12
  military style, 11.12
  numbers in, 3.21–3.27
Decimal numbers, 3.32
  math skill review, **265–266**
Declarative sentences, 6.35
Delivery notation, on letters, 11.31
Descriptive paragraphs, 6.52
Descriptive writing, 8.6
Dewey decimal system, 10.12
Diagonals
  in abbreviations, 1.49
  in dates, 1.48
  in fractions, 1.49
  in reference initials line, 1.50
  spacing, 1.51
  in time expressions, 1.49
  between words, 1.47
Dictionaries, **103**, 10.4
Direct quotation, 12.10
Directories, 10.5
Documentation. *See also* Research
    papers
  bibliography, 12.32–12.34
  of business reports, 12.62
  endnotes, 12.29–12.30
  footnotes, 12.24–12.28
  importance, 12.21
  methods, 12.23
  textnotes, 12.31
Dollar amounts. *See* Money, expressing
DOS commands, **248–249**

Editing
  checklist, 9.10
  conciseness, 9.11
  importance, 9.9
  proofreading, 9.13–9.15
  wordy phrases, 9.12
EEOC (Equal Employment Opportunity
    Commission), 13.12

Election results, numbers in, 3.64
Ellipses
  in quoted material, 1.52
  spacing, 1.53
Elliptical adverb clauses, 6.21
Employment
  advancement tips, 13.17–13.18
  application form, 13.8–13.10,
      Fig. 13-3
  fair employment practices, 13.10
  interview, 13.10, 13.13–13.15
  job search, 13.1–13.3
  letters
    of application, 13.6–13.7, Fig. 13-2
    follow-up, 13.16, Fig. 13-4
  opportunities for, **223**
  performance appraisals, 13.19
  résumé preparation, 13.4–13.5,
      Fig. 13-1
  tests, 13.11
Enclosure notation, in letters, 11.29
Encyclopedias, 1.06
Endnotes, 12.29–12.30, Fig. 12-5
Enumerated items
  parentheses for, 1.67
  periods in, 1.76
  semicolon use in, 1.92
Envelopes. *See also* Business letters
  folding and inserting letters in,
      11.27–11.39
  preparation guidelines, 11.36
  sizes of, 11.35, Fig. 11-7 to 11-9
  window, 11.39
Equal Employment Opportunity
    Commission (EEOC), 13.12
Esq., use of, 4.29
Etc., punctuation with, 1.31
Ethnic and racial references,
    capitalization of, 2.17–2.18
Exclamation points
  with quotation marks, 1.88
  spacing, 1.55
  uses of, 1.54, 6.38
Exclamatory sentences, 6.38
Expository paragraphs, 6.46–6.50
Expository writing, 8.2

Lightface numbers refer to rule sections; **boldface** numbers refer to pages.

INDEX • **289**